REGISTERED AS DISABLED

SALLY SAINSBURY

Lecturer in Social Administration
London School of Economics and Political Science

OCCASIONAL PAPERS ON SOCIAL ADMINISTRATION NO. 35
*Editorial Committee under the
Chairmanship of Professor R. M. Titmuss*

*Published by G. Bell & Sons,
York House, Portugal Street, London, W.C.2*

First published 1970
© *1970 by The Social Administration Research Trust*

ISBN 07135 1619 4

MADE AND PRINTED IN ENGLAND BY
WILLMER BROTHERS LIMITED
BIRKENHEAD

This series of *Occasional Papers* was started in 1960 to supply the need for a medium of publication for studies in the field of social policy and administration which fell between the two extremes of the short article and the full-length book. It was thought that such a series would not only meet a need among research workers and writers concerned with contemporary social issues, but would also strengthen the links between students of the subject and administrators, social workers, committee members and others with responsibilities and interest in the social services.

Contributions to the series should be submitted to the Editorial Committee. A list of earlier papers in this series which are still in print is to be found on the back of this volume.

Richard M. Titmuss

CONTENTS

This small pilot study of 211 persons registered as physically handicapped by the welfare departments of London, Essex and Middlesex was completed in 1965. The object of the study was to explore
the day to day problems of disabled persons. It was sponsored by the
Greater London Association for the Disabled and generously financed
by an anonymous trust.

Many people were liberal with help and advice. Valuable detailed
comment on drafts was provided by Peter Townsend, who introduced me to the subject and supervised the field work, and
Brian Abel-Smith, who supervised the later stages of the project. I
am indebted to them for their encouragement and support. Marie
Brown, Hilary Land, Barbara Rodgers, Thelma Sainsbury, Michael
Humphrey and John Veit-Wilson gave helpful criticism.

The study could not have been undertaken without the co-operation of the welfare departments of London, Middlesex and Essex. I
should like to thank the welfare officers of these departments who
took me on their visits to registered disabled persons.

My main debt, however, is to the 211 disabled persons who allowed me to visit them in their own homes, often for many hours. I
should like to take this opportunity to thank them for their kind
hospitality.

After the outbreak of the last war three separate Acts of Parliament were designed to improve the circumstances of disabled persons in Britain: the Disabled Persons (Employment) Act of 1944, the National Health Service Act of 1946, and the National Assistance Act of 1948. Yet even now, in 1970, it is still difficult to evaluate their effects. There is a dearth of information. Not only is little known about the actual problems encountered by the disabled in their families and in wider society, or about the *efficiency* of the various services introduced to help them. It is even difficult to say how many of the disabled are known to the appropriate services.

The true seriousness of this extraordinary dearth of information dawned on some of those who were involved in discussing the implications for disabled persons of the proposed reorganization of London government in the late 1950's and early 1960's.

The Greater London Association for the disabled explored the possibilities of carrying out research, and commissioned the small pilot inquiry reported in this book. The interviewing was completed in 1965. In this chapter, the problems demanding investigation will be explained. Then the theoretical problems of studying disability will be discussed. Finally, the chosen methods of investigation will be described in some detail.

1. *The Problems demanding investigation*

The problems of the disabled vary widely according to age and clinical condition. First there are problems of mobility and personal self-sufficiency. Which kinds of disabled persons find it difficult or impossible to climb stairs, walk in the street, travel on public transport, dress, use an electric or gas cooker, prepare vegetables and so on? Second, there are problems connected with occupations. Which kinds of disabled person cannot find ordinary paid employment? How many of them can follow, and want to follow, some form of alternative 'sheltered' employment? What forms of occupation are

9

available in the home? Third, there are problems concerned with household and outside social relationships. Which kinds of disabled persons impose particularly severe and emotional burdens upon their relatives? In what way are relationships between husbands and wives, parents and children, and neighbours and friends, affected by disability? What do the disabled themselves *feel* about these relationships?

The answers which can be given here to questions such as these are bound to be tentative, but they may help parents, husbands or wives, friends, doctors, social workers and teachers to *understand* disability. They are also likely to narrow the scope for disagreement about desirable developments in public services. How much priority should the local authorities give to those who are marginally employable, to the severely disabled at home and to the support of relatives who are bearing a particularly heavy burden? Do we need to develop different kinds of services?

2. *Theoretical Problems of Studying Disability*

Theoretically all the crucial questions seem to hinge on whether the disabled should be integrated into society or segregated from it. There are theories of *disengagement*. It could be argued that disability sets in train psychological and social processes similar to ageing. Disabled persons are supposed to 'disengage' from society just as society disengages from them. They are unable to play the roles which are typical for persons of their age and sex and they therefore reconcile themselves to roles which are, from the viewpoint of society, both limited and marginal. They avoid activities which impinge on those of others. They seek to hide their disabilities from the gaze of other people and prefer formal associations outside the mainstream of social life. It is as if in the whirling, ever-changing structure that comprises society the disabled and elderly are gently dislodged from key positions at the centre of the structure and move to the peripheries.

There are also theories of *segregation*. It could be argued that disabled persons have lower levels of activity than, and different needs and interests from, those of others in society. They therefore tend to develop specialized forms of social relationship which emphasize their 'apartness'. Compared with other individuals they are isolated, confining their close relationships to one or two members of their families of marriage or origin, and other disabled persons. They also prefer association from among their number to membership of ordinary clubs and societies. Both sets of theories are important because, depending on the confidence with which they are held, they will tend to govern the evolution of services. Do spastics prefer to live with other spastics, with other kinds of disabled persons or in

10

ordinary households? Do disabled persons prefer to work in sheltered workshops or ordinary employment? These questions show how important it is to explore and test such theories.

The theories can be explored either by examining changes in the life profiles of individuals—patterns of socialization, engagement, and disengagement,[1] adaptation or accommodation—or by examining the structure of contemporary relationships between the disabled and the rest of society. In this report the main emphasis is on the second. The object of the research is thus to describe the roles and social relationships of disabled persons according to their levels of incapacity. These were the theories which governed the approach to the research and also determined the plan of the book.

Compared with the clinical or 'individual' approaches of much of the previous writing about disability in Britain the approach followed in this report is specifically sociological. The concept of 'reference group', for example, is important to the subsequent analysis. A disabled person's attitudes will depend on the frame of reference within which they are conceived. The two most important types of reference group which need to be distinguished are first, *comparative* reference group and second, *membership* reference group. The first is a group with which a person compares himself, or aspires towards. A disabled man may, for example, compare himself with men of his own age in normal employment. The second is a group with which a person identifies himself. A disabled man belongs to a family, for example, and may belong to a class of 'spastics' or 'the blind'. Any person in society will have a multiplicity of reference groups but will restrict himself to using a few for most of the time. Our understanding of disability will develop according to the information we have about the reference groups, and attitudes towards the reference groups, of the disabled.[2]

Needless to say, the comparisons that will be made between an individual and his reference groups are not the only comparisons which will have to be made. Comparisons also have to be made in terms of objective situation and personal life-perspective. The material situation (e.g. housing and income) of the disabled has to be compared with that of others in society. The views individuals hold about themselves, their histories and their futures at different stages of the life-cycle will also have to be compared. Much of this report will therefore represent a very simple fact about the disabled—that they are members of society and, as a consequence, have particular social relationships and aspirations. They are not just individuals with disabilities.

---

1. Cumming, E., and Henry, W. E., *Growing Old: The Process of Disengagement,* New York, Basic Books, 1961.
2. Merton, R. K., and Rossi, A. S., 'Contributions to the Theory of Reference Group Behaviour', in Merton, R. K., *Social Theory and Social Structure,* rev. ed., Glencoe, Illinois, The Free Press, 1957.

One further principle of approach needs to be explained. Disability is usually studied according to clinical type. This is helpful up to a point but is unsatisfactory if a full understanding of the personal and social *consequences* of disability is to be obtained. Some measure is needed of the level of functional capacity. This is a difficult and complicated matter but can be approached by seeking answers to certain groups of questions, for example, the extent to which (i) the individual can care for his person, (ii) manage a house, and (iii) conduct different forms of communication and social relationships. In other words, there are degrees of disability and unless we can compare even broadly the degree to which different persons are 'disabled' it is difficult either to understand their problems or decide what services or monetary compensation they need. Ideally, we want to be able to compare persons who have not only the same but also different clinical disabilities—persons, say, who have a diseased kidney, with those who have pneumoconiosis or a prolapsed disc or an amputated limb.

Much of the official thinking about disability is still extraordinarily limited. The McCorquodale Committee on the Assessment of Disablement repeatedly referred in its report to the principle that assessment should be determined by 'means of a comparison between the condition of the disabled person and that of a normal healthy person of the same age,'[3] but took no steps to apply the principle empirically. The Committee did not obtain information systematically about disabled persons and healthy persons of equivalent age. Nor did the Committee seek to examine the rationale and consistency of current medical assessments. They did not even seek empirical justification for percentage assessments of amputations. For example, they accepted the loss of four fingers and of a leg below the knee (leaving a stump of between $3\frac{1}{2}$ and five inches) each as equivalent to fifty percent disability. In refraining from exploring the functional, psychological and social effects even of different kinds of limb amputation they failed to take advantage of the growing body of knowledge and research methods developed by the social sciences in the last twenty years.

The research described in this report therefore seeks to extend our understanding of disability by employing the concept of 'functional capacity' as well as the concept of 'reference group'.

3. *Methods of Research*

No complete register of disabled persons exists. Those injured in war, in the services, and in industry are known to the Department of Health and Social Security. Those who are thought capable of

3. *Report of the Committee on the Assessment of Disablement* (the McCorquodale Report), Cmnd. 2847. London, H.M.S.O., December 1965, p. 4.

work and are seeking it or have sought it through an Employment Exchange, are registered, if they wish it, by the Department of Employment and Productivity. But these records do not form a satisfactory basis for research into the general condition of the handicapped as a group. There is a third possibility—the registers kept by the local authorities of the general classes of the physically handicapped, the blind and the deaf. Since the research had to be restricted on grounds of cost and since also the blind and the deaf form rather specialized and relatively small groups, it seemed best to concentrate on the registers of the general classes of the physically handicapped.

A random sample was drawn from local authority registers of the physically handicapped in London, Essex and Middlesex which produced a total of 280 persons.

In each area welfare officers visited the people whose names were drawn to seek their permission to be interviewed. Officers of the county welfare departments themselves took the responsibility of offering an explanation of the objects of the survey. They felt that this was likely to reassure individuals who might otherwise worry about the interviews.

It must be remembered that the local authority registers are far from representative of all disabled persons in each locality. Each local authority defines the basis on which its register is to be drawn up and the number per 1,000 population who are registered varies widely.[4] The attitude of an authority towards registration is bound to be reflected in the composition of its register. For example, people were said to be registered in Essex only if it was thought that the county could be of assistance to them, whereas in London the welfare authority tended to register any handicapped person who came to its notice. This means that the registers are not wholly comparable. Second, the interpretation of 'handicap' tends to vary. Greater uniformity in the registration of the handicapped is impossible at present because no satisfactory definition of handicap has been devised. Third, whatever definition of handicap is adopted many handicapped persons are undoubtedly not on local authority registers. The fact that registration is increasing rapidly as services expand makes this plain. For these reasons it is important to emphasize that samples drawn from the local authority registers are not representative of disabled persons in general. They are representative only of the registers from which they are drawn. However, they cover a wide cross-section of the disabled as we shall see.

Seventeen per cent of those in the sample proved to be beyond

---

4. For a brief discussion on the composition of local authority registers, numbers per 1000 population registered in the general classes of the physically handicapped, and expenditure on them per head, see Appendix 3, p. 201.

the scope of the survey for a number of reasons. Some people were dead; some lived outside the area of the local authority; others were in residential homes or schools or in hospital. (See Table 1.) Thus

TABLE 1

Total samples of disabled persons drawn in London, Essex and Middlesex

	London		Essex		Middlesex		All	
	No.	%	No.	%	No.	%	No.	%
Those outside scope of study:								
dead	9	6	0	(0)	4	(6)	13	5
living in residential homes or schools	3	2	2	(3)	4	(6)	9	4
in hospital	4	3	3	(5)	3	(4)	10	4
living outside county	7	5	3	(5)	0	(0)	10	4
Effective sample:	127	84	59	(87)	52	(84)	238	83
Total sample drawn	150	100	67	(100)	63	(100)	280	100

there were 238 persons in the effective sample—that is, registered persons living in their own homes. Of these, twenty-one (nine per cent) refused to be interviewed, and seven (three per cent) were too ill to be interviewed. Altogether, 211 persons were finally interviewed—109 in London, fifty in Middlesex and fifty-two in Essex. (See Table 2.)

TABLE 2

Response to interview in London, Essex and Middlesex

Response	London		Essex		Middlesex		All	
	No.	%	No.	%	No.	%	No.	%
Refused an interview	16	12	2	(3)	2	(4)	20	8
Too ill to be interviewed	2	2	5	(8)	0	(0)	7	3
Total interviewed	109	86	52	(89)	50	(96)	211	89
Total effective sample	127	100	59	(100)	52	(100)	238	100

The interviews took place over a period of a year. About two-thirds of the interviews were carried out by the author. Graduate students in the Department of Sociology at the University of Essex, and medical students interested in social studies at St. Thomas's Hospital, London, helped to complete them in Essex and Middlesex. The average length of the interviews was between two and two-and-a-half hours. Letters of thanks were sent to each person after the interview.

Accounts of the whole of each interview were drawn up independently of the questionnaire. It is from these accounts that examples quoted in the text have been drawn. To preserve the anonymity of the persons interviewed, the names of those to whom such extracts relate have been changed in the text.

14

The main work of interviewing was supplemented by various other assignments. A month was spent with the L.C.C. Welfare Department, and welfare officers were accompanied on their regular visits to the disabled persons. Visits were also paid to three of the area Centres for the handicapped in London, the Welfare Departments of the Essex and Middlesex county councils, and the Chelmsford (Essex) and Southall (Middlesex) area centres for the handicapped. Care was taken to sound out those responsible nationally and locally for different services—the Ministries of Health, Labour and Pensions, local authorities and voluntary agencies—such as the Greater London Association for the Disabled, the Red Cross, Horder Centres for Arthritics, and the Shaftesbury Society. Further information was obtained from a Remploy factory, the L.C.C. workshop at St. Pancras, the Camden Road Rehabilitation Centre, and clubs run for disabled persons by voluntary agencies.

The survey breaks almost entirely new ground. It must therefore be viewed to some extent as a pilot study for later, more systematic, research. The questionnaire was difficult to design, not only because concepts of 'functional capacity' and 'reference groups' proved difficult to define operationally, but also because the handicapped themselves varied enormously in their capacity to understand and answer certain kinds of questions. As a result it sometimes seemed that 'anthropological' reportage was more reliable than certain over-all statistics. Even though the questionnaire was modified after some preliminary interviews, it was still found to be unsatisfactory in the early stages of the main interviewing, and some additions had to be made. For this reason, the reader will find that the response to some questions reported below is slightly smaller than he might otherwise expect.

There are many other deficiencies in the research reported in these pages, and the scale of the work is certainly small. But if the report helps to uncover some of the events, attitudes and relationships which are of major importance to disabled persons then it will have made a modest contribution towards the difficult task of integrating them better into society.

This chapter has a simple object—to describe the main characteristics of the disabled persons interviewed as a basis for subsequent analysis. The first point which must be made is that those interviewed reported a wide variety of clinical conditions.[1] Altogether the 211 persons interviewed suffered from 45 different conditions. In Table 3, the number of persons with different types of conditions is

TABLE 3

Number and percentage of persons reporting particular clinical conditions

Clinical condition	Persons	
	Number	Per cent
Arthritis (unspecified)	38	18
Poliomyelitis	26	13
Amputation	19	9
Multiple sclerosis	18	9
Hemiplegia	18	9
Rheumatoid arthritis	16	8
Bronchitis	13	6
Osteo-arthritis	9	4
Epilepsy	8	4
Coronary thrombosis	8	4
Fractures	8	4
Spastic	8	4
Paraplegia	7	3
Diabetes	6	3
Tuberculosis	5	2
Parkinsons disease	5	2
Others	177	84
N =	211	100

shown. About 31 per cent specified rheumatoid arthritis, osteo-arthritis, or just arthritis. Another 13 per cent were the victims of poliomyelitis,

1. The analysis of clinical conditions must be treated with caution: no check with medical records was possible. However, there is considerable similarity between the proportions of persons in certain categories of conditions in the sample and those in the analysis of the registers nationally. See *Annual Report of the Ministry of Health for the year 1966*, Cmnd. 3326, London H.M.S.O., p. 143, Part 8.

and the number of amputees, hemiplegics, and multiple sclerotics was nine per cent in each instance. Nearly half of the persons interviewed reported more than one condition.

There was a wide variety in age as well as in clinical condition. The ages of the persons interviewed ranged from sixteen to ninety-two years. (See Table 4.) The age distribution in each of the three areas was strikingly similar. However, there were two important features which should be noted. First, there were no children. This was simply a function of administrative registration. Few children were registered by any local authorities. In 1964, at the beginning of the present study, only about three per cent of those registered in England and Wales were below the age of fifteen.[2]

TABLE 4

Age of persons interviewed, registered persons, and population of England and Wales

| Age | Disabled Persons | | | | All Persons In Areas Studied[b] Per cent |
| | Persons interviewed | | England and Wales[a] | | |
	No.	Per cent	No.	Per cent	
0 – 14	0	0	4,402	3	20
15 – 24	4	2			15
25 – 44	31	15	85,070	63	26
45 – 64	89	42			27
65 and over	87	42	44,722	33	12
All	211	100	134,194	100	100
N =	211	100	134,194	100	7,802,780 = 100

[a] Based on the *Annual Report of the Ministry of Health for 1964*, Cmnd. 2688, London, H.M.S.O. 1965.
[b] Based on Reports by the General Register Office, for the Sample Census, 1966, for Greater London, Chelmsford M.B., Chelmsford R.D., and Maldon R.D.

Second, a disproportionate number of the handicapped were in middle and old age. The age groups into which the sample was divided were chosen to correspond roughly to different phases in family life. For those between fifteen and twenty-four one of the main problems is to train for and find a suitable job. Most of those aged twenty-five to forty-four expect to be married and caring for dependent children, whereas most of those aged forty-five to sixty-four no longer expect to have children dependent on them and their opportunities of obtaining new employment have diminished. And those aged sixty-five and over are plainly exposed to the problems of retirement, bereavement and greater physical frailty.

The preponderance of the middle-aged and elderly is brought about by a number of factors. People in these age groups are more liable to disability. Their numbers are also almost certainly swelled

2. See the *Annual Report of the Ministry of Health for the year 1964*, Cmnd. 2688, London H.M.S.O., 1965, p. 127. Table 54.

B

by persons with progressive disabilities who do not feel the need for registration with local authorities until their disability worsens with age. Again, it may be that the services offered by local authorities are of the kind which discourage some of the younger disabled from seeking registration. It is probable that there is a tendency among the younger disabled to register for employment with the Ministry of Labour but not for social services from the local authorities. The numbers per 1,000 population who are registered with local authorities increases with age. Whereas only 0.4 persons per thousand population aged 0 to 15 years were registered in England and Wales, 3.0 persons per thousand population aged sixteen to sixty-four years, and as many as 8.0 persons aged sixty-five years and above were registered.[3] A similar rise with ages in the proportion of persons who are disabled has been noted in other countries.[4]

More than three-fifths of the persons in the sample were women, and they tended to predominate, even when allowance was made for differences between the sexes in age distribution in the general population.[5] There were more disabled women than disabled men aged sixty-five and over, but the ratio was not very different from that in the total elderly population. A more significant difference was found at younger ages, especially among those aged twenty-five to forty-four. In the sample there were proportionately three times as many women as men of this age. (See Table 5.) This can be explained, as above, by the tendency of disabled younger men who are in employment or who still have hopes of employment to refrain from registering with the local authorities. This may be particularly true of men who have wives or other relatives looking after their homes. But this tendency must not be exaggerated. Some men who *are* employed are registered with the local authorities. Moreover there may be numbers of unemployable handicapped men who are cared for by relatives and so not registered. By contrast disabled women are more likely to feel they come within the scope of services which can provide various kinds of help in the home. These are more likely to be sought by her and offered to her than to similarly disabled men. Social norms place emphasis on the need for the house-

3. Based on the *Annual Report of the Ministry of Health for the year 1964*, Cmnd. 2688, London, H.M.S.O., 1965, and on reports of the Registrar General, *Census 1961*, London H.M.S.O.
4. Surveys of the disabled in the U.S.A. and Denmark have shown a similar rise with advancing age in the proportion of people who are disabled. For example, it was estimated in 1956 that 'the older the individual, the more likely he is to be disabled....Two-fifths of the disabled are aged 65 and over...', *Chronic Illness in the United States*, Vol. III, Commission on Chronic Illness, Harvard University Press, 1956, p. 6. A recent survey of the disabled in Denmark has shown that the age distribution of the physically handicapped 'significantly differed from the age distribution of the whole sample because of the extremely high frequency of older persons among the physically handicapped.... The percentage is very small for the lower age groups (for the group 15 to 19 years the number is 1.6 per cent for the men and 1.1 per cent for the women), and then grows larger with increasing age, accelerating increasingly around the 50th year of age. For the highest age group in the study (60 to 61 years), 26.5 per cent of the men and 24 per cent of the women are physically handicapped.' Anderson, B. R., and Madsen, F., *Fysik Handicappede Danmark Book II*, Copenhagen 1964, p. 111.
5. The imbalance between men and women in our sample has not been found to exist among the disabled population of Denmark. See Anderson and Madsen, *op. cit.*, Book II, p. 17, Table 6.

18

wife to be independent. Furthermore, it is possible that women are more likely to be willing to take advantage of the provisions of clubs and centres for the handicapped. This may be partly because the home has been the centre of their existence while disabled men have had a wider experience at work and outside the home of social life, and they may compare clubs and centres for the handicapped unfavourably with their normal recreational activities, such as going with friends to football matches, pubs, or the dogs.

TABLE 5

Age and sex of persons interviewed, and of persons in Great Britain

Age	Sex								
	Men			Women			All		
	Interviewed		Great Britain	Interviewed		Great Britain	Interviewed		Great Britain
	No.	%	%	No.	%	%	No.	%	%
0 – 14	0	(0)	25	0	0	22	0	0	23
15 – 24	3	(4)	15	1	1	14	4	2	15
25 – 44	6	(7)	25	25	19	24	31	15	25
45 – 64	40	(49)	25	49	38	25	89	42	25
65 +	32	(40)	10	55	42	15	87	41	12
Total	81	(100)	100	130	100	100	211	100	100
N =	81		25,319,330	130		26,984,390	211		52,304,720

It must be noted, however, that in December 1964, the general classes of the physically handicapped registered with local authorities in England and Wales were more evenly divided between the sexes than is true of our sample. According to the *Annual Report of the Ministry of Health for the year 1964*, fifty-three per cent of the general classes of the physically handicapped in England and Wales

TABLE 6

Sex and marital status of persons interviewed, and of persons in Great Britain

Marital status	Sex (percentage)					
	Men		Women		All	
	Interviewed[a]	In Great Britain[c]	Interviewed[a]	In Great Britain[c]	Interviewed[b]	In Great Britain[c]
Single	(64)	44	49	39	56	41
Married	(31)	52	31	49	29	51
Widowed	(4)	3	17	11	14	7
Divorced	(1)	1	3	1	1	1
Total	(100)	100	100	100	100	100
N =	81	25,319,330	130	26,984,390	211	52,304,720

a The proportions of persons in different age groups in the sample were not representative of the general population, and have been weighted accordingly.
b The proportions of persons in different age groups and the sexes have been weighted to correspond to those in the total population.
c Based on information published by Registrar General, for the *Sample Census*, 1966, H.M.S.O. London.

19

were women. In the age group sixty-five years and over, however, over three-fifths of those on the registers were women.

Over four-fifths (174) of the persons in the sample were or had been married. Nearly half were currently married (and three-quarters of the men). Nevertheless, more disabled persons (a little less than one-fifth—37) than in the population at large had never been married. Another third were widowed, divorced or married but separated. However, once the age and sex imbalance in the sample is corrected the proportion of single persons is even more striking. (See Table 6.) Even so, the predominance of single persons in the sample was nothing like as great as in institutions.[6] The imbalance between single persons and those who were or had been married was more marked among men than the women in the sample, compared with those in the general population. But the proportion of widowed persons compared with the general population was higher for women than men. In the sample as a whole, the proportion of widowed persons was double that in the nation generally. Thus the persons most likely to be registered as belonging to the general classes of the handicapped by local authorities in the areas studied were those in middle and late years who were single or widowed.

TABLE 7

Social class distribution of persons below pensionable age in the sample, and employed persons in England and Wales

Social Class[a]	Persons interviewed below pensionable age		Employed persons, England and Wales[b]
	No.	%	%
1	0	(0)	4
2	1	(1)	15
3 Manual	37	(38) ⎱	51
3 Non-manual	22	(22) ⎰	
4	19	(19)	21
5	10	(10)	9
Unclassified[c]	10	(10)	0
Total	99	(100)	100

a According to Registrar General's classification.
b Based on figures of the Registrar General, Census 1966, H.M.S.O., London.
c Persons who had never worked, living in households without other persons of employable age.

None of the persons interviewed below pensionable age belonged to Social Class 1, and only one to Social Class 2, compared with almost one-fifth of employed persons in England and Wales. (See Table 7.) This is not perhaps surprising, but it is noteworthy that a majority of those interviewed were classified among those with

---

6. See Abel-Smith, B., and Titmus, R. M., *The Cost of the National Health Service*, Cambridge University Press, 1956; also Benson, S., and Townsend, P., *The Elderly in Long-Stay Institutions*. (forthcoming).

skilled or clerical occupational status. This is much more unexpected. The proportion of persons interviewed in the lower social classes reflected closely that of unemployed persons in England and Wales. It should be remembered that the classification conceals the *fall* in status experienced by some people as a result of their disability. Some persons had been forced into taking less skilled occupations.

Mr. Thompson was in his late fifties and suffered badly with bronchitis. He started life as a blacksmith, shoeing horses for a brewery. He then went into engineering. As his bronchitis became worse he found that he had to take less demanding work. Gradually he found that he had to spend an increasing proportion of every winter away from work because of his bronchial attacks. He was eventually reduced to light casual labour. His present job consists of sweeping the floor of a nearby factory.

Where the onset of a disability makes an immediate impact on a person's capacity for a particular type of work, that person may drop at once to a lower social class.

Mr. Atkinson is fifty-three. His career as a reasonably successful actor was terminated by the onset of polio when he was in his thirties. When he recovered he managed to run a theatrical agency for a time. He soon found that the strain was too great, and he was forced to take work requiring less responsibility and effort. His last job was that of a clerk in a local bookmakers office.

The predominance of persons in Social Class 3 probably reflects the more articulate demand for services among persons of this class than those in lower classes, not greater need.

Summary

The disabled persons interviewed varied widely in type of disability, age and social characteristics. Nearly a third suffered from forms of arthritis and nearly a tenth suffered respectively from multiple sclerosis, hemiplegia and amputations.

Almost two-fifths were aged sixty-five years or over and more than another two-fifths were aged forty-five to sixty-four. Few were in their twenties and none were children. A half were married but a fifth were single. Since a majority were or had been married, it can be said that the population interviewed tended to reflect the type of services provided by local authorities—which help women in the home more than men seeking work, and older people who are more likely to be reconciled to the organization of activities and services by others than younger people, particularly men with wives and children. However, once the age imbalance in the sample is corrected it is clear that in the areas included in the study, single and widowed persons were more likely than married persons to be registered with their local authority.

Compared with the general population, the Registrar General's Social Classes 1 and 2 were under-represented, and Social Class 3 over-represented, among the persons interviewed. This was partly due to a smaller chance of middle-class persons (in professional and managerial occupations) getting certain forms of chronic disability (such as bronchitis and tuberculosis). But the fact that a number of the disabled had experienced downward social mobility should be noted.[7] The disproportionately large number of persons in Social Class 3 using welfare services was probably a reflection of more articulate demand among persons of this than lower classes, not a reflection of greater need.

---

7. Almost one-fifth of those who were employed at the time of the interview had experienced downward social mobility. Over the sample as a whole the proportion would be smaller because of the large number of women who derived their social status from their able-bodied husbands. See the interesting parallel analysis by Goldberg and Morrison of the disproportionately large number of persons in Social Class 5 who enter hospital because of schizophrenia. They showed that when admissions were analysed in terms of parental occupations there was no excess of schizophrenia in Social Class 5. Goldberg, E. M. and Morrison, S. L., 'Schizophrenia and Social Class', *British Journal of Psychiatry*, Vol. 109, No. 463, 1963.

3. INCAPACITY—ITS MEASUREMENT AND EFFECT ON MOBILITY

The persons interviewed suffered from a wide variety of clinical conditions, as we have seen. How far is it possible to compare the extent to which they are 'disabled'? Is it meaningful to compare individuals who are suffering from the effects of poliomyelitis with those who have bronchitis, osteoarthritis, Parkinson's disease and epilepsy? And even among individuals with the same type of disability is it possible meaningfully to distinguish the *degree* to which they are disabled? This chapter will describe a measure which allows us to give positive, if qualified, answers to both these types of question. It is argued that concepts of 'functional capacity', operationally defined, are necessary to the exploration and understanding of disability. After describing the measure and the results of applying it to the persons in the sample the problems of *progressive, fluctuating* and *occasional* or 'suppressed' disability will be discussed and the mobility problems of the disabled will be described.

1. *Government Attempts to Define and Measure Disability*

No satisfactory definition or measurement of handicap has yet been devised. Most definitions themselves beg definition. For example, the conditions of eligibility stipulated by the Department of Employment and Productivity for admission to and retention on the Register of Disabled Persons are that the applicant must :

(1) be substantially handicapped on account of injury, disease (including a physical or mental condition) arising from imperfect development of any organ or congenital deformity, in obtaining or keeping employment or work on his own account otherwise suited to his age, qualification and experience; the disablement being likely to last for twelve months or more.

(2) desire to engage in some form of remunerative employment or work on his own account in Great Britain and have a reason-

able prospect of obtaining and keeping such employment or work on his own account.[1]

No social or other criteria have been laid down as to how a person should be judged to be sufficiently handicapped for inclusion on the Register. No attempt has been made to ascertain empirically what actions, degree of exertion, and so on, are required in different kinds of premises, and how these relate to different kinds and degrees of disability. The interpretation of 'substantially handicapped' is said to depend largely on the medical evidence available. Such evidence is carefully considered by a Disablement Resettlement Officer in relation to a person's employability as well as on the basis of physical injury, impairment or loss of activity. Medical advice is available to the D.R.O. through the Regional Medical Service of the Department of Health and Social Security, the hospital services and general practitioners. The D.R.O. may also obtain advice and guidance from the local Disablement Advisory Committee which includes a doctor amongst its members. However, the medical advice available to the D.R.O. is based on an outline of a person's capabilities which a person's medical practitioner believes he should *avoid* in his employment.

Assessments of disability are also made by the Department of Health and Social Security in awarding war pensions and industrial injuries benefits. These assessments are said to be based on comparison between 'the condition of a disabled person and that of a normal healthy person of the same age. Assessment on this basis measures the general handicap imposed by loss of faculty. Loss of faculty may be defined as the loss of physical or mental capacity to lead a normally occupied life and does not depend on the way in which the disablement affects the particular circumstances of the individual. A normally occupied life includes work as well as household and social activities and leisure pursuits.'[2]

No attempt has been made, however, to discover empirically the conditions which constitute normal employment, household, social and leisure pursuits, and therefore, no attempt can be made to assess how far people with different kinds of disability depart from this norm.

Assessments of disability according to schedules compiled by the Department in terms of percentages of disablement are limited to certain kinds of disability, mainly amputation of limbs. The percentages are determined by the site of amputation. Thus an arm amputated 'below shoulder with a stump less than 8 inches from tip of acromion' and 'amputation of both feet resulting in end-bearing stumps' are both

1. See, The Register of Disabled Persons, *Ministry of Labour Gazette*, July 1964, London H.M.S.O., p. 280.
2. Ministry of Pensions and National Insurance. *Report of the Committee on the Assessment of Disablement.* December, 1965. London H.M.S.O., Cmnd. 2847, p. 4.

assessed as producing ninety per cent disability. Even within the limited scope of the schedules this system produces odd equivalents : the loss of three fingers, the 'amputation of one foot resulting in end-bearing stump', the amputation through one foot proximal to the meta-tarpo-phalangeal joint', and the 'loss of vision of one eye' are each assessed as producing thirty per cent disability.[3] It is difficult to see how these different kinds of disablement can be said to impair equally 'the normal occupied life', especially when the factors con-stituting the normally occupied life remain undefined and undiscov-ered. As a result, the schedules of handicap as applied by the Depart-ment of Health and Social Security bear no direct relationship to what people can actually do. Some persons considered to be 100 per cent disabled and granted pensions accordingly manage to find suit-able work, whereas others classified as fifty per cent or sixty per cent disabled are unable to do so.

Apart from the schedules, the percentage of disability is medically determined for the Ministry, and the various factors that are taken into account have not been studied systematically nor data assembled and presented.

The only guidance given by the Ministry of Health (from 1968 the Department of Health and Social Security) to local authorities when deciding whether a person is suitable for registration is that that person should be considered to be 'substantially and permanently handicapped'.

Britain is not alone in finding it difficult to devise a satisfactory definition and measure of physical disability. In the United States, for example, the disability provisions of the Social Security Act are clumsy. Initially, disability was defined within the meaning of the Act as being 'inability to engage in any substantial gainful activity by reason of any medically determinable physical or mental impairment which can be expected to result in death or to be of long-continued and indefinite duration'. In the absence of any empirically verified criteria by which disability could be evaluated in relation to ability to work, evaluation guides were produced listing 130 impairments. For each impairment were shown the 'clinical and laboratory findings that usually exist when the condition has become so severe that most persons so afflicted would be unable to engage in substantial gainful work'.

It was found that the definition did not answer specifically such questions as: What is 'long-continued and indefinite duration?' What constitutes 'substantial gainful activity?' What is 'medically deter-

3. From provisions of *Royal Warrant of 19th September, 1964*, Cmnd. 2467, London H.M.S.O. From 21 March 1966, some assessments were changed in accordance with suggestions made by the McCorquo-dale Committee. But the principle is unchanged, and equivalents remain odd. *Ministry of Social Security Annual Report 1966*, Cmnd. 3338, London H.M.S.O., p. 5.

minable?' Further definition was required to explain these key terms. Thus 'long-continued' was 'interpreted to exclude any impairment that can be expected to improve to such an extent in the reasonably near future that it would no longer prevent the individual from engaging in substantial work. Moreover, if by reasonable effort and with safety to himself the individual could achieve recovery or substantial reduction of the symptoms of the condition, the impairment would not meet the 'long-continued and indefinite requirement'.[4] It is obvious that some of the key phrases in *this* elaborated definition are likely to be open to different interpretations. For instance, what is meant by 'the reasonably near future', a 'reasonable effort', and a 'substantial reduction of the symptoms of the condition'?

The most difficult phrase in the definition was found to be 'inability to engage in substantial gainful work of any type, and not merely the kind of work the applicant had usually engaged in'. Moreover, there had to be '(1) a reasonable expectation that a medically determinable condition of serious proportions exists that will continue indefinitely and (2) a finding of a present inability to engage in any substantial gainful work because of such impairment'. Again, this elaboration does not help very much. For instance, what exactly is 'a reasonable expectation', and a 'condition of serious proportions'? No objective criteria for answering these questions are provided.

It is admitted that 'the governing factor in determining ability or inability ... is the actual capacity for gainful work as shown by the physical and mental demands of the job, the hours of work, the nature of the duties, the amount of earnings, and the continuity and duration of the effort'. Nowhere, however, was an attempt made to establish how capacity in these terms may be measured. No means were provided for estimating objectively the demands of the job, or the continuity and duration of the effort involved.[5]

2. *The Problem of Definition*

The problem might be summed up as follows. An individual is 'disabled' if he cannot engage in the activities, participate in the relationships and play the roles which are normal for someone of his age and sex. If we are to measure disability we therefore need first to list the activities, relationships and roles which are 'normal'. These might be grouped as *activities* which (a) maintian personal existence (e.g. eating, drinking, evacuating, walking, climbing, washing, dressing); (b) are necessary to managing a home (e.g. cooking, cleaning, making a cup of tea); (c) are necessary to household rela-

---

4. Our discussion here depends heavily on Hess, A. E., 'Old Age, Survivors and Disability Insurance: Early Problems and Operations of the Disability Provisions', *Social Security Bulletin*, U.S. Department of Health, Education and Welfare, December 1957, Volume 20, Number 12.
5. Hess, Arthur, E., *op. cit.*

tionships (e.g. sexual, marital, parental); (d) are necessary to social relationships outside the home (e.g. visiting, travelling, becoming one of a crowd, making friends, being neighbourly) and (e) fulfil instrumental roles inside and outside the home (i.e. occupational activities, whether in paid employment or in relationship to the roles performed at home). Plainly there is room for argument about the activities which are to be included in the list and how far they are independent of, or duplicate each other. Whether or not they are 'normal' or 'common' activities should also be treated, ideally, as a matter for empirical validation.

Second, after listing the activities, we need to allow for the degree to which individuals are capable of carrying them out, or do carry them out. Thus a score of 0 might represent the fact that an individual is capable of undertaking a particular activity without difficulty, a score of 1 might signify that he has difficulty and a score of 2 might signify that he is incapable of undertaking the activity at all. Plainly this kind of ordinal scale can only give a crude indication of 'degree' of capacity.

Third, a system of weighing the different activities has to be developed. Should each activity have equal weight? Should *each* be scored 0, 1 or 2 as above? No doubt we could show that some activities are more important to the individual, and the empirical use of a scale reflecting importance might justify a differential weighting system. Weighting may also be affected by the problem mentioned above of including two or more items in the list of activities which duplicate each other too closely.

Finally, individuals have to be rated according to the system devised. The main difficulty here is whether the measure is equally fair or appropriate to people who differ in sex and age and social circumstances. The particular cluster of activities undertaken by an individual tend to be related to his individual age, marital status and social status, as well as his physical environment. Moreover, there are other difficulties, such as the necessity to rely on *reported* as distinct from *observable* capacity for some of the activities listed, and the difficulties are occasional, fluctuating or progressive.

These difficulties have been discussed at greater length elsewhere.[6] They have been emphasized here simply to call attention to the complexity of the concept of 'disability' and the impossibility of establishing wholly satisfactory scientific criteria of measurement. But a crude index which can be used as a basis for comparison is far better than no index at all. In fact, it is inescapable. In medical and social work practice as well as in common speech, assumptions are continually made about those who are 'severely', 'moderately', or

5. Townsend, P., *The Last Refuge*, London, Routledge, 1962, pp. 257–261, and 464–476.

only 'slightly' disabled. In developing an index we are doing no more than trying to systematize and rationalize professional and common usage.

3. *A Measure of Personal and Household Incapacity*

In the present study a list of activities was drawn up (see Figure 1)

FIGURE 1

A MEASURE OF INCAPACITY

Capacity to perform activity

Activities	Without difficulty 0	With difficulty but without help 1	Not at all or only with help 2
I *Personal Tasks*			
1) Go out of doors on own			
2) Go up and down stairs			
3) Get about house on own			
4) Wash down or bath			
5) Dress and put on shoes			
6) Cut own toenails			
7) Get in and out of bed			
8) Brush and comb hair			
9) Feed self			
10) Go to toilet on own			
II *Household Tasks*			
1) Clean floors			
2) Make a cup of tea			
3) Cook a hot meal			
4) Do the shopping			
III *Physical and Mental Faculties*			
1) See (even with spectacles)			
2) Hear (even with hearing-aid)			
3) Speak			
4) Organize thoughts in lucid speech			
5) Sit or move without falls or giddiness			
6) Control passing of urine			
7) Control passing of faeces			
8) Manage other special disabilities without help			
9) Co-ordinate mental faculties in performing personal services			

and for each person interviewed an attempt was made to establish whether each activity could be performed without help, with difficulty but without help, or only with help. The activities are broadly those which most people expect to undertake in the course of a normal week. In practice none of them are standardized according to _depends or access_

environment. Scoring is based on the individual's ability to perform the activities in the context of his home environment. This means that the scores assigned for a particular activity may be different for two people with an identical degree of disability. For example, one woman may receive a score of 2 for being unable to go to the lavatory unaided because she is unable to negotiate the steps down to the lavatory. On the other hand, another similarly handicapped woman, who is unable to climb stairs, receives a score of 0 for the same activity because there are no steps down to her lavatory. However, there are a number of activities in the list which are independent of the physical environment, and it should be remembered that the environment may make it harder for some activities but easier for others to be performed. A modern flat may have difficult access. A comfortable and prosperous owner-occupied home may be difficult to heat and clean and far from the shops. A house in a working-class street may have a W.C. in the back yard but it may be near to transport and shops.

One point should be made clear about the number of activities in the list. For purposes of broad approximation in general surveys of a population the items in the first two sections would be enough. But in classifying a minority of individuals as between 'severe' and 'moderate' incapacity, for example, it was found that attention had to be paid to general physical and mental faculties. (See Table 9.)

Another problem of standardizing the measure is as between men and women. Sometimes men who were interviewed did not know whether they could do certain household tasks simply because they had never been required to do them. This was particularly true of cooking a hot meal. However, most men felt able to distinguish capacity from customary role expectations.

A few of the people interviewed eagerly demonstrated how they managed to do certain activities. But generally people's affirmation of what they could and could not do had to be accepted. In a long interview consistency of response was found to be important in judging reliability. Self-reports were not, however, invariably accepted. When it was evident that a person was over- or under-estimating his capacities, a note was made and after subsequent consideration, the rating was changed. A few individuals seemed to be trying to appeal to the emotions of a spouse or another relative who was present at the interview by suggesting that they were more handicapped than they were. Others seemed to fear that their independence or privacy might be threatened by bureaucratic social services and tended to exaggerate their capacities. But the great majority seemed to report honestly and realistically. Changes were made to fewer than four per cent of the self-assessments. All this shows that there is no simple procedure which can be adopted in obtaining approximately reliable ratings of disability and also shows how much must inevitably rest on the perceptiveness of the interviewer.

In estimating capacity husbands or wives or relatives were not always reliable witnesses. They tended to overestimate handicapped persons' capacities, just as the latter sometimes underestimated them. On the whole, however, the predominant impression was that both disabled persons and their relatives were generally realistic about their capacities.

In Table 8, the personal and household activities included in the

TABLE 8

Percentage of Disabled Persons unable to perform personal and household activities even with difficulty

| Activities | Unable to perform Activities even with Difficulty | | |
	Men	Women	Men & Women
Clean floors	(74)	70	72
Go up and down stairs	(67)	70	70
Do shopping	(70)	66	68
Cut toenails	(60)	65	64
Go out of doors	(57)	60	57
Cook a hot meal	(59)	32	42
Wash down (or bath)	(41)	28	33
Make a cup of tea	(33)	20	25
Dress and put shoes on	(25)	18	22
Go to the lavatory	(27)	19	22
Get in and out of bed	(17)	15	16
Get about the house	(15)	13	14
Brush and comb hair	(7)	7	7
Feed Self	(2)	2	2
N =	(81)	130	211

capacity index are set out in rank order according to the proportion of persons who were unable to perform the activities even with difficulty. Between three-fifths and three-quarters of the people interviewed could not clean the floors, get up and down stairs, shop, cut their toenails, and go out of doors unaided. On the other hand, only thirteen per cent were unable to get about the house unaided, and only two per cent were unable to feed themselves. Altogether, only fourteen per cent of the persons in the sample were able to perform *all* the fourteen listed activities even with difficulty.

4. Degree of Overall Incapacity

How many of the disabled persons interviewed were severely incapacitated in performing personal and household activities?

After carrying out the enquiry it seemed reasonable to categorize the persons interviewed into four groups according to scores achieved on capacity for the personal and household activities listed in sections

I and II of Figure 1. The maximum score possible—28—was divided equally between the four groups thus :

0 — 7   slightly incapacitated
8 — 14   moderately incapacitated
15 — 21   severely incapacitated
22 and above very severely incapacitated

Although the index of personal and household activities did indeed seem to reflect the general capacities of most of the persons interviewed, they did not accurately reflect those of all. For example, there was sometimes a marked difference in overall capacity between two persons having roughly the same score up to this point in the index. On the basis of further questioning about mental and physical faculties (see Section III of Figure 1) a small minority had to be transferred to other usually more 'severe' categories of incapacity (see Table 9).

TABLE 9

Persons with different degrees of incapacity, according to the index of personal and household tasks only, and of general physical and mental faculties as well

| Degree of Incapacity | Persons incapacitated according to | | | |
| | listed personal and household activities only[a] | | all listed activities[b] | |
	Number	Percent	Number	Percent
Slight (0 – 7)	31	15	27	13
Moderate (8 – 14)	67	32	65	31
Severe (15 – 21)	79	37	76	36
Very Severe (22 & over)	34	16	43	20
N =	211	100	211	100

[a] Activities listed in section 1 and 2 of Figure 1.
[b] Activities listed in all three sections of Figure 1.

Some of the people who had a comparable facility in tackling the chosen personal and household activities varied widely in their faculty to tackle other activities—usually because of disabilities such as deafness, blindness or mental impairment.

Mrs. Johnson, aged sixty-seven, lived alone in the basement flat of a large house in London. She suffered from epilepsy and angina but managed to look after herself without help. 'Except on very bad days I can do all for myself. I get all my stuff at the corner shop, and I get as far as the fish and chip shop down at the main road. I won't have no one to help me. The basement steps are a bit of a job because there's no rail and one of the steps is broken. But I manage not so bad. I don't say anything. I don't often get fits now. I had one last week when I was visiting next door. They used to call the doctor when I got like it, but they just put me on the bed now. You should see the bruises I have next day. It all started eight years ago when I was knocked down in the road. The worst part was having to give up work. I've cleaned all my life. Mind you, it's not being able to see that's really done me. I was not too bad before my eyes started to go. Now I can't read anything. I can see you a blur when you stand in front of the light by the window. The lady came from the welfare yesterday to see about registering me blind. They're going to teach me to read, and perhaps they'll get me a talking book.' Score on Personal and Household Activities: Difficulty going out of doors (1), going up and down stairs (1), getting about the house (1), cutting toenails (1), cleaning floors (1), shopping (1); total 6. Score on Section III of Figure 1: unable to see (even with spectacles) (2), difficult to hear (even with hearing aid) (1); total 3.

Overall score: 9.

Below are examples of each of the four categories of incapacity.

Slight incapacity

Miss Multer, aged twenty-one, lived with her parents and younger sister in a new block of council flats in South London. She worked as a laboratory technician in the Scientific Civil Service. 'I had polio when I was a few months old, but it did not affect me much. I went to ordinary schools, and when I left I got this job. I am trying to get my A-levels at the moment. I don't have trouble doing anything really. My one foot is a bit stiff and turns in slightly, but it doesn't bother me. I could probably get that better if I did my exercises, but I can't be bothered. It's so much trouble for so little in return. Progress is very slow. They have given me a non-slip bath mat but I don't use it because I can never convince myself that it won't slip. I go to work in the normal way—by bus and tube. I don't have any trouble at all, really.' Has difficulty cutting toenails (1).

Total score: one.

Moderate incapacity

Mr. McKenna, aged fifty-six, lived with his wife, son and daughter in a block of new council flats in South London. Mr. McKenna worked as a lift attendant. 'I was wounded in the War in January 1944. I was so badly wounded that they kept on operating—my leg, it was. Then I got knocked down in 1952. That made it so bad that they had to amputate. I've had bronchitis as well for just over two years. Then I had a cartilage removed in the knees. I've had bad trouble in the knees lately. Now they've given me a new leg. It's rigid, so I've got to walk stiff-legged. I've had to have a very heavy leg. Going up and down stairs beats me now. It's the bronchitis. With this stiff leg I can't bend, so the wife has to do the floors and that. I can't carry shopping because I have to have crutches when I'm out. It's a bit of a struggle to get down to the car, but once I'm in that I'm alright. I'm okay indoors on the level because I've got my crutches. Washing down is a bit of a bother but I'm all right as long as there's someone here in case I do something silly. My wife has to help me cut my toenails, but she cuts them too short. I find I can swing myself out of bed with a bit of an effort. I can make a cup of tea because I can lean on something. The hot water's a bit dodgy though. Still, I'd make a cup of tea if I was dying. I can cook in the frying pan and that—but nothing in the oven, of course.' Unable to clean floors (2), do the shopping (2), cut toenails (2). Has difficulty going up and down stairs (1), washing down (1), getting in and out of bed (1), making a cup of tea (1). Total score: ten.

Severe incapacity

Mrs. Guierson, aged thirty-seven, lived with her husband and three years old son in a flat in a new council estate in London. 'I've got multiple sclerosis. It started ten years ago. I found I had double vision when I was working in a cinema. I went into hospital in 1956. It started in my eyes and then worked down to my stomach, back and legs. My arms aren't quite so good now. I think it's getting worse personally. Some days it's worse than others. Today I've got the shakes, but last week I was lovely. I've only been in the chair a year. It's a blessing really. I can do so much more. I can't go out of doors without my sister or my husband takes me. And I can't walk, let alone manage the stairs. My husband has to help me wash down and cut my toenails. I can't go to the toilet because there aren't any rails there yet. We've been waiting for them to come from the council for six weeks. My sister has to do the floors and that, and she takes me shopping in the wheel chair. I get about the house fairly well in the chair, but I take the paint off the doors because they are so narrow. The only place where there's enough space to turn properly is the sitting room. I manage to dress myself if I take my time, but knickers are difficult, so I don't bother indoors. I have to use a hoist and the baby's cot to get myself out of bed. I usually fall back two or three times before I finally manage it. I can do my hair, but I shake like anything. It's the same with cooking, though I don't do anything fancy. My trouble is that I've got no sense of balance. If I try to stand up I just fall down. I even fall around in the wheel chair first thing in the morning. The trouble is that you forget how to walk. So I have a little practice with my husband in the evening.' Unable to go out of doors on own (2), go up and down stairs (2), wash down (2), cut toenails (2), go to the toilet on own (2), clean floors (2), do the shopping (2). Has difficulty dressing and putting on shoes (1), getting in and out of bed (1), brushing and combing hair (1), cooking a hot meal (1).

Total score : 18.

Very Severe Incapacity

Mr. King, aged forty-one, lived with his mother in a semi-detached suburban house with a front and back garden. He worked at home putting rubber in bottle tops for a local firm. He spoke with difficulty. 'I'm a spastic, I used to get fits of convulsions when I was young. The doctor put it down to teething. Then I had a very bad fit at nine months, so Mum took me down to Great Ormond Street and they decided I was spastic. I didn't grow till after I was five. I had an operation: that weakened my stomach and didn't do any good. Mum has to do everything for me and I hate it. I can't go outside without Mum pushes me in the chair. I can't stand, let alone go up and down stairs. I shall be able to get about the house a bit when I get my new wheel chair. It's self propelling. I've only got a big push chair now. Mum has to give me a blanket bath, dress me, and cut my toenails. She helps me to get in and out of bed, too. I can't lift my arms up very far, so she has to do my hair. I can feed myself, but I'm so slow that it all gets cold, so Mum feeds me at dinner time. I haven't got an appetite anyway. I can't use the lavatory, so Mum helps me with the commode. She has to do all the housework. Really all I can do are a few things which aren't difficult with my hands. This job takes me all my time and it makes my wrists ache. I shake a lot, but all spastics do that.' Unable to go out of doors on own (2), go up and down stairs (2), get about the house on own (2), wash down (2), dress and put on shoes (2), cut own toenails (2), get in and out of bed (2), brush and comb hair (2), go to toilet on own (2), clean floors (2), make a cup of tea (2), cook a hot meal (2), do the shopping (2). Has difficulty feeding self (1), speaking (1).

Total score : 28.

As many as fifty-six per cent (119) of the persons interviewed were severely or very severely incapacitated, but only thirteen per cent (27) were slightly incapacitated. (See Table 10.).

There was a clear correlation between age and extent of incapacity. Only a third of those younger than forty-five were severely or very severely incapacitated, compared with more than half of those aged forty-five—sixty-four and more than two thirds of those aged sixty-five and over. (See Table 10.) Either fewer of the younger registered disabled are severely incapacitated or more of them are in institutions. Moreover, very few (four) of the persons aged sixty-five

TABLE 10

Disabled persons of different age with different degrees of incapacity

Degree of Incapacity (score on index)	under 45 years		Age 45–64 years		65 years and over		All	
	No.	%	No.	%	No.	%	No.	%
Slight (0–7)	12	(33)	11	(13)	4	(5)	27	13
Moderate (8–14)	10	(30)	31	(34)	24	(28)	65	31
Severe (15–21)	6	(17)	31	(34)	39	(44)	76	36
Very Severe (22 & over)	7	(20)	16	(19)	20	(23)	43	20
N =	35	(100)	89	(100)	87	(100)	211	100

and over were only slightly incapacitated.

Generally speaking, the differences between the sexes were not marked. However a higher proportion of men than women were severely or very severely incapacitated—sixty-three per cent (51) compared with fifty-two per cent (68). To some extent this difference may be explained by the higher proportion of men than women in the sample aged forty-five to sixty-four years, though it must be remembered that a slightly higher proportion of women than men were aged sixty-five years and above. It may be that more women than men who reach an advanced stage of disability are obliged to enter institutions. More older women than men are widowed and tend to be living alone. If they become severely incapacitated it is difficult for them to continue living at home.

In 1961, 20 per 1,000 (6.9 per 1,000 were men and 13.1 per 1,000 were women) of the total population aged sixty-five and over were living in non-psychiatric hospitals (N.H.S., voluntary and private). Of all men aged sixty-five and over 18.1 per 1,000, and of all women 21.2 per 1,000 were living in such institutions. It must be remembered that of a total population aged sixty-five and over sixty-two per cent were women and thirty-eight per cent were men. For the influence of marital status on the likelihood of aged women as compared with men entering non-psychiatric institutions (i.e. residential homes, and hospitals other than psychiatric hospitals), see Table 11.

There was a clear correlation between degree of incapacity, and the extent to which people went out. Almost nineteen per cent (40) of the persons interviewed said that they went out twice a year or less. None of those who were slightly incapacitated experienced much difficulty in getting about, and they all went out frequently. But almost a quarter (15) of severely incapacitated, and nearly half (20) of very severely incapacitated persons said that they went out twice a year or less.

TABLE 11

Age, sex and marital status of persons aged 65 years and above, in non-psychiatric institutions

Marital Status	General population aged 65 and over (%)		Pop. of non-psychiatric institutions aged 65 and over (%)		No. per 1,000 of each marital group in elderly pop. living in non-psychiatric institutions	
	Men	Women	Men	Women	Men	Women
Unmarried	7.9	16.1	18.7	25.3	42.8	33.4
Married	69.6	33.8	42.7	15.8	11.1	9.9
Widowed/ Divorced	22.5	50.0	38.6	58.9	3.1	25.0
Total	100	99.9	100	100	18.1	21.2

Source: Registrar General, in the Report of the *Census, 1961* (Census figures for England, Wales and Scotland).

5. *Multiple Disabilities*

In developing the overall degree of the functional incapacity of registered disabled persons it is important to stress that inferences have not been made from clinical conditions alone. This would be inappropriate since a high proportion of disabled persons had two, three, or more conditions. About forty-eight per cent had more than one clinical condition, and twenty-one per cent three or more. Even these figures are almost certainly an underestimate. They are based on information supplied by the respondents themselves, and although alternative possible conditions were carefully prompted, some people had their main disability at the forefront of their minds and did not want to think about, or suppressed the thought of minor disabilities. Once or twice another condition came to light later in the interview.

6. *The Incapacitating Effects of Different Clinical Conditions*

How great was the incapacity of persons with different clinical conditions? Paraplegics and those with Parkinson's Disease were the most incapacitated in the sample, although they were relatively few in number—only five. Practically all of them were severely or very severely incapacitated. So were nearly three-quarters of those with multiple sclerosis, who were nearly a tenth of the sample. After these three groups—paraplegics, those suffering from Parkinson's Disease, and multiple sclerotics,—the other groups with a disproportionately large number of severely or very severely incapacitated persons among them were hemiplegics and those suffering from fractures. By contrast, relatively few amputees and epileptics were severely incapacitated. The numbers in the sample were too few to lend themselves to statistical analysis but the differences suggest the value of the functional type of analysis which had been adopted.

7. *Progressive Disabilities*

A large number of persons in the sample had to accept the fact that the extent of their incapacity was likely to increase. Almost three-fifths (121) said that their disability was progressive. Wide variations in the rate of progress both between different clinical conditions and between persons with the same clinical conditions were reported, but these were difficult to assess systematically.

To know that one's physical capacity is inferior to that of others of the same age is daunting enough in itself. But to adjust to the prospect of steady deterioration is an enormous challenge, because, for young and middle-aged persons at any rate, it is so rare.

Some people, such as those with arthritis and bronchitis, found that incapacity increased gradually while others found it increased in sharp steps. The latter sometimes related to cold spells of weather. Some people with disseminated sclerosis reported marked fluctuations over time, saying that occasionally, after depressing spells of more comprehensive incapacity, they reverted to a condition similar to that when the condition had first been diagnosed. Arthritics sometimes associated sharp increases in incapacity with periods spent without adequate exercise in hospital for treatment, often for ailments other than the main condition. In no circumstances did individuals themselves associate increases in incapacity with family troubles, though in a number of instances onset of disability was dated from such events as the death of a spouse, child or parent.

However incapacitated, the majority of people with progressive disabilities continued to want to go to the shops and meet friends. For some of them the physical effort involved was so great that it was difficult to take pleasure in such activities. A very small minority, consisting of some of those who were severely depressed, wanted to cut themselves off from life outside. They found that any social contacts tended to emphasize their disability.

On the whole, few of the people with progressive disabilities would own to experiencing severe depression. Most agreed that they were depressed occasionally but felt that this was probably no more than what the majority of normal people experienced. They were intent on making the best of their increasing loss of independence. One man expressed a common attitude when he said: 'I don't let it get me down. I think that if you use what powers you've got to their limits, you don't get depressed so much.'

Those with disabilities which were obviously more quickly progressive than most, more readily admitted to frequent and severe depression. The realities of considerable and increasing loss of independence were not easily digested. For most, the hope of gaining effective medical treatment was given up. But although some people tried to reconcile themselves to increasing incapacity, everything in their nature and in their history rebelled against it. There were moments when they were swept by sudden and irrational hopes of cure. They did not believe in miraculous cure and yet almost yearned for it. Some had turned to spiritual advice and were now spiritualists, while others attended faith healers.

Depression was experienced particularly by middle aged women who were severely handicapped and lived on their own. Their mental state appeared to be related to their fear that further loss of independence would probably result in their removal to a hospital or a residential home. The following example is perhaps peculiarly ironic in showing how far an ex-nurse, with long (private) hospital experience was prepared to go to avoid institutionalization.

Miss Answell, aged sixty, lived in a semi-detached house in a residential part of Middlesex. 'It's very difficult even to talk now. I'm just a nuisance to myself and everyone else. The trouble is, I don't want to go to hospital until the very last minute. I've just had a bad experience of hospitals. I was having the district nurse in, but they could only come once a day. I had awful bed sores, so the doctor sent me to hospital. I was in a geriatric ward for five months and my bed sores got no more treatment there than they did with the district nurse. The doctor only came round a few times, and when he did my bed sores were never mentioned. So I left and came home. I got myself a full time nurse and a woman to do the cleaning and get me a few meals. The nurse lives here with me with full board and rent free. In addition I pay her £12 a week. The daily gets five shillings an hour. The nurse is very good in some ways. She is keen to get the bed sores cleared up, and they are gradually getting better. But she knocks off at 4.0 p.m. I only call her after that in emergencies. This is the only arrangement that enables me to stay in my own home. But I phoned my bank manager up today and he told me that I've only got £60 left. He's coming round to see me. I don't know what I shall do. There's the house. That could be sold. But where else can I live? I'm sick with worry. I don't want to be taken away yet. I could go on living like this for some time. When I get too bad I shall be at the mercy of those people in the hospital. That's why I don't want to move until the last minute.'

Some married women with quickly progressive disabilities also experienced severe depression, usually because they had largely given up the roles of mother and housewife to husbands who already had a paid job outside the home. On the whole, men were less inclined to become severely depressed. But a number had become depressed at the prospect of loss of employment through increasing incapacity. A progressive disability was particularly frightening for a man who was trying to retain employment in order to maintain his dependent family.

The fear of increasing dependence on others, and changes in marital and parental roles tended to be greater among women than men, and greater in middle age than in old age. Most older men who had become disabled were retired already, and suffered little more from role deprivation on becoming dependent upon their wives than other men of their age. And even those women with progressive disabilities who were elderly tended to attribute their misfortunes to their age and resign themselves accordingly.

> Mrs. Gipson, a large, white haired woman aged eighty, had rheumatoid arthritis, which was progressing quickly. 'Well, duck, there's nothing you, nor I, nor anybody else can do about it. And that's that. It's got to be faced.'

It may be that the elderly accept progressive disability more easily than younger people because the disabled form a much larger reference group among the aged than is true of other age groups.

It is impossible to draw a hard and fast line between progressive and non-progressive disabilities. An amputation is usually quoted as an example of a non-progressive disability. Yet among the amputees who were interviewed there were a number who suffered more than previously from sore stumps and phantom pains. Another example often quoted is poliomyelitis. Yet a number of people who had had polio said that their capacity became more limited as the years went by.

8. *Fluctuating Incapacity*

The incapacity of some people varies little from week to week, or between summer and winter. But other people's abilities fluctuate extremely. It seems that disability can fluctuate according to clinical condition (e.g. multiple sclerosis) or according to climatic condition and season (e.g. bronchitis). Such functions can produce serious problems for the housewife or anyone trying to work outside the home.

> Mrs. Masterton, aged thirty, lived with her husband in a new council flat in North London. Her speech was impaired and she spoke slowly and with great deliberation. Throughout the interview she spent her time attempting to peel potatoes for her husband's evening meal. She had little grip on the knife and her headway was slow. Mrs. Masterton could walk only by clinging on to walls and furniture. 'You've found me at a bad time. A very

bad time. I've been like it for a fortnight now. The doctor's been to see me. I can't do anything in the house really. I expect I shall get over it. I've been like this before. I can't even dress myself properly. That's why I haven't pulled my stockings up. I got them to my knees and then I couldn't be bothered. They've gone right down now though. My husband will have to do the dinner. He's been coming home at midday to get me something and to see that I'm all right. He's been doing the housework and getting the shopping too. I hope it doesn't last much longer because he's missing so much overtime. We need the money: we bought all new furniture to come in here. I get very depressed when I'm like this.' Mrs. Masterton's score on the index of functional incapacity at the time of interview: unable to get out of doors on own (2), go up and down stairs (2), wash down (2), cut toenails (2), get in and out of bed (2), clean floors (2), cook a hot meal (2), do shopping (2), had difficulty getting about the house (1), dressing and putting on shoes (1), brushing and combing hair (1), making a cup of tea (1), speaking (1), sitting and moving without falls or giddiness (1). Total score: 22. On the basis of what Mrs. Masterton said it was possible to estimate roughly what her normal score was: difficulty going out of doors (1), going up and down stairs (1), washing down (1), dressing and putting on shoes (1), cutting toenails (1), getting in and out of bed (1), cleaning floors (1), shopping (1). Total score: 8.

Disabilities such as chronic bronchitis and asthma tend to be aggravated by the weather. Some people were prevented from going to work when it was frosty, wet or foggy, and even those who spent their days in and around the house found that their activities were curtailed.

Mr. O'Keefe, aged sixty-seven, lived with his wife at the top of a tall block of flats in a crowded area of North London. 'The wife goes out to work all day. She has to, to keep us. I like to do some odd jobs in the house and get the shopping and that for her. I'm all right if I take it slowly and the lift's in order. Of course, I'm really done for if the wretched thing breaks down while I'm out. I've had to wait an hour or more sitting on the steps while they mended it. But when it's raining the going's too hard and I have to stay in. Then the wife has to give up her dinner hour doing the shopping. Once October's in, it's a dead cert that I'll be in bed for weeks. The wife has to stay at home to look after me, and then we're back on National Assistance. And if she's been home a month or more she's lucky if her job is still there for her. She's in a laundry now. Even when she goes back she never knows how long it will be before she's got to chuck it in again to look after me.' Score at the time of interview : unable to go up and down stairs (2), has difficulty going out of doors (1), cleaning floors (1), shopping (1).

Total score : 5. During the winter Mr. O'Keefe's score increases considerably for many weeks at a time: unable to go out of doors (2), go up and down stairs (2), clean floors (2), cook a hot meal (2), do shopping (2); has difficulty getting about the house (1), washing down (1), dressing and putting on own shoes (1), getting in and out of bed (1), making a cup of tea (1).

Total score : 15.

Obviously the estimates made here of the variation in incapacity provide only a very rough guide. They are based entirely on the subjective evidence of the respondents. Some people may have under-estimated their 'normal' level of incapacity in order to minimize the extent to which they differed from 'normal' people. Others may have exaggerated, perhaps unwittingly, the fluctuations in their level of incapacity in order to make present misfortunes seem 'temporary'. Only with careful checks over long periods of time against standard activities could more accurate information concerning such fluctuations be obtained. Strangely enough the course of disability has not been systematically charted, so far as we are aware.

Some forms of incapacity are occasional or 'suppressed'. Epilepsy seldom incapacitates in the sense that people cannot undertake every-day personal and household tasks. But it can be handicapping socially. An epileptic fit is a disturbing experience for some people when first witnessed and epileptics often go to extreme lengths to avoid having a fit in public.

Mr. Kendle, aged forty-two, was a messenger lift attendant who lived with his mother at the top of a tall block of council flats in a poor and densely populated area of South London. 'I only get fits now about once a week. It's due to a war wound. I can do everything for myself. There's nothing wrong with me really. But there are social disabilities. I'm all right with friends I know very well. They don't bother if I have a fit. They know what to do. But I can't call in a pub, say, on the way home from work without them. I did once, and I had a fit. They called the police because they thought I was drunk. There was no one there to explain, you see. Then I can't drive a car. Now, driving a car is a normal occupation in our society. But rightly, I'm debarred from it. This means that I have to leave for home early when I'm out visiting, unless there's someone with a car going my way. I've been engaged twice in the last five years. I'd like to get married—it's only natural. Both the girls were all right when I told them about epilepsy, but once they had seen me have a fit, that was it. They thought I would be a hopeless liability. It's not as if I'm a cripple. I go to work and I get a fair wage. What will they do if anything happens to their husbands so as they can't go out to work, and they've got to stay in all the time and look after them? After all, it can happen to the best of people.'

9. *Difficulty with Upper and Lower Limbs*

A person's difficulties varied according to which limbs were affected by the condition. The sample divided into four groups: those whose disability affected their lower limbs; those whose upper and lower limbs were affected; those whose upper limbs alone were affected and those whose limbs were not affected at all. The first was by far the largest; altogether there were 130 people in this category. The second, with both upper and lower limbs affected, contained 59 people. The third, with upper limbs alone affected contained only six persons, most of whom were amputees. There were sixteen people in the final category.

It was of some interest to find that those who had no arms or hands were much better with mechanical aids than those having no lower limbs or having difficulty with their lower limbs. A large array of aids, such as special eating utensils, long-handled combs and 'permanent' collars and ties, had been developed and were being used by persons in the sample. One man spent a happy hour demonstrating how the various attachments to his artificial arm worked. 'I can even peel potatoes with one of the gadgets', he said. 'The only thing that beats me is doing up buttons.'

The lack of really satisfactory artificial legs and aids to mobility—despite the far larger numbers having difficulties with legs than with arms—was repeatedly drawn to our attention. All but one (16) of the persons with artificial legs who were interviewed had a great deal of trouble either because their stumps were sore, or because they suffered from phantom pains. They all found walking difficult, both indoors and out of doors. Slippery pavements in wet weather were a special hazard. Climbing stairs was difficult and even dangerous. Some people preferred to come downstairs backwards. Those who still had their own legs but could use them only to a limited degree found some tasks impossible. Leg supports or substitutes, such as crutches or wheelchairs are remarkably cumbersome. For the chair-bound, there are no neat aids for getting up and down stairs, getting through narrow doorways, or into small bathrooms and kitchens, or making a bed in a confined space. A housewife who cannot move without crutches is prevented in some types of accommodation from cooking, making tea, lighting fires, and so on. An armless person can usually find an aid which enables him to cope with his environment. Usually, the problem for the legless person is how to have his environment altered in such a way as to enable him to attempt certain ordinary personal and household tasks.

Those in the sample whose upper limbs only were affected by their disability were distinguished from two other groups—those whose lower limbs were affected and those whose upper and lower limbs were affected—and their capacities were compared. The first point is that the task which created difficulty for the greatest number of those whose upper limbs alone were affected, was making a cup of tea, which ranked only eighth in importance for the other two groups. (See Table 8 for the list of tasks). By contrast, the difficulty of negotiating stairs ranked ninth in importance, compared with first and second respectively for those whose lower limbs only, and those whose upper and lower limbs were affected. Otherwise there was little difference between each of the groups in the ranking of tasks according to the numbers having difficulty performing them.

Second, those whose upper limbs only were affected by disability tended to be less incapacitated than those whose lower limbs only were affected, though their numbers in the sample were so small that no firm conclusions could be drawn. (See Table 12.) The figures

TABLE 12

Percentage of persons with different limbs affected by their disability who had different degrees of incapacity

Extent of Incapacity (Score)	Limbs affected by disability			Limbs not affected by disability
	Lower only	Upper only	Lower and upper	
Slight (0–7)	7	(50)	8	(38)
Moderate (8–14)	42	(17)	23	(37)
Severe (15–21)	36	(33)	41	(25)
Very severe (22 and over)	15	(0)	28	(0)
Total	100	(100)	100	(100)
N =	130	6	59	16
Mean score	18.8	11	22.1	11.3

in the second and fourth columns of Table 12 are illustrative only of what might prove to be the pattern established after more extensive research. However, the differences between those whose lower limbs only and those whose lower and upper limbs were affected by disability are interesting and important.

10.   *Mechanical Aids*

Not long ago obtaining any aid or artificial limb was the primary difficulty for the disabled. After the introduction of the National Health Service the supply of artificial legs (including pylons) and of artificial arms more than doubled between 1949 and 1964. However, the supply of arm appliances, (i.e. gadget attachments) has remained below the level for 1949. The repair of artificial limbs has increased even more sharply than their supply since 1949 : the repair of artificial legs through the National Health Service has more than quadrupled, while that of artificial arms has increased by more than five times.[7]

Annual Reports of the Ministry of Health reflect the change from concern with the adequacy of the supply of artificial limbs to concern with their development and improvement. For example, the Report for 1949 states that 'the appliances provided ... are of good quality and functionally efficient. No grant in aid is made to patients wishing to obtain a more costly appliance; nor does the Service undertake to pay for appliances obtained by the patient under private arrangements direct from suppliers'.[8] By the following year a more liberal attitude had developed: 'The standard quality of appliance has been good. In respect of certain artificial limbs, a National Health Service patient can, if he desires, select a more expensive article by contributing part of the cost.'[9] The Roehampton Limb Service Headquarters has contributed to the improvement of artificial limbs. The Ministry's Report for 1954 stated, 'Development of new ideas to improve artificial limbs was continued at the Limb Service Headquarters at Roehampton. Particular attention was paid to better methods of fitting sockets and to the special requirements of children with congenital deformities and the elderly; this research work continues.'[10]

In recent years the development and improvement of artificial limbs has been stimulated by pressure groups acting on behalf of certain categories of disabled persons. These groups have not only agitated for research into and the production of improved artificial limbs, they have also stimulated research and production by publicizing advances made in other countries. Conspicuous in this work has been the group led by Lady Hoare, which seeks to further the interests of thalidomide children.

The state provision of motorized and other aids to mobility has increased enormously since the introduction of the National Health Service. This is true both in terms of the different kinds of aids available and the kinds and numbers of people to whom they are supplied. Between 1949 and 1964 the supply of vehicles increased ten times. At present ordinary cars are available under certain circumstances besides carriages, chairs, and tricycles.

7. See, *Report of the Ministry of Health for the year ended 31st December 1954*, Cmnd. 9566, London, H.M.S.O. p. 181, and *Annual Report of the Ministry of Health for the year ended 1964*, Cmnd. 2688, London, H.M.S.O. p. 167.
8. *Report of the Ministry of Health for the Year ended 31st March 1949*, Cmnd. 7910, London, H.M.S.O., 1950 p. 252.
9. *Report of the Ministry of Health for the Year ended 31st March 1950*, Cmnd. 8342, Part 1, London, H.M.S.O. p. 6.
10. *Report of the Ministry of Health for the Year ended 31st December, 1954.* Cmnd. 9566, Part 1, London H.M.S.O., 1955, p. 18.

Originally such aids were available mainly to those who were able to work but were prevented from doing so by lack of public or private transport. The Department is willing in some cases to provide mechanical aids for recreational purposes. Even now the supply of cars is limited to certain groups of disabled persons. (See p. 86.) In practice the rule that vehicles may be supplied only when a garage is available appears to have been waived. Many disabled persons in densely populated areas were quite unable to comply with this rule.

11. *The Value of Mechanical Aids*

The present investigation sought to establish individuals' capacity, whether or not they used mechanical aids. It is true that some would have been rated as very severely incapacitated but for the aids upon which they depended. In the event they were only rated as slightly or moderately incapacitated. There were individuals, for example, who made such good use of wheelchairs, crutches and cars that they were astonishingly mobile. Others became dextorous in the use of hand 'tools'. But the availability of aids was not satisfactory. Many people in the sample would have achieved greater independence if certain kinds of aids had been more generally available. A later chapter will discuss needs. Here we shall discuss the *use* of aids.

There are a wide variety. So-called 'surgical' aids may consist in anything from a boot to a corset. In some instances local authority welfare departments provide simple aids and gadgets, such as pick-up sticks. Handicapped people often invent gadgets for themselves. These include long-handled combs, special eating utensils and pick-up sticks. Some people turn certain mass-produced articles to new uses—prams were used for support and to carry shopping, for example.

Because of the multiplicity of aids and gadgets the use of them by members of the sample cannot all be considered here. Two normal functions will be considered by way of illustration, namely going out of doors and getting about the house. Only about a third of those in the sample were able to get about outside the house without any aid. Of these, over two-thirds managed to do so only with great difficulty. Over a quarter were dependent on a wheelchair and a similar proportion depended on sticks or crutches only. About one in ten depended on a car (of whom over half used sticks and crutches as well). This figure, of course, refers to those who used rather than those who *needed* to use cars. Cars were found to be available to proportionately fewer people in Middlesex and Essex than in London.

A smaller proportion—only fifteen per cent—used a wheelchair for getting about in the home. Another forty per cent either had no need of aids or did not use them if they did. Yet just under two-thirds of those without aids found difficulty getting about the home on their own. It was felt that some of these could have benefited from aids to mobility.

Altogether it seemed that aids made a major 'contribution' to the functional capacity of as many as thirty to forty per cent of the sample. There were individuals, for example, whose score in the index of functional incapacity would have been fifteen or more but for wheelchairs, sticks, and so on, but which were in fact only eight to ten. The average index score was 16.5, and it is estimated that without aids the figure would probably lie around 21.3 (See Table 13.)

TABLE 13

Percentage of disabled persons with varying degrees of incapacity when using and not using aids

Extent of Incapacity (Score)	Including use of aids	Not including use of aids[a]
Slight (0–7)	11	6
Moderate (8–14)	36	10
Severe (15–21)	36	18
Very severe (22 and over)	17	66
Total	100	100
N =	211	211
Mean score	16.5	21.3

[a] The second column is only crudely approximate. It is based on the scores of a sub-sample of 50 persons whose capacities and circumstances were specially evaluated.

12. *Independence*

Throughout this chapter the functional incapacity of disabled persons has been discussed in terms of personal independence. In stressing the desirability of a disabled person attaining the greatest degree of independence possible, present medical as well as social thought and practice has been followed. Yet there is a danger of over emphasizing the adjustments which are expected of the disabled, and forgetting those which society itself needs to make. Welfare and medical provisions, though important, are not enough. For example, help must be offered spontaneously as well as sought. Many disabled people do not like asking for help, but appreciate receiving it.

One man said: 'You've got to accept the fact that you're not like most other people, and you need help. Once you've got that most of your troubles are over. I enjoy a little bit of help, even when I don't really need it. People mean it kindly. And you don't always feel like making the effort to manage on your own. But it has to be offered, you see. I don't like asking.'

Another man said: 'Well, of course I like them all to help me, don't I? After all, what else are relatives and friends for? It's when you're like I am that you find out who your friends really are.'

Most people were able to rationalize their loss of independence satisfactorily.

A woman with multiple sclerosis said: 'I thought when I had to have help that I was losing my independence. Then I thought about it a bit and realized that we all depend so much on one another anyway that the question really didn't arise. After all, I always depended on bus drivers and dustmen and so on. If it comes to that, in a sense, the welfare officer who comes here depends on the disabled for her employment, if you see what I mean. So do you, too. When I got that far, I began to enjoy myself again.'

This statement seems to offer the key both to understanding disability and devising social action to assist. Help is pleasant to receive only when the person who offers it really accepts the fact of disability. However, many disabled people reported that some of their acquaintances found it difficult to know what attitude they should adopt.

One woman said: 'It's one of my criteria for judging people when I first meet them now. If they can't look at me, I know that our relationship is going to be awkward.'

In saying that the disabled should be as independent as possible, it is easy to forget the tremendous expenditure of energy and time which this frequently entails. If a disabled person feels slightly 'under the weather' or has to face extra demands on his time, he just cannot approximate his normal performance.

Miss Didcott, aged thirty, said, 'No one appreciates how tiring it is trying to look after yourself and going out to work. If I feel the least bit ill I have to miss certain things. To sum it up, you spend three times as long doing something as a normal person, and you do it half as well. I think it's a mistake for doctors to keep telling you that you can do things as well as anyone else. I know this is meant to boost morale, but it can work the other way. No one knows what a let down it can be to be told that you are quite normal, and then to do a thing and discover that it's taken you twice as long and you've only done it half as well as you used to. Then if you don't feel well, or if anything extra crops up, it's very difficult to cope with the normal things. Last weekend, for instance, I was going out. I had got home late from the office, so I was pushed for time. Just as I was going to leave, the woman

I live with suggested that, as she had the vacum cleaner out, I should run over my bit before I left. That little bit extra so upset me that by the time I got to the train I found I couldn't get up the steps. I just sat down on the steps and waited till someone came and lifted me up. Normally I can manage perfectly well.'

Some of those who were interviewed felt that they would give up doing certain things for themselves if they had the choice, and they did not feel this would threaten their individuality or freedom. Some resented their relatives and friends for expecting too much of them. They felt under continuous strain to emulate 'normal' physical activity.

13. *Summary*

In the present investigation 'disability' was explored first in terms of capacity to manage personal and household tasks. A measure was devised which took account of twenty-four activities or tasks, ranging from 'cleaning floors' to 'feeding oneself'. Additional questions were devised relating to physical and mental faculties. The measure is of course crude but makes possible a comparison between disabled and 'normal' persons, and between disabled persons suffering from one type of disability and those suffering from another type of disability.

So far as individual activities are concerned, between three-fifths and three-quarters of the sample could not clean floors, get up and down stairs, shop, cut their toenails and go out of doors unaided. By contrast, only thirteen per cent were unable to get about the house unaided, and only two per cent were unable to feed themselves.

Altogether as many as twenty per cent of the persons in the sample had to be categorized on the basis of information on this index of activities as very severely incapacitated. Another thirty-six per cent were severely incapacitated. Only thirteen per cent were slightly incapacitated. On the whole the differences between the sexes were small, though a smaller proportion of women than men were very severely incapacitated.

Incapacity tended to increase with age. Only a third of those younger than forty-five were severely or very severely incapacitated, compared with more than half those aged forty-five to sixty-four and more than two-thirds of those aged sixty-five and over.

Altogether, forty-five clinically defined conditions were represented among the sample. About forty-eight per cent had more than one condition, and twenty-one per cent had three conditions or more. Those suffering from paraplegia and Parkinson's disease were the most incapacitated in the sample, followed by those with multiple sclerosis and hemiplegia. By contrast, relatively few amputees and epileptics were severely incapacitated.

48

As many as three-fifths of those interviewed said they had a progressive disability. The rate of progress appeared to vary considerably both between persons with different clinical conditions, and between persons with the same clinical condition. Quite apart from the consequent psychological and social problems, which will be discussed later, major problems of adaptation in managing everyday personal and household activities were posed. In this study it was difficult to draw a distinction between progressive and so-called 'nonprogressive' disabilities, because even people who had had amputations and poliomyelitis tended to encounter more problems as time passed. Yet even for some whose disabilities were more 'quickly' progressive than most there were periods of recovery or restoration.

There are *fluctuating* and *suppressed* disabilities as well as progressive ones. Internal or external conditions may vary from time to time, or from season to season. Some persons in the sample with chronic bronchitis were much more incapacitated in the winter than in the summer. Some persons with multiple sclerosis found that their condition and therefore their capacities, varied disturbingly from time to time. Others may be able to measure this variation over time, for it is a phenomenon of great importance.

Some evidence was found that, compared with those whose lower limbs were affected by disability, those whose upper limbs were affected were both less incapacitated and better served by aids. Altogether only about a third of those in the sample were able to get about outside the home without any aid. Twenty-nine per cent used a wheelchair, nine per cent used a car or tricycle, and twenty-nine per cent used callipers or sticks or crutches only. Inside the home fifteen per cent used a wheelchair. Another forty per cent used sticks and/or callipers but forty-five per cent used no aids in getting about.

Much of the emphasis placed by medical personnel and social workers on 'independence' appears to be misplaced. Many of the persons interviewed felt that they would function more effectively if their incapacity was honestly recognized, so that 'normal' members of society were not inhibited from spontaneously offering help.

D

Little information is available on the impact of disability on income and resources. Yet it is clear that certain questions relating to disability and income are crucial to any assessment of the financial, employment, and welfare provisions for the disabled. For instance, how does the impact of disability on income vary according to the stage in life at which the onset of disability occurs, and according to the degree of incapacity? How important are factors such as type of employment, social class, education and locality in determining the effect of disability on income? So far little attempt has been made to establish the economic effects of disability on the family and social position of the disabled. Nor is it yet clear how far disability affects the style of living and household resources of families which contain disabled persons.

The only large-scale systematic study of the incomes of the disabled is that produced from the analysis by Brian Abel-Smith and Peter Townsend of data made available by the Ministry of Labour's Family Expenditure Surveys of 1953-54 and 1960.[1] This study revealed that a disproportionate number of low income households contain disabled persons.

However, no field work has been carried out on a comparable scale to document the financial consequence of disability. There have been a few studies which provide some financial data, but they tend to be small in scale or restricted to certain clinically defined categories of disabled persons.[2] Moreover, the definitions of income used have been narrow. Nevertheless, the studies broadly confirm the view that disabled persons tend to have low incomes.[3]

Although the present study involved in a wide range of disabled persons, the number is too small for any but tentative conclusions.

---

1. Abel-Smith, B., and Townsend, P., *The Poor and the Poorest*, Occasional Papers in Social Administration, Bell, 1965.
2. See, for example, Neilson, M. G. C., and Crofton, E., *The Social Effects of Chronic Bronchitis; a Scottish Study*, the Heart and Chest Association, 1965. Also, Lee, M., *The Residue of Poliomyelitis*, Office of Health Economics, Survey 1, 1966. For a crude analysis of income and expenditure, see Stacey, L., and Guthrie, D. (eds.) *A study in poverty. The day to day accounts of five disabled people*, Action for the Crippled Child, March 1966.
3. See also, Viet-Wilson, J., *The Chronic Sick*. (Forthcoming). A study of disabled heads of households.

Furthermore, the data cannot be used to assess the effect of disability on resources over time. In addition, no analysis can be made according to type of household.

The purpose of this chapter is to trace the history of income maintenance, as well as to describe current income and certain assets of respondents, and household income. Resources will be analysed to assess how far the level of income of the disabled persons interviewed compared with the general population and varied according to source. Six main topics will be discussed. First, the development of the provision of resources for disabled persons will be traced. Then, sources of income will be analysed. Next the variations in amounts payable through state benefits to different categories of disabled persons will be considered. Fourth, levels of personal income will be analysed. Fifth, the effect of the lower income levels on the lives of the persons interviewed will be described. Finally, household income will be assessed in relation to the National Assistance basic scale operating at the time of the interviews, and the proportion actually derived from state benefits.

Far more is known about the resources of the elderly than younger disabled persons.[4] Furthermore, for most people a reduction in income is inevitable on retirement. Therefore, most of the succeeding analysis will be confined to the incomes of persons below pensionable age.

However, it is useful to consider briefly first the development of the provision of resources for disabled persons generally. Current methods of allocating resources will be described later in this chapter and other relevant chapters. It is the object of the following account only to try to explain the variety of principles on which provisions are now made.

1. *The development of the provision of resources for disabled persons*

Broadly speaking, provisions fall into three main categories. First, there are those which have developed mainly from the poor law and the work of the voluntary societies which supplemented it. Second, there are cash benefits included in the national insurance scheme which derive from the private insurance schemes of the last century. And finally, there is compensation for damages. Outside this mainstream of development, special provisions have been available since 1916 for the small minority of disabled persons who have been incapacitated by injury or disease sustained as a result of service in the armed forces. As we shall see later, provisions in these different categories are not necessarily exclusive.

---

4. See, for example, Townsend, P., and Wedderburn, D., *The Aged in the Welfare State*, Occasional Papers in Social Administration, Welwyn, 1965.

Until the insurance and compensation schemes of the last century, the only resources available to most disabled persons who were unable to find employment, were those provided under the poor law. From its early days, the poor law distinguished between the unemployed and the unemployable—'the impotent and aged poor' as distinct from the able-bodied poor.[5] Although a distinction had been drawn in previous legislation between the able bodied and other poor persons, it had generally expressed only pious hopes for the relief of the latter, and concentrated on the brutal suppression of the former.[6] However, until the great codification of the Poor Law legislative provisions, such as those of 1547,[7] 1549,[8] reiterated a general concern for the 'impotent poor', but the period was chiefly remarkable for experiments in the relief of the needy carried out by some of the large progressive municipalities. The codification provided the administrative machinery for the relief of the impotent poor which was largely to persist until the nineteenth century. The principles on which its relief measures were based are with us still. The principle was to make provision for the control of those elements of the population which were unable, or refused to conform to the requirement that they maintain themselves and those dependent on them. The object was to protect society. Provision was to be made in three ways—the parish was to provide work for those who were able to undertake it, maintenance for others, and shelter for those who needed it.[9]

Although experiments in the provisions of relief continued, emphasis was placed on minimum cash maintenance allowances and shelter. Responsibility for outdoor relief passed in 1929 to Public Assistance Committees set up by counties and county boroughs, thence in 1948 to the National Assistance Board, and finally to the Supplementary Benefits Commission in 1966.

Supplementary Benefit, like its predecessors, National Assistance, Public Assistance and Poor Relief, is a means tested cash payment. Under the poor law, payments were made only to applicants who satisfied the 'destitution test': savings were expected to be exhausted before relief was granted. The introduction of a variety of disregards, by which certain types of income were ignored in the calculation of relief gradually modified the destitution test.

5. For example, an act for the punishment of sturdy vagabonds and beggars, *27 Henry VIII, c. 25*. The legislation of 1536 was probably based on a paper in the possession of Thomas Cromwell outlining proposals for the eradication of poverty. Its author, who was clearly indebted to Vives for many of his ideas, went further than the subsequent Act in suggesting provisions for seeking out the impotent poor, taking the sick to hospital (at public expense if necessary) and providing free medical treatment. Although the Act implemented many of the suggestions made in the paper, it failed to provide for adequate administrative machinery. See, Elton, G. R., An early Tudor Poor Law, *Economic History Review*, Second Series, Vol. 6, 1953–4.
6. See, for example, An act concerning the punishment of beggars and vagabonds, *22 Henry VIII, c. 12*.
7. *1 Edward VI c. 3.*
8. *4 Edward VI, c. 16.*
9. *39 Elizabeth c. 3.*

Because of the difficulties of definition it is impossible to assess the proportion of disabled persons who were given relief under the poor law. In 1893, the Charity Organization society could provide no estimate, and it was content to apply to Britain German estimates of the incidence of epilepsy—about one per thousand of the population. A survey of more than 50,000 school children showed that about five per thousand of them suffered from some physical disease or deformity other than those affecting the eyes. Of these disabled children, two-fifths attended poor law or certified industrial schools.[10] However, more reliable estimates are available for the number of blind persons among the general population. For example, the Census of 1871 revealed that there were 2,890 blind persons in the Metropolis, of whom about seventeen per cent were probably in Metropolitan Poor Law Institutions.[11]

In 1948 local authorities retained their responsibility for providing places in residential institutions, while responsibility for medical treatment passed to the National Health Service. But by 1948, the emphasis was shifting from indoor to outdoor relief in kind. For the most part, the local authority services making provision for relief in kind were based on those which had been developed by voluntary societies to supplement the Poor Law cash payments during the previous century. In the second half of the nineteenth century some voluntary societies had begun to undertake case work among disabled persons living in their own homes, and to distribute aids and gadgets. For example, the Invalid Children's Aid Association appointed a 'lady visitor' for each of its twenty-seven districts in London; in all, the Association had 200 visitors by 1893. A nurse describes her duties:

'I make friends with the mother as a preliminary to being allowed to give the child a good wash, and then a flannel nightgown and red bedjacket are recognized by all concerned as a great change for the better. Possibly a cot and blankets are lent, and a wicker guard or bed-cradle is placed in position to keep the weight of the clothes off the limb. One poor little boy I found, who used to lie with his knee up to keep the clothes from pressing on his thigh. I give the mother hints as to food, and furnish her with a feeding-cup and other appliances required by the child's position....'[12]

It is interesting to compare this account with the work currently

---

10. Charity Organization Series, *The Epileptic and Crippled Child and Adult. A report on the present conditions of these classes of afflicted persons, with suggestions for their better education and employment*, 1893, pp. 108–9.
11. 'By courtesy of the Local Government Board the Committee have been furnished with statistics which show that in July 1875, 493 blind persons were inmates of Metropolitan Poor-Law Institutions.' Report of a Special Committee of the Charity Organization Society, *Training of the Blind*, 1876, p. 5.
12. Charity Organization Series, *The Epileptic and Crippled Child and Adult; a report on the present conditions of these classes of afflicted persons, with suggestions for their better education and employment*. London, 1893, pp. 123–124.

carried out by local authority welfare officers. (See Appendix 1). Permissive powers were given to local authorities to set up such schemes themselves, and to register the disabled persons with whom they were in contact under Section 29 of the National Assistance Act, 1948. It was not until 1960 that the establishment of special schemes for disabled persons became mandatory. Moreover, the domiciliary services which were developed by local authorities mainly to enable elderly incapacitated persons to remain in their own homes—for example, home helps, chiropody and bathing services and meals services—have been extended to benefit younger disabled persons too. Together they form part of an extensive system of relief in kind. Like supplementary benefit, most of these services are means tested. But whereas cash payments are based on a single means test by the central government, each local authority devises its own means test for the provision of services.[13] And as we shall see, local authorities vary enormously in the standard and extent of their provision.[14]

The third aspect of the Elizabethan Poor Law was the parish stock of hemp which provided work for those who could not find employment. By the nineteenth century, little attempt was made under the poor law to provide work for the disabled. The experience of most disabled persons was said to accord with that of epileptics, which was described by the C.O.S. in 1893:

> 'The life of an epileptic may soon be told. As a child, he is not educated. As a young man, he fails to obtain employment, or, obtaining it with difficulty, he keeps it only on sufferance. As years advance and strength decreases he retires to the workhouse or to the asylum.'[15]

Yet the desire to offset the cost of those who were unable to work in full time open employment was as strong as it had been earlier. In fact, the mounting cost of poor relief was increasingly feared. It was argued that the burden of relief as much as a mass of uncontrolled poor threatened the order of society. For the general population the answer was held to be national education and vocational training.[16] However, where special provision was required for disabled persons, it was left largely to the voluntary bodies to produce a solution. For example, the Charity Organization Society, if only to justify its own belief that all but the morally weak could become self-reliant, interested itself in the problem of educating, training and employing disabled persons. A principle which was becoming increasingly popular in some continental countries in the second half of the nineteenth

---

13. See, Reddin, M., 'Local authority means-tested services', *Social Services for All.* Fabian Tract 382, 1968.
14. See Chapters 8 and 9, and Appendix 3.
15. *The Epileptic and Crippled Child and Adult; a report on the present conditions of these classes of afflicted person, with suggestions for their better education and employment,* Charity Organization Series, London, 1893, p. 17.
16. For the fears which motivated pressure for reforms in education and vocational training, see, for example, the evidence given to the *Select Committee on the Education of Destitute Children,* 1861.

century was adopted by the C.O.S.: certain types of disabilities require their own specific methods of social training. Following closely on congresses held in Vienna and the United States, the C.O.S. produced a report in 1876 on the condition of the blind.[17] The report advocated more infant and industrial training for the blind. It was felt that organizations for the blind should seek to reproduce normal factory conditions in their workshops, and that where possible, the blind should work among sighted persons. In this respect, the report drew heavily on the experience of Saxony and the United States.[18]

There followed in 1877, a report on 'idiots, imbeciles, and harmless lunatics',[19] which again, emphasized training and education. However, it was not for another twenty years that a study was produced on the condition of epileptics and other physically handicapped persons. Once more the C.O.S. advocated education, training, and employment, preferably in homes and colonies, on the Continental, particularly the Swedish pattern. Thus voluntary bodies were urged to take the blind, subnormal, epileptic and crippled persons away from their lives of dependence in the workhouses, and train them to maintain themselves. Segregated from the community in general as they were in the workhouse, some groups of disabled persons were now to be segregated from others. Indeed it could be argued that though the workhouse population was segregated it was *more* of a communtity, (i.e. a motley collection of people of all ages) than the segregated population of the disabled. The principle of developing special techniques to meet the needs of certain groups of disabled persons initially affected the organization of local authority services. Under its influence, voluntary effort on behalf of disabled persons had fragmented, until separate organizations existed to work on behalf of disabled persons with particular disabling conditions. Thus fragmentation was already built into the structure of all services for the disabled when they were taken over by the local authorities, not merely those related to education and training. Certain categories of persons were catered for separately—the blind, deaf, mentally handicapped, mentally ill, and the general classes of the disabled. Only recently has it become possible to begin to integrate services once more. However, integration may be more difficult for voluntary societies: it is possible that it is easier to raise money for a particular condition than for disabled persons generally.[20]

The education of disabled children is among the general education responsibilities of local authorities. Following the C.O.S. reports,

---

17. Report of Special Committee of the Charity Organization Society, *Training of the Blind*, 1876, p. 19.
18. *Ibid.*, p. 10.
19. Report of Special Committee of the Charity Organization Society, *The Education and Care of Idiots, Imbeciles, and Harmless Lunatics*, 1877.
20. It is impossible to assess personality and other factors which are likely to affect the success of individual charitable organizations. But it may well be that, say, guilt associated with a particular group of disabled persons explains the relative success, for example, of Lady Hoare's appeal on behalf of thalidomide children, compared with those appealing on behalf of autistic children.

little was immediately provided at a national level for the education and training of the disabled. The Elementary Education Act, 1893, went some way towards meeting demands for the education of the blind and deaf. In 1899, the Elementary Education (Defective Children) Act encouraged education authorities to provide schools for educationally subnormal and epileptic children, and made their attendance at such schools compulsory. Those deemed ineducable attended training centres provided by local authorities under the National Health Act. Over the last few decades it has become clear that sporadic education remains the lot of many physically handicapped children. The provision of special schools for the disabled is beset by all the problems of assessing needs, defining disability, and so on. Moreover, provision for small minorities raises the difficulty of the satisfactory distribution of schools, particularly at the secondary level: the situation has drawn complaints of 'the extreme dearth of facilities designed specially to bring grammar school education within the reach of the physically handicapped.'[21] In remote rural areas the problem is particularly difficult.[22] It is probable that those disabled persons who are most succesful in maintaining jobs are clerical or skilled manual workers,[23] but ability to secure such jobs is at least in part determined by the standard of education achieved.

The state has now largely taken over from voluntary organizations the provision of vocational training schemes. Most of the training available became the responsibility of the Ministry of Labour (since 1966 the Department of Employment and Productivity) under the Disabled Persons (Employment) Act, 1944, and the Employment and Training Act, 1948. In addition, within the employment exchange structure, special facilities have been established for those disabled persons who wish to take advantage of registration and the services of the disablement resettlement officer in seeking work.

Furthermore, to ensure the employment of at least some disabled persons, those firms employing twenty or more persons are required to employ a 'quota' of disabled persons, amounting to three per cent of their employees. Certain types of work have been designated to be carried out by the able-bodied only if no disabled person is available: at present only the work of passenger lift attendants and car park attendants is so designated.

Local authorities are empowered as part of their responsibility to establish welfare schemes for the disabled, to provide sheltered employment for those who are unable to work in normal conditions. But most local authorities have concentrated on providing diversionary

21.Clarke, J. S., *Disabled Citizens*, George Allen and Unwin, 1951, p. 123.
22.See Montgomerie, J. F., *The Handicapped Person*, The Scottish Council of Social Service, 1958 pp. 14–15.
23.Ferguson, T., and Kerr, A. W., *Handicapped Youth: a report on the employment problems of handicapped young people in Glasgow*, O.U.P., 1960.

occupation for the disabled in centres. Some approved voluntary organizations, too, provide sheltered employment. But by far the most important source of sheltered work is Remploy Limited, a non-profit making company. In the mid-forties it was estimated that there were about 12,000 severely disabled people unemployed, and that 136 factories were required to provide work for them. In 1949, however, it was decided that only ninety were required, and these have been built since 1952. Remploy Limited receives a considerable government subsidy.[24] Those with approved schemes may receive payments from the Department of Employment and Productivity in respect of expenses incurred. Maintenance allowances are paid by the Department to trainees and grants are made towards meeting trading losses and expenses incurred in training and employment, as well as for approved capital expenditure.

The cash benefits provided for the disabled under the National Insurance Act—sickness benefit and industrial injuries benefit and disablement benefit—grew out of a desire to provide for those who were unable to earn a living without forcing them to experience the indignities associated with the poor law. Until 1897, the only sources of support for the destitute apart from the poor law were benefit clubs, charities, and damages for those who had been injured and could successfully prosecute for negligence. But the first Workmen's (Compensation for Accidents) Act made special provision for persons injured at work : it was now sufficient to prove that he had been injured as the result of an accident 'arising out of and in the course of employment', unless it could be shown that the injury was due to his own serious and wilful misconduct. The principle according to which compensation was paid was loss of earnings; thus the amount of compensation paid was not necessarily related to the degree of disability. Neither the state nor the workman contributed to the scheme: compensation was entirely the responsibility of the employer. The trade unions were opposed to the system which was financed through private insurance because it was felt that it was inevitably weighted in favour of the insurance companies and the employers.

A further drawback was that only certain industries were covered by the scheme.[25] When Beveridge reviewed the scheme, he advocated grafting it on to the proposed scheme for national insurance, and replacing the Workmen's Compensation Act by a scheme involving compulsory contributions by, and complete coverage for, all employed persons. Another departure from the principles of workmen's compensation was involved in the scheme embodied in the National Insurance (Industrial Injuries) Act of 1946: the basis for compensation

24. See Remploy Limited, *Annual Review and Accounts.*
25. For an analysis of the disadvantages of the Workmen's Compensation scheme, see Young, A. F. *Industrial Injuries Insurance,* Routledge and Kegan Paul, 1964.

for injuries which resulted in long term disablement was degree of disability, as it was for war disability pensions, and not loss of earning power. But, like other national insurance benefits, payments were also determined by need. Need was assessed according to the cost of living while a supplementary allowance was devised to compensate for loss of earnings.

The social insurance scheme onto which the industrial injuries scheme was eventually grafted was first established in 1911. Friendly, and other Approved Societies administered a system of health insurance which provided cash benefits and medical treatment for those covered by the scheme. In addition, the Board of Trade administered a limited scheme of unemployment benefits. The schemes of social insurance were gradually expanded until the national scheme was established by the National Insurance Act, 1946. Administered by the Ministry of National Insurance until 1953,[26] and thereafter by the Ministry of Pensions and National Insurance until 1966 when it became the Ministry of Social Security, the scheme has been the responsibility of the Department of Health and Social Security since 1968. For younger disabled persons, the most important benefits are probably those for sickness and unemployment. These and the other main benefits included in the scheme are contributory, and are payable only in cases where the contribution record satisfies the Minister's requirements. The main benefits under the national insurance scheme are payable according to need in so far as special allowances are made for dependents. Since 1966, an earnings related supplement has been payable for up to six months to persons receiving unemployment, sickness or injury benefit. Unlike the cash payments and other benefits which have developed from the poor law, unemployment and sickness benefit are not means tested : they are payable irrespective of savings and other personal income. However, an earnings rule determines whether dependance allowances may be paid to recipients in respect of a spouse and children.

Pensions for those suffering from injury or disease as a result of service in the armed forces were introduced during the First World War. The scheme, which also provided for medical treatment and artificial limbs, was administered by the Ministry of Pensions, which was established for the purpose in 1916. In 1953, the Ministry of Pensions was amalgamated with the Ministry of National Insurance for the purposes of paying pensions, while its medical responsibilities were undertaken by the National Health Service.

Although the principles devised for the payment of pensions to the war disabled were adopted for the industrial injuries scheme, war pensions, like family allowances, are not paid out of an insur-

26. For an account of the development of the administrative machinery devised for the scheme of national insurance, see King, G. S., *The Ministry of Pensions and National Insurance*, Allen and Unwin, 1958.

ance fund, but from money voted annually by Parliament. The difference has been justified thus: 'The war pensions scheme is part of the conditions of a man's service in the armed forces and has nothing to do with insurance....'[27] In 1948, welfare officers were appointed to the Ministry's main offices and the hospitals administered by the Ministry. Their purpose was to ensure that war pensioners received the relevant rehabilitation and resettlement services. In addition, members of local War Pensioners Committees and other volunteers visit those who are unemployable in the hope of interesting them in craftwork and hobbies.

Other cash payments are made to disabled persons which are outside the development of the poor law and national insurance schemes—namely, compensation for damages. A man may claim for damages were it can be proved that an injury has been caused by a breach of the Factory Acts or by negligence. The object of the payment of damages is to help to compensate for an injury and to try to prevent accidents in the future. But the burden of proof lies with the injured person. In fact most claims for damages are settled by agreement between the parties before the case gets to court, because legal proceedings are expensive and often take a long time to finalize.[28] Using a sample of 297 contested cases, the Winn Committee found an overall average delay of 37 months from accident to judgement. There are other difficulties attached to the process of compensation for personal injuries. Because of the limitations of the Factory Act, some injuries may result in a successful claim for damages whereas others, which result from similar circumstances, do not. Judges have a scale by which compensation is assessed, but there is no clear rationale for the scale.[29] Moreover, in spite of the difficulties of prognosis, in the assessment of compensation account has to be taken of the way in which the injury might develop. The payment of compensation in lump sums involves other difficulties: some account must be taken of the possible effects of inflation; and it is difficult to advise on the best method of investment. Yet in the final analysis, these are payments made by society at large, because in most cases defendants are insured.[30] Moreover, only a small proportion of persons injured in accidents are able to claim damages.

It is important to note that one major group of disabled persons receive no cash benefits as of right—housewives who are not eligible for sickness benefit, are not disabled as a result of disease or

27. King, G. S., *The Ministry of Pensions and National Insurance*, Allen and Unwin, 1958, pp. 14–15.
28. For a brief introduction to the rights of persons injured at work, see Thompson, R., and Thompson, B., *Accidents at Work*, Twentieth Century Press, London, 1968 (Third edition). For general background on awards for damages, see Ison, T., *The Forensic Lottery*, Staples Press, 1967.
29. See Clark, G. de N., Compensation for Personal Injuries – Damages and Social Insurance, *Law Society's Gazette*, July 1967.
30. For an analysis of the problem involved in the present system of compensating for personal injuries see Clark, G. de N., Compensation for Personal Injuries – Part II, *Law Society's Gazette*, August 1967, and Part III, *Law Society's Gazette*, September 1967.

injury arising out of employment or service in the armed forces, and cannot claim damages. It is true that such a housewife may obtain resources in kind from the local authority: for example, she may be supplied with a ramp and receive help in the home. But unlike cash benefits, the provision of resources in kind is not standard. Moreover they are usually means tested according to locally determined criteria, which take into account her husband's income.

2. *Sources of personal income*

What were the financial circumstances of the persons in the sample? Only twenty-six per cent (29) of persons below pensionable age derived most of their personal income from earnings. Of these, about two-thirds were entirely dependent upon earnings. The remaining third received state benefits as well. A further three per cent (7) of the sample were employed part-time, usually at home. With the exception of two housewives, they received state benefits as well as part-time earnings. However, as we shall see, home work was merely a means of supplementing state benefits. Only a third of the men in the sample below pensionable age derived all or most of their personal income from earnings. But the proportion of women was even smaller—less than a fifth.

As many as fifty-four per cent (65) of persons below pensionable age derived all or most of their income from state benefits. Almost three-quarters of the men (35) but less than half of the women (23) belonged to this category.[31]

State benefits available to disabled persons are not uniform either in terms of the methods of assessment or the amounts of money provided. Eligibility for the different benefits is determined by the cause of disability. Benefits fall into three main categories.

First there are the specific disability awards, war disablement pensions and the benefits available under the industrial injuries scheme. Only a small minority of persons in the sample (seven per cent) received these benefits. Injury benefit is a flat rate benefit awarded to persons whose incapacity for work results from an industrial accident or prescribed disease 'for a maximum period of six months from the date of the accident or the development of the disease'.[32] Industrial injuries disablement benefit is a long term benefit for disablement or disease 'arising out of or in the course of employment'. Except where there is no incapacity for work, or in cases of pneumoconiosis and byssinosis, its payment usually follows a period of injury benefit. Degree of disability is determined by medical

---

31. By contrast, income from state retirement, old age and widows' pensions, and other state benefits amounted to 7.9 per cent of household income for all households at the time. See Ministry of Labour *Family Expenditure Survey Report for 1965*, London H.M.S.O., p. 20.
32. Since October 1966 recipients of injury benefit, like unemployment benefit are paid a wage-related supplement for the first 6 months off work.

boards and expressed in percentages of disability. Medical assessments of disability take no account of loss of earnings, though a claimant may be entitled to supplementary allowances to meet certain specified needs including loss of earnings. Recipients of disablement benefit and its supplements other than unemployability supplement, may also claim other benefits of the national insurance scheme to which they are entitled, such as sickness benefit. The allocation of service disablement pensions follows a broadly similar pattern.

The majority of persons receiving industrial injury disablement benefit are assessed at only twenty per cent disability. Indeed, there are almost nine times as many people receiving benefits of between twenty and fifty per cent as there are between sixty and one hundred per cent disability. Although no systematic studies have been undertaken to compare assessments of percentage disability with degree of incapacity, it seems reasonable to suppose from the information available that only persons assessed at fifty per cent disability or more are seriously incapacitated. It may be that persons with service disabilities are more generously assessed than the industrially injured: a far higher proportion of war disablement pensions than industrial injury disablement benefits are for disabilities assessed at 100 per cent.[33]

The second category of disabled persons below pensionable age who are entitled to state benefits are persons in receipt of sickness benefit. People who have been normally employed may receive benefit if their contributions satisfy the Ministry's requirements. Unlike the specific disability benefits, in the payment of sickness benefit no attempt is made to place a cash value on the degree of disability.[34] Moreover, payment ceases on the recipient's return to employment. In fact, sickness benefit was the most important single source of income for younger persons in the sample. As many as thirty-two per cent (36) of the people below pensionable age received sickness benefit. Understandably, the majority of these (26) were men. All but two of the men who received sickness benefit were married. Thus, more than half (41) of all the married men interviewed below pensionable age were dependent upon sickness benefit as the major source of their income.

The third category of state benefit recipients were those in receipt of national assistance. National assistance[35] is payable as the main source of income to persons between the ages of sixteen and retirement where they are unable to work through sickness or disability, and are not in full-time education, nor housewives dependent on a husband's

3.Based on figures published in *Ministry of Social Security Annual Report, 1967.* Cmnd. 3693, London H.M.S.O., pp. 89 and 99.
4.Since October 1966 an earnings related supplement is payable for the first six months for which sickness benefit is received according to contribution record.
5.From October 1966, national assistance became supplementary benefit.

earnings, and are not entitled to sickness or other benefits. National assistance is also payable where necessary to raise the income of those dependent upon other benefits to the officially determined minimum levels of income. Altogether, eleven per cent of persons below pensionable age (13) were dependent upon national assistance. Almost all were single persons. Thus, for about a quarter of all young unmarried persons (42) in the sample, national assistance was the main source of income.

The five remaining younger persons in the sample (four per cent) who were not dependent housewives derived their main income from other sources: two women were dependent on income from property; two women received widow's pensions and claimed no other support; and one woman received maintenance for herself and her two children.

There are two important groups of younger disabled persons who are entitled to no state benefits: the first are married women who are not normally employed, or whose contribution record does not entitle them to indefinite continuation of sickness benefit—for example, those who have opted out of the payment of National Insurance contributions; the second group are disabled dependent children. As many as eighteen per cent (20) of younger persons in the sample received no personal income. All were married women. Altogether, two-thirds of the married women in this age group (29) were without a personal income.

3. Variations in amounts payable through state benefits to different categories of disabled persons

The amounts of income from state benefits available to the various categories of disabled persons are far from uniform. As we have seen, the amounts paid to the industrially injured and war disabled vary according to percentage disability. Flat rates are payable according to contribution record for sickness and unemployment benefit,[36] regardless of degree of disability. Recipients of national assistance (now supplementary benefit) receive flat rates too, though extra discretionary allowances are available to those of them who have certain special needs. In addition, supplementary allowances are available to the war and industrially injured to meet the special needs arising from their disability. A greater variety of supplementary allowances are available to the war disabled than the industrially injured. For persons receiving sickness benefit and national assistance there are no regular supplementary allowances of this kind to meet the special needs which may arise from disability. However unlike other benefits, war and industrial injury benefits do not usually

---

36. Since 1966, a wage related supplement has been payable for the first six months of sickness according to contribution record, to recipients of sickness and unemployment benefit.

include supplements for dependents. Furthermore, war and industrial injury pensioners who are not employed may receive disablement benefit and supplementary allowances in addition to any sickness benefit to which their contributions may entitle them. Moreover, a higher proportion of war and industrial injury benefits than of other benefits is disregarded in the assessment of national assistance. The inequalities extend beyond the normal working life: unlike sickness and unemployment benefits industrial injury benefit and war disablement pensions continue to be drawn after retirement.

Some of the differences in the amounts of state benefit payable according to cause of disability to a married non-employed man (100 per cent disabled with two dependent children aged eleven and nine years), are shown in Table 14. But persons dependent upon sickness

TABLE 14

The benefits which were available to a non-employed married man, assessed as 100 per cent disabled (wife not working) who had two dependent children aged 9 and 11 [a]

| Allowances | Type of benefit received | | | |
	War disabled	Industrially injured	Sickness benefit	National assistance [b]
	£ s. d.	£ s. d.	£ s. d.	£ s. d.
100% disabled man	6 15 0	6 15 0	4 0 0 ⎫	6 5 6
Wife	2 10 0	2 10 0	2 10 0 ⎬	
Child aged 11	1 2 6	1 2 6	1 2 6 ⎭	13 6
Child aged 9	14 6	14 6	14 6	7 0
Unemployability	4 7 6	4 0 0	None	None
Constant attendance	2 15 0	2 15 0	None	None
Comforts allowance	1 0 0	None	None	None
Total payable [b]	19 4 6	17 17 6	8 7 0	9 6 0 (+ housing cost)

[a] Based on information supplied in the *Report of the Ministry of Pensions and National Insurance for the year 1965*, Cmnd. 3046, H.M.S.O., London.
[b] National assistance was available to those receiving other benefits whose resources were below the national assistance minimum level.

benefit or national assistance may receive less than half the amount paid to an industrially injured person with the same degree of disability and number of dependents. Yet together, sickness benefit and national assistance were the most important sources of income for persons below pensionable age in the sample: only seven per cent received war disablement or industrial injury benefit compared with forty-three per cent who received sickness benefit or national assistance. Thus, cause of disability may result in a difference of as much as fifty per cent in payments derived from state benefits.

In comparing the income payable through state benefits it must be remembered that the average wage in the area at the time of the interviews was £16.75.[37] Furthermore, a man assessed as being 100 per cent disabled who successfully claimed damages at common law, may have been awarded as much as £25,000 by the court.

4. *Levels of personal income of disabled persons*

Regardless of source, on average, the personal weekly income of the younger disabled people who were interviewed was well below average weekly earnings for persons in all occupations in the South East at the time.

On average, wage earners were by far the best off among the persons interviewed. In analysing income derived from wages, no account has been taken of earnings obtained from home work. The earnings of younger persons engaged in home work ranged from eighteen shillings to £2 17s. 3d. per week, and averaged only £1 12s. 8d. per week. Thus, for the persons interviewed, home work was not a substitute for a job in open employment, but merely a means of supplementing a state benefit.

Even for those fortunate persons who were able to find full time employment outside the home, wages were not high. The earnings of persons in full time employment ranged from £5 0s. 0d. to £48 0s. 0d. per week, but the average was only £12 2s. 0d. compared with £16 7s. 0d. for the South East generally.[38] It was ironic that low wage earners tended to be less incapacitated than others. Whereas almost half of those whose earnings were below the average for the group as a whole were slightly incapacitated, this was true of only three tenths of persons whose wages were above this average. However two-fifths of wage earners were women, and in no case was a woman's earnings as high as the average for the group as a whole. Earnings for women ranged from £5 0s. 0d. to £10 6s. 0d. while the average was only £6 17s. 0d. whereas the mean for women of all occupations in the South East was £9 4s. 0d.[39] However, only two-sevenths of employed men earned less than the average for the group, the range being from £6 0s. 0d. to £48 0s. 0d. Even so, earnings for men averaged only £16 11s. 0d. compared with £20 5s. 0d. for men of all occupations in the South East at the time.[40] Yet two-thirds of disabled persons in full time employment were the principal sources of income for their households.

On the whole, people were grateful to find work, and tended to be unwilling to express discontent with low wages. Nevertheless, it was the view of some people that there were employers who exploited the disabled by deliberately paying low wages.

Even so, on average, weekly earnings were higher than the weekly

37. See Ministry of Labour, *Family Expenditure Survey, Report for 1965*, London, H.M.S.O., p. 8.
38. See Ministry of Labour, *Family Expenditure Survey, Report for 1965*, London, H.M.S.O., p. 8.
39. *Ibid.*, p. 7.
40. *Ibid.*, p. 6.

incomes of those who depended largely on disability pensions. The number of younger persons in the sample who received disability pensions was too small for firm conclusions to be drawn. War disablement pensions averaged £2 15s. 6d. per week, and industrial injury benefits £4 6s. 0d. Little systematic evidence is available of the circumstances in which supplementary allowances are made to those receiving war or industrial injury benefits. The conditions which determine the award of supplementary allowances are spelt out in the Ministry's annual reports. But it is difficult to evaluate the basis on which awards are made in practice. Even the full allowance would not cover the cost of constant attendance. The experience of some persons in the sample showed that attendance during the day was likely to cost £12 a week in addition to the provision of rent free accommodation and free meals. Nor was the allowance an adequate recompense for a wife who had to stay at home to look after her disabled husband rather than go out to work. For her it involved a loss not only in terms of income, but of companionship outside the home.

For persons in the sample, most disability pensions amounted to only small sums. But even a pension for twenty per cent disablement raised the income of a man with average male earnings for the sample as a whole by ten per cent.

These findings are in line with the position nationally shown in the facts presented by the Ministry. Most people who receive state disability pensions receive only small amounts. The supplementary allowances available to the seriously disabled war pensioners and industrially injured do not represent either the cost of employing help or the sacrifice of a wife from not going to work. But compared with other, non-employed disabled persons, recipients of war disablement pensions and industrial injury disablement benefit were well off. The average weekly income of those mainly dependent on sickness benefit and national assistance was less than half the average weekly earnings of persons in the sample. Yet together, these two benefits were the main source of income for almost half (49) of the persons in the sample below pensionable age. Predictably, persons dependent mainly upon national assistance received on average a lower weekly income than any others.

However, the above analysis under-represents the extent of poverty among persons in the sample judged by national assistance scales: it fails to reveal the total number of persons whose income was supplemented by national assistance to bring it up to officially defined minimum levels of income. Almost one-third of the younger persons in the sample (33) derived all or part of their income from national assistance. None of the persons below pensionable age receiving war disablement pensions or industrial injury disablement benefit received national assistance. But half of those dependent upon sickness benefit, as well as those who received unemployment benefit had their income supplemented by national assistance. As might be expected the proportion of elderly persons receiving national assistance was even higher—fifty-seven per cent. In the sample, as a whole forty-two per cent (90) of the disabled persons received, or were dependent on husbands who received, national assistance.

About five per cent of persons in the sample (12) were probably entitled to national assistance, but refused to apply for it. The most common reason given for not applying was the desire to be independent. Particularly among older people, there was a reluctance to admit the need for help of this kind. They found it difficult to relate their own situation to the poverty they had seen in their youth. Occasionally, family feeling against the necessary enquiry into the household's financial arrangements forced the disabled person to reject national assistance.

> Mrs. Greenfield, aged forty-four, lived with her parents and brother in Middlesex. 'I've had this trouble since childhood. It's petit mal. Once every six weeks I drop whatever I'm holding. If I'm sitting down I look strange. But I come to in about a minute. It happens in the evening mainly. I'm on drugs all the time, they have helped. But they make me a little slow and sleepy. I feel disheartened at times. I would like to feel occupied and useful, but can't get out to work. I get 10s. a week widow's allowance, and there's no disability pension. I did get £2 17s. 6d. national insurance until last Friday. People ask me why I can't stay with my parents for ever. But I must have some means of earning my own money. I had national assistance once. It was better then. But had to give it up. My mother didn't like people prying about. She said I should be able to get it straight from the post office.' (Slightly incapacitated.).

There are occasions when the choice before a family which has an alternative source of income to national assistance is to agree to the family being broken up or to swallow pride and accept national assistance. Among the twenty disabled married women in the sample below pensionable age who were eligible for no benefit in their own right was one whose husband was forced to stay at home to look after her. As a result, the family was now dependent upon national assistance instead of the husband's formerly above-average wage.

Allowances additional to the basic scale are available to those receiving national assistance, who have special needs. Grants obtained by persons in the sample included exceptional needs grants for clothing, and discretionary allowances for fuel, special diet, and window cleaning. Everyone who received a grant or allowance was grateful for the additional income but commented that it was inadquate to meet the purpose for which it was granted. Three people reported having received a clothing grant at some time. In each case grants were said to amount to £5. In another case, the same amount had been paid in a grant to two people.

Mrs. Perkins, aged forty-nine, lived with her chairbound husband in a council flat. 'We've been completely on the assistance since I had to give up my little job as a doctor's receptionist. It got too much for me. Of course, we've never been able to replace anything that's worn out in the house. Most of the furniture my husband has made out of boxes I get for him. That table was the last thing. The assistance buys the food, and what's left seems to go on heating and light. Last winter my husband didn't have a coat. I didn't have a coat. And I have terrible trouble with my callipers: they tear all my stockings. So I got on to the assistance bloke and asked him about it. I can't go without stockings and a coat and my husband couldn't go without a coat. As it is I have terrible trouble with his trousers. There's one shop round here that sells extra large ones. And then I have to let pieces into the waistband. Well, he made a fuss about it. We wrote up. And then he came again. In the end they gave us a clothing grant, and do you know how much it was? £5! What can you do with that? So I got my husband one thin coat for £4 15s. 0d. and there was enough left over for a pair of stockings for me.
(Severely incapacitated.).

Unfortunately, the analysis of discretionary allowances is imprecise : few people were sure how their weekly benefits were made up.[41] Discretionary allowances for fuel were granted throughout the winter months to some of the people in the sample. No extra allowance was made to persons living in clean air zones where fuel tended to cost twice as much as ordinary coal. Many people felt that the Board's policy of paying fuel grants only in the winter months was shortsighted: coal was cheaper in the summer months and stocks for the winter were best obtained then.

Many disabled persons faced great practical difficulties in their attempts to practice stringent economy. Some persons in the sample received an extra allowance because they required a special diet. In most cases recipients had been advised to eat white meat or fish and sieved vegetables. Even so, to manage required careful shopping. But few recipients were able to do their own shopping, far less to look for bargains. Some people found themselves too exhausted by the general process of cooking to go to the extra trouble of sieving such fresh vegetables as they could afford. Yet even with their extra allowances they could not afford tinned sieved vegetables.

.Precision was impossible: the conditions which determined eligibility for these allowances were secret.

In many cases, extra allowances were merged with the general household income because the basic allowance was so small. Everyone required fuel in winter. But most people tried to do without the special diet and the window cleaner, and used the extra money to meet these special needs to help pay for the ordinary household requirements.

It must be remembered that the discretionary allowances described above were granted to persons who, in the main, had lived at the officially determined minimum level of income for many years. Indeed, a few had lived on national assistance alone all their adult lives. They had been unable to save for times of need, or to collect the possessions which most people regard as normal requirements for a comfortable home.

It is true that for most people the onset of disability occurred later in life, usually in middle age. Therefore they had already acquired household equipment. But middle age is the point of life at which most people look forward to replace old household equipment. They have more money because the children are no longer dependent. In addition, they can usually expect to be able to afford many of the things which they originally had to forego to support a young family. The onset of disability prevents this. Sickness benefit and national assistance did not allow for the renewal of household equipment.

There were other people who reported that the onset of disability had occurred while their families were still dependent. They spent all their savings ensuring that their disability would not deprive their children of the normal choices.

Mr. Matthews said 'We set our hearts on buying a house with a garden. We saved hard. Then I got a tumour on the brain. I was in a wheel chair for years. We decided that if the children were to have all they should we'd have to give up the idea of the house. So although there was only sickness benefit, we went on holiday together every year, and we kept the girls on at school 'til they were eighteen. I was determined they'd miss nothing because of me. They're both settled nicely now. But there isn't a penny left, and we're still stuck here with the stuff we had when we were married. I started back to work last year. I'm back at the bench. But I'll never make that money up. I'm sixty next year. I've only got another five years.'

Most people laughed when they were asked if they had any savings. One woman said 'I've had 8s. 6d. in the post office for twenty years. I wonder how much interest it's amassed.' As many as three-quarters (158) of the persons in the sample reported savings of less than £50. Almost four-fifths (168) said that their total savings were below £100. Only eight per cent (16) of the people interviewed had savings o more than £500: in four cases where savings were of this order, the money was acquired through actions for damages at common law. Of course, assets were not restricted to savings. Almost a quarter (50) of the people in the sample were themselves owner-occupiers. Almost half (23) of those who owned their own houses also had savings of more than £100. Thus 11 per cent of the persons interviewed were markedly more affluent than the rest.

Most people found that their capacity for participation in general and social activities was restricted both by disability and their limited financial resources.

Mr. Martin said, 'The old lady can't get out at all now. It's the basement steps, her legs won't carry her. I can get down to the end of the road, but I don't go often now. My mates at the factory see me, they ask when I'm going to have a night out. The most I can have now is my baccy. You can't give up every bit of pleasure. The old lady and me have worked hard all our lives. I can't afford a night out. I just can't do it. Oh, they don't expect me to pay, you understand. But your pride won't let you take all the time. So I don't go down the end of the road any more. I go to the news-agent's on the corner for my baccy and the paper every Sunday morning.'

In fact, there were people who became reconciled to incapacity because their lack of resources limited their activities.

Mrs Gipson said, 'I used to mind staying in with that chair here. It seemed such a waste. Then my niece came round and took me up Spitalfields market in the chair. I couldn't buy anything. It was all too expensive. I felt miserable. So now I'm quite happy to stay indoors. I have to save up for everything I need, and the home help brings in what she thinks. I don't feel so bad then.'

On the whole, the limitation of resources was accepted as the inevitable consequence of incapacity. But a few people reported open disagreements with the assessments made by N.A.B. officers.

Only occasionally did anyone point out that the reduction of the disabled to officially determined minimum levels of income was in itself absurd: disability tends to increase expenditure above the normal level for anyone who attempts to take part in the usual daily activities.

Mrs. Hawkins said, 'People don't realize how expensive it is to be disabled. You have to go to the nearest shops, not the cheapest. And you can't run round comparing prices. You can't even buy large economy sizes of anything because the money isn't there. I've got tins labelled 'gas', 'electric', 'rent', and 'coal', up here in the cupboard. As soon as I get the assistance I share out the money—I've worked it out. My main worry is to pay off those. Then what's left over goes mainly on food. Coal costs a lot. I need it for Dad. He must be kept warm, these places are damp. If we went to the pictures even, we'd need a taxi. Imagine that on what we've got.'

Even where people were not dependent upon state benefits, disability caused economic difficulties. For example, disabled housewives who were dependent upon their husband's earnings were usually unable to supplement the family income by getting a job. Moreover, they, too faced the problem of being unable to shop carefully.

To some extent, degree of incapacity determined the source, and therefore the amount of personal income of the disabled persons in the sample. Whereas half of the persons below pensionable age who were assessed as being slightly or moderately incapacitated had found employment, this was true of only an eighth of severely or very severely incapacitated persons. But employment opportunities and cause of disability are factors of considerable importance in determining levels of personal income. Although the majority of wage earners were only slightly or moderately incapacitated, it is also true that a little more than a fifth were severely or very severely incapacitated. On the other hand, of the seven people who received disability benefits, four were only slightly or moderately incapacitated. Likewise, it was striking that of the forty-nine persons who were dependent upon national assistance or sickness benefit, almost half (24) were only slightly or moderately incapacitated.

5. *Household income*

Personal income is not always a good indicator of standard of living. Average household income was low—£12 4s. 1d. compared with a national average of about £24 13s. 0d.[42] But household income varied widely, as did family commitments among people in the sample. For example, some households depended entirely on the income of the disabled person, whereas in other households there were several sources of income. Household income expressed as a percentage of the basic national assistance scale provides some indication of the standard of living of persons in the sample in relation to the officially determined minimum levels of income.

As many as forty-eight per cent (100) of the households represented in the sample reported resources of below 140 per cent of the basic national assistance scale, compared with eighteen per cent in the United Kingdom generally.[43] Whereas about five per cent of households nationally had incomes below the basic national assistance

42. Ministry of Labour, *Family Expenditure Survey, Report for 1965*, H.M.S.O., p. 20.
43. Abel-Smith, B., and Townsend, P., *The Poor and the Poorest*, Occasional Papers in Social Administration, Bell, 1965, p. 39. (Based on figures for 1960.)

scale, this was true of fourteen per cent of households in the sample. Of course, there was a disproportionate number of elderly persons in the sample, and this might be expected to inflate the proportion of low income households. But an above average number of younger persons in the sample belonged to low-income households. Ten per cent of persons below pensionable age belonged to households where the total income was below the basic national assistance scale, compared with five per cent of households nationally. The proportion of households represented by younger persons in the sample where the total income was below 140 per cent of the basic national assistance scale was nearly as large as for the sample as a whole—forty-seven per cent.

On the whole, households containing employed persons had a higher standard of living than those of persons who derived most of their income from state benefits. Only two of the twenty-nine employed persons in the sample were found to belong to households with a total income of less than 140 per cent of the basic national assistance scale, compared with more than half of the people dependent upon state benefits.

For many of the households represented in the sample, state benefits were an important source of income. Only twenty per cent of households received no income from state benefits. But for fifty-five per cent of households, state benefits provided more than half of their total income. State benefits were the only source of income for almost two fifths (80) of the households in the sample. To some extent, the degree of reliance placed by households on state benefits as a source of income is explained by the disproportionate number of elderly persons in the sample. But more than two-fifths (46) of younger disabled persons lived in households which derived half or more of their income from state benefits, while for more than a quarter (31) the household was entirely dependent on state benefits for its income.

As might be expected, most low income households were dependent for all, or most of their income on state benefits. Almost half (54) of the households in which fifty per cent or more of the total income was derived from state benefits (113), had a household income which was below 110 per cent of the national assistance level, while for a further ten per cent (23) household income was less than 120 per cent of that level. All but two of the seventy-four households which depended entirely on state benefits had total incomes of less than 130 per cent of the national assistance level. But not all low income households were largely dependent on state benefits. As many as two-fifths (13) of the households which received no support from state benefits had total incomes of less than 140 per cent of the basic national assistance scale. Indeed, the income of three of these households was below the level they would have received if they had been

71

dependent on national assistance. In each of these households the disabled person was a housewife who was unable to work and there were three or more dependent children.

The analysis of personal and household income presented here is unrealistic in a number of ways. First, it takes no account of debts, such as current hire purchase obligations and certain kinds of assets. More important, no attempt has been made to include income in kind. Many people received extensive services in kind from relatives, friends, neighbours, the local authority, and voluntary organizations. Such services ranged from help in the home to the provision of free holidays and interior decorating. The extent of help received by persons in the sample will be discussed in later chapters. Moreover, it must be remembered that it is likely that persons with relatively low incomes are especially liable to see advantages in registration with the local authority.

6. *Summary*

The current system of provision of resources for disabled persons is not comprehensive. An important group of disabled persons not entitled to any payment in their own right are housewives who are not covered by insurance for sickness, unemployment or industrial injury benefit. Moreover, the system is anomalous as between different types of income maintenance. While national assistance (supplementary benefit) like the outdoor poor relief of which it is the descendant is a means tested payment, sickness and unemployment benefit are paid only to those whose national insurance contributions comply with the regulations. On the other hand, industrial injury disablement benefit, which is part of the national insurance scheme, is paid to those covered by the scheme, regardless of contribution record. Furthermore, payments under the industrial injury scheme, unlike other national insurance benefits, are made according to the same method of assessment as war disablement pensions. Perhaps even more important than the differences of principle on which payments are made is the fact that there may be a difference of as much as fifty per cent in the amount of benefit received by two men with identical capacity, disability, and family responsibilities, and commitments, depending on the benefits to which they are entitled. The system has grown up largely in response to the pressures of particular interests and situations. For example, unemployment and sickness benefit grew out of the private insurance schemes of the last century, whose object was to circumvent the degradation attached to the receipt of poor relief; the industrial injuries scheme was developed from the system of workmen's compensation which was established in 1897 as a result of trades union pressure; the benefit scheme for persons disabled as a result of service in the armed forces was established in 1916 in response to conscription in the First World War. There has been no rational attempt to assess the relationship between need and disability.

Most of the registered disabled persons included in the present study received incomes which were below the average wage. This is a reflection of their main sources of income. Only a minority (13 per cent) of the persons interviewed were wage earners. The majority depended upon state support of various kinds. Resources were limited not only because personal incomes tended to be low, but also because savings were low. Only a minority (20 per cent) of the persons interviewed had savings of more than £100. Furthermore, most people had few capital assets. The proportion of owner-occupiers in the sample was below the national average. Moreover, household equipment often required replacement but limited resources made this impossible. Household income too tended to be below the national average. The proportion of persons in the sample who lived in households where income was below the basic national assistance scale, and where it was below 140 per cent of that scale was almost three times the proportion for the United Kingdom generally. Indeed, more than half of the households included in the sample derived half or more of their income from state benefits. But low income households were not confined entirely to those which were largely dependent on state benefits. About two-fifths of households which received no income from state benefits had total incomes of less than 140 per cent of the basic national assistance scale.

Employment is important for social as well as financial reasons. The purpose of this chapter is to explore three topics. First, the number of employed persons in the sample, their degree of skill and status, the types of jobs acquired, hours and rates of payment. Second, the importance of age and family position in finding and keeping employment will be analysed. The influence of family pressures on the attitude of disabled persons to work, and the attitude of society to disabled workers, will be considered. Finally, an attempt will be made to probe the effectiveness of the present provisions for helping disabled persons to work. Is the degree of incapacity an important factor in determining capacity to find and keep a job, and type of employment obtained? How do the disabled find jobs? How far are jobs suitable? Is rehabilitation effective? How great is the problem of transport? What is the demand for employment among the disabled? What types of work are required? The conclusions drawn from such a small sample are necessarily tentative. But it is hoped that a description of the experiences of persons in the sample will help to indicate the problems of the disabled in finding and keeping employment.

1. *Disabled persons in employment*

Altogether more than half (109) of the persons interviewed were of employable age. Of the sixty-six non-employed persons in the sample below pensionable age who had been obliged to give up their job because of disability, all but one said that giving up work was the worst consequence of disability.

As might be expected, the general level of employment is an important factor in determining the proportion of disabled persons in jobs. A Ministry of Labour enquiry carried out in October 1964 showed that those outside the 'labour reserve' among the unemployed were, in the main, elderly or disabled. Furthermore, 'in relation to

1. 'Second Inquiry into the Characteristics of the Unemployed', *Ministry of Labour Gazette*, Vol. LXXIV, No. 4, April 1966, London, H.M.S.O.

he total regional labour force this . . . group tends to be relatively largest in Regions where unemployment is highest.'

The unemployment rate among the disabled is far higher than in the community as a whole. Since 1964, the unemployment rate among persons registered as disabled by the Ministry of Labour (since 1968 the Department of Employment and Productivity) has generally been about four times higher than among the population as a whole.[2] Even this is probably a serious underestimate. The Ministry's study showed that eighty per cent of the 104,000 men who were unemployed for six months or more prior to the survey 'had personal handicaps, again largely age or physical or mental condition.'

Yet legislation requires the Department of Employment and Productivity, local authorities, and private firms to accept some responsibility for the employment of the disabled. The Department runs Industrial Rehabilitation Units and retraining schemes, registers if they wish it, disabled persons who seek employment through its Employment Exchanges, and provides Exchanges with Disablement Resettlement Officers who place disabled persons in employment. Sheltered employment facilities for those who are too incapacitated to work in open employment are provided in ninety factories run by Remploy Limited, a state subsidized agency. Local authorities have permissive powers to promote similar schemes, and to organize home working schemes for persons who are unable to work outside their own homes. Finally, the quota and designated employment systems compel many employers to accept a small number of disabled workers. The quota system requires employers of twenty or more persons to accept a three per cent quota of disabled workers. Two kinds of employment—those of electric passenger lift attendant and car park attendant—have been designated in which a normal person may be employed only if a disabled person is not available for the job.

Only twenty-nine per cent of the persons in the sample under pensionable age were employed. For a number of reasons, the persons below pensionable age who were interviewed were not representative this category of disabled persons generally. First, there were many disabled persons on the Ministry of Labour registers who were not registered with the local authority. Less than half of the employed people interviewed and only a few of the non-employed were registered with the Ministry of Labour. Second, since both local authority and Ministry of Labour registers appeared to be incomplete, it is likely that there were some employed disabled persons who were not registered at all. These qualifications must be borne in mind in the subsequent analysis.

The Piercy Committee stated in its Report : 'The Ministry of Lab-

---

Based on information published in the *Ministry of Labour Gazette*, London., H.M.S.O.

our's policy as regards placing disabled persons in employment i based on the Report of the Tomlinson Committee, which took th view that the only completely satisfactory form of resettlement for a disabled person is employment which he can keep on his merits as a worker in normal competition with his fellows.'[3] Yet only twenty two per cent (27) of those below pensionable age were in open em ployment, and these accounted for the majority of employed dis abled persons: only one person was in sheltered work, while eigh were employed at home.

The numbers were too small to determine the effectiveness of th quota and designated employment schemes. Only three people wer in designated employment: two men were passenger electric lift at tendants, and one was a car park attendant.[4] Few people knev whether they were employed as part of their firm's quota.[5] Som people suspected that firms made up their quotas by employin people with relatively minor disabilities. One woman's experienc gave support to the suspicion. In the absence of any meaningfι definition of disability, perhaps it is not surprising that this shoul sometimes happen.

Only one employed person was engaged in sheltered work—a ca penter in an L.C.C. factory. Most sheltered employment schemes ar run by Remploy Limited, while a few are provided by voluntar organizations and local authorities. Most schemes run at a cor siderable loss. In an effort to boost the morale of disabled workers an to keep down costs, attempts are made to maintain the standards an conditions of open employment.

Sheltered schemes are so few that most employees have to trav some distance to work. Yet the people who need sheltered workin conditions are those who are capable of more than diversiona occupation, but are unable to undertake a normal day's work or a lor journey. This was true of twelve non-employed people and six hon workers—almost nine per cent of the sample, most of whom wei middle aged skilled engineers who were capable of doing their pr vious jobs in favourable working conditions. Others requested light a sembly work. In spite of this unmet demand, at least one shelter€ workshop in Central London had vacancies which it was unable fill at the time.

Almost a quarter of employed persons (eight) did home work. Al though some people were too incapacitated to attempt any other kir of work, there were others who were prevented from working in op€

---

3. *The Rehabilitation, Training, and Resettlement of Disabled Persons*, Cmnd. 9883, London H.M.S.O., 19. para. 182.
4. According to the Ministry of Labour's Survey of designated employment, August 1964, 2,260 out the 2,769 passenger electric lift attendants were disabled; 2,175 of the 2,583 car park attendants we disabled. Information kindly supplied by the Ministry of Labour.
5. On 1 July, 1966, 65,576 firms were liable to employ the three per cent quota of disabled worke Of these, 33,915 in fact satisfied the quota. From information kindly provided by the Ministry Labour.

or sheltered employment mainly by lack of transport. No one managed to earn more than £5 a week from home work. Average earnings were about £3 per week. None of those employed at home earned more than three shillings an hour. Apart from being poorly paid, much of it was of a seasonal nature. For example, people engaged in the manufacture of seasonal decorations said that they were usually short of work from early December to March.

According to the Piercy Report, the main agencies which provide home work are 'local authorities, voluntary organizations, and Remploy Limited'.[6] But of the home workers in the sample, only one obtained work through Remploy Limited, and one through a local authority. The rest depended directly upon local manufacturers for work. A Middlesex welfare officer stated that a major difficulty in organizing home working schemes was the lack of obligation felt by homeworkers to maintain a consistent rate of production. Yet most home workers were satisfactorily employed directly by manufacturers. Perhaps the intervention of the local authority is the factor which prevents people from adopting a responsible attitude towards delivery dates. If so, it may be that the proper role of local authorities is that of a referral agency acting on behalf of a local firm.

The average weekly wage of persons in full time employment outside the home was £12 2s. 0d. The average for men was £16 compared with £19 in London and the South East generally. People were asked to estimate their hourly rate of pay. Wages ranged from 3s. 0d. to 8s. 0d. per hour. Over a third of those who were employed outside the home earned between 5s. 7d. and 8s. 0d. an hour. All were skilled workmen, most of whom were engaged in engineering. Almost two-thirds earned between 3s. 0d. and 5s. 6d. per hour. On average they expected to earn about £9 per week. For the most part the group consisted of persons in clerical work and semi-skilled and unskilled manual jobs.

Only persons engaged in home work earned less than 3s. 0d. an hour. Clearly the Piercy Committee was correct in stating that 'in making strenuous attempts to command a living wage, the disabled person (engaged in home work) may well work long hours.'[7] Nor were low earnings always determined by degree of incapacity. Of course, the absence of the element of competition may slow the rate of production of home workers.

The range of employment available to home workers was limited. A few people performed part of the process in the manufacture of springs. Others packed toys. Whatever the job, it required hard work to earn a few pounds.

---

6. *The Rehabilitation Training and Resettlement of Disabled Persons,* 1956, London, H.M.S.O., para. 229.
7. *Ibid.,* para. 231.

Nor were rates of pay uniform for the same job. In one instance the difference in the renumeration of two people doing the same job was 100 per cent. Of two people who made flower holders one was paid 3s. 6d. per dozen, while the other received 1s. 9d. per dozen.

The Piercy Committee stated that low wages were the result of the high cost of administering home working schemes. Yet most of the home workers interviewed had found their own jobs and were employed directly by a local manufacturer. Some people even saved their firms' carriage costs because they, or a friend or relative, collected the work and delivered the finished article to the factory.

In most cases home work was little more than paid occupational therapy which provided a small supplement to the household income. But in the absence of suitable sheltered or open employment, home work remained important. It was disturbing to find that lack of transport, not degree of incapacity, forced some people to accept home employment.

Employers, managers, and the self-employed were under-represented in the sample. Only one man was self-employed : he owned a small engineering establishment in Essex. No professional persons were among those interviewed. But there was no significant difference between the proportions of employed persons in the sample and in the area generally, in Social Classes 3 and 4. Most employed persons in Social Class 3 were skilled manual workers; two-fifths were clerical workers, most of them severely disabled women. However, the proportion of unskilled manual workers in Social class 5 among the employed persons interviewed was twice the proportion among employed persons nationally. But one-fifth of the employed persons interviewed had experienced downward social mobility, all of them having moved between grades of manual work. The same tendency was not observable among clerical workers, although the numbers involved are too small for firm conclusions to be drawn. It must be remembered that there are relatively few training and retraining schemes for disabled persons, and legislation tends to encourage the placement of disabled persons in menial jobs.

The majority of persons in Social Classes 4 and 5 had poorly paid factory jobs—light assembly work, packing, storekeeping and factory cleaning were the main occupations. Most persons in such employment tended to drift from job to job, hoping for a few extra shillings, lighter work, or employment nearer home. Some of those who had been disabled early in life, had drifted from school into unsuitable employment, and frequently changed their jobs. Semi-skilled and unskilled jobs provided little in the way of prospects and therefore often failed to hold people. Thus people tended to change their jobs frequently, and to be dissatisfied with their conditions of work.

2. *Employment and the family*

The proportion of persons in work declined with age. Four-fifths of those between the ages of sixteen and twenty-five years were employed, compared with one-third of those aged twenty-five to forty-four years, and only two-ninths of other persons below pensionable age. It is likely that schools and youth employment officers are vigilant to ensure that where possible young disabled persons obtain a job on leaving school. Moreover, employment opportunities for the young are more abundant than for those who are forced to seek a new job in middle age. Yet the likelihood of becoming disabled increases with age. Finally, some persons with long standing disabilities who had been accustomed to work, experienced with advancing age a decline in capacity, and thus found it increasingly difficult to work.

Mrs. Baker was a widow in her early fifties. As a child she had polio which affected her arms and legs. 'I've always worked, and I've been in this factory packing hair nets now for years. But it's no good. I can't lift boxes like I used to. And they don't like it. I've been worried stiff just lately. I know I shall have to leave.'

It seemed possible that some of the younger employed persons would experience similar difficulties later in their lives.

Altogether half of the fully employed persons interviewed had dependent relatives. A higher proportion of men than women below pensionable age were employed—two-fifths, compared with less than one-fifth. Clearly, the pressures, financial and social, are greater on men than women to obtain employment. Moreover, most of the younger disabled women interviewed could consider paid employment only in addition to their role as housewives. Most found that they were exhausted by housework alone. But men who were deprived of their role as breadwinner tended to feel depressed and hopeless. In all cases where roles had been reversed—where non-employed men stayed at home and were dependent upon working wives—men said that this was the most serious blow to morale.

Mr. Grantham, aged fifty-six, had been an engineer until Parkinsons disease had seriously curtailed his mobility. 'I'm very lucky that my wife was clever enough to pass the civil service examinations. It means that she's got a secure job and a decent wage. But it shouldn't be. It's against nature. It's the worst thing I've got to live with. A man should provide for his family. I did until four years ago. But now I've got to depend on my wife. It isn't right. I sit here thinking about it when she's out during the day, asking "Why should it happen to me?". But there you are. What can you do about it?'

Of course, the problem was most acute in cases where the wife was forced to adopt the roles of both breadwinner and housewife. (For a fuller discussion of this and related problems see Chapter 7). The pressures to remain in employment were greatest on men with dependent children. Anxiety was particularly acute where fathers had progressive disabilities: in such circumstances men become obsessed with the fear that they would be forced to give up work before their children became independent.

Anxiety remained even when adolescent children began to work. Most fathers had been forced by disability to undertake low-paid jobs for many years, and as a consequence families had few ressources. Moreover, the children were rarely settled in their jobs, and their wages tended to be low.

Mr. Reynolds, an ex-docker, was on the verge of tears. 'I'm at my wits end. I don't know what to do. How mother manages I couldn't tell you. She doesn't get much from the kids because they've only just started work. I only get twelve quid a week. As it is we haven't had a holiday since my accident. This job is no good for me. The doctor told me so. It's all that climbing and lifting. In wet weather my leg plays up so that I've got to stay at home. Even if I went I'd never manage the wet pavements. They won't put up with this for long. No firm would. I've been to the labour exchange today but they say there's nothing doing for me. You couldn't get me into Remploy, could you, love?'

Officially, a disabled man is fully rehabilitated only if he maintains a job in open employment. But about half of the disabled persons of employable age interviewed reported some experience of discrimination among workers and at management level. It appeared that certain conditions arouse more prejudice than others—epilepsy is an example. Workmates may be more intolerant than managements. On the other hand, there were a few instances in which workmates were prepared to protect the disabled person from the management.

Mr. Kendle said, 'It's my old firm I work for. At first they wouldn't take me back when they knew I had been injured. But I threatened to expose them in the Sunday papers. It's a big firm and they enjoy a good reputation, so they took me back. I never told them that I suffer from epilepsy. My workmates know, of course. They look after me and cover up for me when I have a fit. They won't tell anyone.'

However, most people felt that their colleagues at work were indifferent to or irritated by disabled workers.

The majority of persons interviewed felt that only the most gifted disabled persons avoided relegation to menial jobs. To some extent, popular prejudice in this respect receives official encouragement from the designated employment scheme. There were a number of persons among those interviewed who had been assigned to lower-paid posts than those for which they had trained.

However, some firms were very helpful, and even made attempts at rehabilitation.

Miss Fenwick's present employer knew that failure to maintain jobs in the past had led her to give up employment for ten years until she obtained her present position. 'Sometimes I get over-anxious when the work piles up. I want to go fast and I find I can't even do it like I normally do. I get that concerned and depressed about it. My boss always knows what's up. He takes one look at me and says "You shouldn't worry so much. It's not the end of the world. You go home for the rest of the day and forget about it. You'll be all right tomorrow." And he's always right.'

Employment provisions for the disabled

All but two of the employed disabled persons interviewed said that their employment opportunities had been affected in some way by disability. But degree of incapacity is not necessarily the only, or even the main factor involved in determining a person's chance of obtaining employment. It is true that the majority of persons in full time employment were only slightly or moderately incapacitated. On the other hand, some severely disabled persons were employed.

Miss Tanner, aged twenty-one, had polio five years ago and was able to move indoors only with the aid of callipers and sticks. She had help with dressing herself and getting in and out of bed. Because of her sticks she was unable to carry anything, but she could cook sitting down. Miss Tanner worked as an accounts clerk. She travelled to work in a Ministry tricycle. At work she was allowed to take a friend with her when she went to the lavatory because she could not manage on her own.

Many employed persons experienced considerable mobility difficulties. A seventh of those in open employment (4) were chairbound, while about a quarter (7) depended upon a car to get to work. Altogether, one third of persons in open employment required a walking aid even indoors, while one sixth (5) were unable to walk up or down stairs. As might be expected, a far higher proportion of home-workers had mobility difficulties. For example, all of them required a walking aid out of doors. Homeworkers were generally more incapacitated than persons in open employment: most of them were severely or very severely incapacitated. Yet there were four persons in open employment who were severely or very severely incapacitated, while two moderately incapacitated persons worked at home.

Both Mr. Grant and Mr. Duncan had multiple sclerosis and were twenty-one years old. Both lived with their families in residential areas of Middlesex. Mr. Grant, who was severely incapacitated, worked as an engraver. He was unable to get about out of doors without his Ministry tricycle, and he required an aid to get about indoors. Mr. Duncan had been told that he would never work outside his own home, and he was resigned to this. In spite of the obvious limitations of the local market, he had been encouraged by the hospital to settle down to basket making for the neighbourhood. The hospital supplied him with materials. Mr. Duncan was moderately incapacitated.

Thus it seemed likely that some home workers were capable of open employment. Indeed, a few said that they would like full time employment, but required transport to and from work.

One-third of non-employed persons below pensionable age (42) said that they would like work. Two-thirds of them required an aid to get about indoors and out of doors, and almost half were unable to walk up and down stairs. Although these proportions are slightly higher than for employed persons, almost half of the non-employed persons seeking work were only slightly or moderately incapacitated, while four were severely incapacitated.

A general tendency to underestimate the capacity of disabled persons, prejudice against the employment of the disabled, and lack of transport facilities appeared to be factors which limited employment opportunities. It seemed probable, too, that education and type of training were important. It was noticeable that manual workers experienced greater employment difficulties than others.

How do disabled persons obtain employment? The Tomlinson Committee stated that the majority of people who become disabled return to their former employment. Only one-sixth of employed persons in the sample were able to return to their former jobs. A further four were employed by their old firms but in different work. Almost three quarters, including those who were disabled in childhood, had to find new jobs.

According to the Piercy Committee, the Disablement Resettlement Officer plays a vital role in the resettlement services.[8] Yet only five per cent of persons below pensionable age obtained work through the D.R.O. Most of these people felt that the service was a good one, and a few were enthusiastic.

The wife of a man who was very severely disabled by a stroke in his forties, exclaimed : 'Oh, the Disablement Resettlement Officer was wonderful, wasn't he, Ron?' He got the job and told us a

8. *Op. cit.,* paras. 179 and 180.

about the Ministry car and all that. Ron thought he would never work again, but he told us not to worry. He's a marvellous man.'

Those who had applied unsuccessfully to a D.R.O. for a job were either resigned to the absence of help, or laughed at the expectation of aid through official channels.

A fifty year old man, whose left leg had been amputated expressed a common reaction: 'They said they couldn't help me. They said there was nothing doing then. So I went and found myself a job.'

D.R.O.'s are challenged by a difficult problem.[9] Current assessments for employment are medical evaluations provided by G.P.'s based on schedules issued by the Ministry of Labour. Even with a more positive test, and further analysis to determine the suitability of the work environment, it is likely that there will still be some people who will fail to display their full potential.

Eleven of the persons interviewed had found their jobs through social clubs, welfare officers, and medical social workers, compared with five who obtained employment through D.R.O.'s. Some people had never thought of going to a D.R.O. A few preferred to avoid the humiliation of asking for official help. On the whole, the D.R.O.'s service was acceptable because it worked within the familiar routine of the Labour Exchange. But over half of employed persons (20) had found their own jobs, mostly through advertisements in the local press, or the recommendation of friends. Perhaps the disabled person, intent on getting work, initially overestimates and thus extends his capacity.

It was not easy to obtain suitable employment. Four people said that their jobs were unsuitable. All four found their work physically distressing. But the chances of finding more suitable employment appeared to be remote.

A storekeeper said, 'I have to climb up and down ladders all the time, and push and heave things about. My right leg is amputated from the knee and the stump gets very sore sometimes. I've got arthritis in the other leg too, and I depend on that to get me about.'

Most people felt that acceptance by workmates was essential. Rejection by only one person among many could lead to acute unhappiness. Such unhappiness had driven several people from employment for a number of years.

---

9. A D.R.O. in Central London was asked about a moderately incapacitated woman who had not been found a job in six months. He replied: 'I don't know this case personally, but such circumstances often arise even in my district which has the longest list of employers in the country. Although her present job is unsuitable, it may well be better than anything else that's available.'

Employment difficulties varied according to the age at which disability occurred. Persons below the age of thirty required suitable jobs which offered chances of promotion, but only half of those in this age group had been successful in obtaining such employment. Older people were anxious to retain their current jobs until retirement. Special problems beset those who became disabled during their working lives. On returning to work, fear of how workmates will react, and how the boss would handle the situation had to be overcome.

Mr. Brown said, 'I had stuck out to get back my old job, but when it came to it I was a bit scared. After all, I looked quite normal when my workmates saw me last. Now I can't move without sticks, callipers and a steel corset. And I hadn't got on very well with the boss before. No one was used to seeing really handicapped people around the place: the most they had taken were people with one eye, or a finger off, or something. Well, when I got there they all stood round in a circle looking at me, and no one seemed to know what to do. Then the boss came along, and all he said was, "Hullo, Brown, it's nice to see you back". That was just right. If he had asked me how I was or anything I would have felt awful. As he was going out of the door, I slipped on a patch of oil and down I went. No one knew whether to help me up or what. I felt daft. The boss came back and said, "And you can get up from there. I don't pay you for lying down all day". That was fine—everything was back to normal.'

Those who were unable to return to their former jobs had to accustom themselves to starting at the bottom again in a new work environment, and to the likelihood that they would be unable to rise to the position for which they had planned. Some people returned to their old trade but had to take lower grade work. Most of those who were disabled in middle age had spent their savings and superannuation to provide educational and social opportunities for their children. Thus they faced retirement with fewer resources than planned. Even the skilled men who returned to work which specifically required their skills and forged ahead surprisingly quickly found it impossible to make up for the chances of promotion lost during years of hospitalization, convalescence, and rehabilitation.

Certain conditions presented special employment difficulties. The problem of maintaining a job was particularly acute for persons with progressive disabilities. They faced the inevitability of a steady decline in their employment prospects, rather than the promotion for which they had worked. Fluctuating disabilities sometimes demanded long absences from work. Thus anxiety about losing a job was ever present.

It seemed likely that the employment prospects of some of the disabled persons interviewed would have been more hopeful with re-habilitation and training for suitable employment. A few firms run their own rehabilitation schemes, but by far the biggest contribution to industrial rehabilitation and resettlement is made by the Depart-ment of Employment and Productivity. The number of persons attending courses at the (then) Ministry's Industrial Rehabilitation Units on 21 February 1966 was 1,716.[10] About eighty per cent of those who finish courses each year find employment, or go on to further vocational training, at, for example, Government Training Centres. The Tomlinson Committee envisaged that persons who were unemployable as a result of disability would, if they wished, attend a training course to fit them for open employment.[11]

Only two of the persons interviewed had attended a rehabilitation unit, though others had been given the opportunity of attending at a unit. Some people were unwilling to leave home to attend residential courses. Delays were reported in gaining admission to Units. Some people who were unable to bear the financial burden of long unem-ployment or the boredom of remaining at home, preferred to give up their chance of a place in a Unit and take the first job which looked possible. However, there were people in the sample—about half of the non-employed who desired work, as well as some persons already in employment, who thought that they required industrial re-habilitation and training, but had not been offered places at Units of Centres.

Mr. Thompson found that bronchitis brought his engineering job to an end. He then looked forward to being taught a new skill. 'Training? Ha! They sent me down to this factory, the Labour Exchange did, and gave me a bucket and a mop and told me to get on with washing the floors. I've been doing that ever since.'

None of the persons interviewed had been to a Government Train-ing Centre.

It seems clear that there is an unmet demand for industrial re-habilitation and retraining. It may be that because of the problems presented by functional incapacity, greater emphasis should be placed on teaching non-manual skills in retraining schemes for disabled persons than is the case at present. How many more disabled persons would find employment if they attended training courses? How many more would be able to maintain their original jobs or under-take work with comparable pay and prospects if they went to a Unit? These are important questions, but further research is required to provide answers.

10. *Ministry of Labour Gazette*, Vol. LXIV, No. 4, April 1966, London, H.M.S.O.
11. *The Rehabilitation, Training and Resettlement of Disabled Persons*, London, H.M.S.O., 1956, para. 66.

Transport difficulties limited the employment opportunities of many of the persons interviewed. Two people had been unable to accept offers of suitable jobs because no transport was available. About half of the employed persons in the sample went to work by public transport. Most of them found it difficult to board buses and trains during the rush hour. For many people the daily journey by public transport was the most alarming aspect of participation in 'normal' life. People with artificial legs, crutches, or sticks, found that the hazards of travelling to work increased in wet or icy weather. Others, for example, bronchitics and asthmatics, were adversely affected by wet or foggy weather.

Three categories of disabled persons are eligible for tricycles which are supplied free by the government—those with double amputation of the lower limbs, one being an amputation above the knee, those who have lost the use of the lower limbs, and those who require personal transport to and from work. Persons disabled as a result of service in the armed forces who belong to these categories are entitled to an adapted car. A small number of other disabled persons may be eligible for a car rather than a tricycle—for example, disabled widows with the sole care of a young child, and those who live with a second disabled person who is also entitled to a government vehicle. The government pays insurance, licence and maintenance on all vehicles provided to disabled persons.

One sixth of employed persons used Ministry vehicles to get to work. One man, with poor circulation, said that his tricycle was so cold during the winter that he had to strap hot water bottles around himself. Some people said that tricycles were too light to cope with a heavy wind.[12] Only one man, a war pensioner, had been given a car. He said that it was a great improvement on his tricycle. 'The mini is steadier, easier to control, and it's got a heater.'

Three main criticisms were levelled at Ministry allocation of vehicles. First, people who experienced increasing difficulty in using public transport—usually because their disability was progressive—found it hard to convince the Ministry of their need for a vehicle. Two people obtained Ministry vehicles only after they had been involved in accidents on public transport. Second, some people could not convince the Ministry that only the lack of a vehicle prevented them from working. This was true of as many as ten for the forty-two people who desired employment. All but three of them depended upon state benefits and therefore were unable to buy a car. They were particularly bitter because they knew that some disabled persons obtained Ministry vehicles purely for social purposes. Third, the delivery

12. Tricycles have recently been described by the Consumers' Association as 'fairly disastrous'. The recently developed new version of the tricycle has been welcomed by the Association as meeting many of its criticisms. *Which?* August 1969. Published by the Consumers' Association. It has been estimated recently that 'the difference in capital cost between providing a tricycle and a small car would only be £30 per year (£40 for an automatic-gear change car.)' *The Lancet*, September 6, 1969, p. 529.

of Ministry vehicles usually involved a delay of at least six months. In two cases, firms had been unable to hold positions open for this length of time for the disabled persons concerned. The garaging rules which often caused delays in congested urban areas have since been relaxed.

Altogether, a little over six per cent of the total sample, who did not have private cars for work had had their applications for a vehicle rejected by the Ministry. If the sample were representative of all persons on local authority registers, about 8,000 more registered disabled persons would have required Ministry vehicles to get to work.

The three people who owned cars were skilled engineers receiving the highest wages of those in the sample. No maintenance allowance is available to those who are eligible for government vehicles but choose to purchase their own, though they are entitled to payment up to a maximum of £90 for adaptations.

Some employed persons who were unable to use transport on their own were taken to work each day by friends or workmates. Three non-employed people would have been able to work if such help had been available. One woman had been forced to give up her job because the friend who had previously taken her to work could do so no longer. No one benefited from the transport provided privately by a firm, yet the Piercy Committee had hoped that a greater supply of works' transport would enable more disabled persons to work outside the home.

What were the characterisitics of the persons who were seeking employment and what kind of work did they require? Degree of incapacity was not the only factor which limited employment opportunities. Although half of those seeking work were severely or very severely incapacitated, there were equally incapacitated persons among those already in employment. The majority of persons seeking employment were between forty-five and sixty-four years of age, but the age group with the highest proportion of persons desiring employment was twenty-five to forty-four years. No one under the age of twenty-five was without work.

More than half (19) of the persons seeking work were women: a smaller proportion of women than men were already employed—twenty per cent of women below pensionable age compared with forty per cent of men. The mobility of some of those seeking employment was severely limited. As many as one-third were chairbound compared with only one-seventh of employed persons. The employed as a group were more mobile out of doors partly because more than half of them had Ministry or other vehicles compared with only two of the people seeking work. Where people were sure of obtaining a vehicle they could search confidently for a job beyond their own locality. A quarter of those seeking employment required a Ministry vehicle to get to work, but a further tenth would have been unable to drive a vehicle themselves.

Over two-fifths of those seeking employment did not require special working conditions. All of these wanted full time employment. And all but two of them were able to travel any distance to work, provided they had their own transport. A further fifth, however, required work, mainly of an unskilled or clerical nature, within ten or fifteen minutes of home. Two-fifths of those seeking employment required home work, although a few of them could have been taken to part-time open employment if transport were available.

All but four of the persons seeking work were unskilled.

4. *Conclusion*

There is a dearth of information about the effects of disability on employment opportunities in general. What difficulties beset disabled persons who attempt to operate within the normal work environment? Could more be done to adapt the tools and work amenities used by disabled persons? How far are special transport provisions required? The middle aged disabled person faces particularly difficult problems: we need to be able to distinguish more clearly those problems caused specifically by disability from the general employment problems of this age group.

We need to know far more about how current employment provisions operate in practice, and how far they meet the needs of the consumer. What are the appropriate training courses for persons with different kinds of conditions and different degrees of incapacity? Which training schemes best satisfy the needs of local industry? How far are training courses accessible and attractive to family men and women, many of whom have severe mobility difficulties? The quota scheme appears to require careful vetting. In spite of high unemployment among the disabled, a large minority of firms fail to meet their quota. Some have exemption agreements with the Department of Employment and Productivity. The identity, though not the number of firms which fail to satisfy the quota remains secret. We need to know what kind of firms these are. Do they cluster regionally? Do some kinds of firms lose more than others by implementing the system? Likewise the designated employment scheme requires careful assessment: what is the demand for this type of work? Few of those interviewed were satisfied either with the status or the pay of the present categories of designated employment. The role of sheltered employment requires investigation. How many of those currently employed in sheltered workshops could be absorbed into open employment? With the need for subsidies honestly recognized and the provision of adequate transport facilities, could more severely disabled persons be employed in sheltered conditions? To ensure a more

en spread of sheltered work, should local authorities take over the
ajor role in its provision? This raises the whole question of the role
local authorities in the employment field. Is there a case for ex-
nding their present responsibilities to include a placement service
orking closely with the D.R.O. in the employment exchange?
ould they operate as agents for securing home workers for manu-
cturers?

The possibility of new provisions needs to be explored. Is there a
ed for a government subsidy to encourage the adaptation of the
ork environment, the provision of transport facilities, and the em-
oyment of disabled persons?

Summary

More than half (109) of the persons interviewed were of employ-
le age, but less than a third of these were in work. The proportion
persons in employment declined with age. Although degree of in-
pacity was a crucial factor in determining whether persons were
uployed, there were severely incapacitated persons in employment,
hile some moderately incapacitated persons were unable to find
itable work.

The difficulties of obtaining employment caused some disabled
rsons to undertake home work. Yet home work rarely provided
ough money to be regarded as anything more than paid occu-
tional therapy.

No firm conclusions about the employment facilities provided for
sabled persons can be drawn from this study. Few people had ex-
rience of rehabilitation and training schemes, designated or shel-
red work. Most of those who were employed had obtained work
thout the assistance of the D.R.O. It appeared that some D.R.O.'s
ay tend to underestimate capacity. Employers, too, were said some-
nes to be unwilling to accept the disabled person's subjective esti-
ate of incapacity.

That so few of the persons interviewed had been in contact with
e employment services suggested that provision may not meet need.
uis conclusion is supported by the fact that a further twenty-five
r cent of those below pensionable age wanted work. In terms of
capacity they did not compare unfavourably with many of those
eady in employment. Some people were kept from work by lack
transport facilities. A further thirteen per cent of those below pen-
nable age needed a Ministry vehicle, while four per cent required
be taken to work. Few of those seeking work were skilled, and most
pressed an interest in the possibilities of training.

Most handicapped persons faced serious employment difficulties.
en skilled persons in open employment usually experienced a drop
earnings and status after the onset of disability.

An attempt will be made in this chapter to assess the extent
which housing restricted the activities of the disabled persons i
terviewed. Four main topics will be explored. First, the housing ar
enities of the persons interviewed will be compared with those of t
general population of the areas studied. Second, the impact of hou
design on the lives of the persons interviewed will be described. Thir
the practicability of adaptations will be discussed, and finally t
effect of rehousing schemes will be considered.

An analysis of the households of the persons in the sample in ter
of tenure provides a framework for comparison. The tenure patte
of the dwellings in the sample was strikingly different to that
dwellings generally in the areas studied. Whereas almost half of t
dwellings in Greater London and Essex were owner occupied,[1] l
than a quarter (49) of the persons interviewed lived in homes whi
they or their families had bought or were buying. On the other har
more than half (109) of the persons interviewed rented their acco:
modation from the local authority, compared with only a quarter
the general population in the area. The proportion of persons in t
sample and in the area generally who lived in privately rented acco:
modation was the same—a quarter. This is unexpected in view of t
fact that more than half—105—of the persons interviewed lived
single or two-person households where at least one person was abc
pensionable age: it was among this section of the general populati
that a disproportionately large number of persons lived in priv
rented accommodation. Thus the preponderance of council tenants
the sample was even more marked than a simple analysis
dwellings by tenure would suggest. Of course, in consideration for
housing the severely disabled belonged to a priority group in
areas studied. But other factors may help to explain the high p
portion of persons renting dwellings from the local authority. It

1. Data relating to Greater London and Essex are based on statistics of General Register Office, Sa:
Census 1966, London H.M.S.O.

ossible that council tenants are more likely than other disabled persons to become known to those administering welfare services. Moreover, recent housing studies suggest that the majority of council tenants belong to Social Class 3,[2] and as we have seen, a disproportionately large number of persons in the sample were in this category.

Two separate but related housing problems emerged in the course of the study. First, many of the persons interviewed lived in dwellings which were *inadequate* in respect of certain facilities. Second, there were many dwellings which were *unsuitable* for persons with certain conditions.

Inadequate housing

Adequacy was assessed according to the presence and use of the standard facilities within a dwelling, for which corresponding Census data were available,—flush W.C., fixed bath, piped water, hot water, stove and sink.[3] Only fifty-three per cent (113) of the persons interviewed compared with sixty-eight per cent of dwellings in Greater London and Essex had sole use of an indoor flush W.C., fixed bath, piped water, and hot water. A higher proportion of those living in council accommodation than others had sole use of the four amenities —almost three-quarters (76) compared with almost two-thirds (28) of owner occupiers, and less than one-fifth (9) of those in privately rented accommodation.

The proportion of persons in the sample having sole use of a fixed bath and an inside W.C. was about the same as the proportion

TABLE 15

Use of amenities by persons interviewed and in London and Essex

Amenities		Persons interviewed		Dwellings in London and Essex [a]
		No.	Per cent	Per cent
Piped hot water	Own	144	69	81
	Shared	2	1	5
	None	65	30	14
Fixed bath	Own	159	77	73
	Shared	5	2	12
	None	47	21	15
Inside W.C.	Own	161	76	75
	Shared	10	5	12
Outside W.C.	Own	30	14	9
	Shared	8	4	3
No W.C.		2	1	1

N = 211   100   2,625,150 = 100

[a] Based on statistics of the Registrar General, *Sample Census 1966*, London, H.M.S.O.

See, for example, Cullingworth, J. B., *English Housing Trends*, Occasional Papers on Social Administration, Number 13, 1965, p. 26. In 1962, an analysis of a sample of households by tenure and occupation showed that 44 per cent of council tenants were foremen and skilled workers, and another 7 per cent were clerical workers and shop assistants.
Based on statistics of General Register Office, *Sample Census 1966*, London, H.M.S.O.

of dwellings having these amenities in the areas studied. (See Table 15.) But only sixty-nine per cent (144) of the persons interviewed had sole use of piped hot water compared with eighty-one per cent of dwellings in Greater London and Essex. Considerably lower proportions of persons in the sample than of dwellings in the area generally shared piped hot water, fixed baths, and inside W.C.'s. But the proportion of persons interviewed without these amenities was far higher than of dwellings in Greater London and Essex. In addition, as many as six per cent (12) of the persons interviewed had no sink or piped cold water of their own, while four per cent (8) did not have the sole use of a stove. Thus a higher proportion of the dwellings of the persons interviewed than in the area generally lacked amenities.[4]

More of privately rented, than of council or owner occupied accommodation in the sample lacked amenities, and more had inadequate facilities. About three-fifths (32) of privately rented dwellings but only a quarter (26) of council and one-fifth (10) of owner occupied accommodation did not have sole use of piped hot water. More than three-fifths (35) of privately rented accommodation, but only two-sevenths (14) of owner occupied and four council dwellings were without the sole use of a bath. As many as three-fifths (35) of privately rented, compared with a quarter (12) of owner-occupied and only eight council dwellings in the sample were without the sole use of an indoor W.C.

Almost half (50) of the persons interviewed whose dwellings were inadequate lacked only one of the standard facilities, and two thirds of these lacked piped hot water only. But more than a fifth (13) had no inside W.C. of their own, and another sixth (8) had no bath. The absence of even one standard facility, particularly the lack of an indoor W.C., presented considerable difficulties for severely disabled persons.

> Mrs. Sanger, aged 78, had arthritis in her legs. She lived in an old terraced house in a quiet residential area of Middlesex. "Going to the lavatory is really dangerous. You see, the path is broken all along, especially by the wall. That's the frost. I've timed it. It takes me two minutes in fine weather, three in the rain because I'm scared of slipping, and even longer when there's ice. Sometimes I feel I take my life in my hands when I come out here."
> (Housing deficient: no inside lavatory. Mrs. Sanger severely incapacitated.)

But more than one-fifth (48) of the persons interviewed lived in dwellings which lacked two or more standard amenities, while five

---

4. See *Report of the Committee on Housing in Greater London*, Cmnd. 2605, H.M.S.O., 1965, p. 109 (Milner Holland Report), and Cullingworth J. B. *English Housing Trends*, Occasional Papers on Social Administration, 1965, p. 21, Table 3.

per cent (11) lacked all four—sole use of piped water, piped hot water, indoor W.C., and fixed bath. As in the area generally, and the country as a whole, privately rented dwellings lacked more standard amenities than others.[5] As many as three-fifths (32) of privately rented dwellings in the sample, compared with less than a quarter (11) of owner-occupied, and only two per cent of council dwellings lacked two or more amenities. And all dwellings in the sample which lacked all four amenities were privately rented.

Where dwellings were seriously inadequate, the difficulties and frustrations which household activities involved were far greater than they need have been. Consequently, people found that simple household tasks engaged all their energy. The problem was particularly acute for those who lived alone.

Mrs. Morris, aged fifty-five, had multiple sclerosis. She lived alone in the front room of a terraced cottage in an industrial area of Middlesex. 'I've got this one bed-sitting room. There's no bathroom and the lavatory is outside. I have to share it with the five other people in the house. It's a bit awkward because there are two steps up to the kitchen and I'm not good at those. I don't like having to go through when they're all in the kitchen. And when I get there there's usually somebody else there. There's no hot water. I bring all the water I need from the kitchen in this pail. I have to boil it in the kettle on the fire. I do all my cooking on that open fire. The doctor saw me once and he was horrified. I could share the kitchen out the back, but I would have to carry everything up and down the steps, and I'm liable to have an accident. Anyway, with five of them out there you can't move. The wall (between their room and hers) moves when you touch it. (The interviewer pushed the wall and it moved.) There's damp along those two walls, especially the outside one. You can see it up there where the paper is hanging down. The plaster is coming off and it is all going green. Look at the wall underneath the window. There are holes all the way along the bottom. You can see the daylight coming through, can't you? (Light could be seen through the holes.) He tacked boards on the outside last winter to stop the cold coming through. I have to have the coal fire all the year round to cook on. And look how black it makes my pans.'
(Housing deficient: Shared sink, no stove, shared outside W.C., no fixed bath, no hot water, damp. Mrs. Morris severely incapacitated.)

It is true that where a disabled person has to look after a family, some help could be expected from other members of the household.

See *Report of the Committee on Housing in Greater London.* Cmnd. 2605, London, H.M.S.O., 1965, p. 109 (Milner Holland Report); and Donnison, D. V., *The Government of Housing*, Hammondsworth, Penguin Books, 1967, p. 186.

But inadequate housing imposed an additional strain, particularly on mothers of young children.

Mrs. Fulmer, aged thirty-three, had rheumatoid arthritis. She lived with her eight year old daughter in one room of a tall terraced house in Paddington. 'We only have this one room. We have to sleep, eat and do everything in here. It's very awkward really because my daughter has to go to bed at eight o'clock and it means that I can't have the wireless on or anything after that, and I can't read because I have to turn the light out. I try to go to bed at the same time but my back pains so much when I lie down that I have to get up again and wait until I'm really tired. I've only got one ring to cook on. I don't have any water here. There's a tap on the landing upstairs—four other families use that sink. Of course, there's no hot water. Usually I get my little girl to bring down enough water to last me until dinner time. But if I run out I have to go up and get it myself. I can't carry the kettle or walk upstairs. I have to crawl up on my hands and knees and drag the kettle from one step to another. The lavatory is downstairs in the yard. I don't like having to ask my daughter to do things all the time. She ought to be playing. But I don't think she minds. She seems to accept it, I couldn't manage the other two here as well all the time. It's much too inconvenient. I feel very sorry that they can't be with us, but they are too young to manage on their own. They will have to wait until we get another place. I used to try to look for somewhere else, but I got worse two years ago. The council put me on the list a year ago, and the welfare officer is doing her best.'

(Housing deficient: no kitchen, no fixed bath, shared W.C., no hot water. Mrs. Fulmer very severely incapacitated.)

However, it was not only the disabled person who was affected by the difficulties which arise through inadequate housing. The lack of basic amenities often placed an enormous burden on relatives or friends who looked after them. Occasionally the additional strain imposed by inadequate housing threatened to break up the household.

Mr. Timpson, aged seventy, was a retired farm worker, and lived with his seventy-one year old sister in a cottage in a rural area of Essex. He had been unable to walk for the last five years, and also had some trouble with his arms and with speech. He depended entirely upon his sister to wash, bath, and dress him. In addition, his sister had to do all the cooking, housework, and shopping. She had to get water from the pump in the garden. All the cooking was done by calor gas. There was no flush lavatory, no electricity.

and of course, no bath. She said, 'I don't know how much longer I can go on for.'

(Housing deficient: no hot water, no fixed bath, no W.C. Mr. Timpson very severely incapacitated.)

Mr. Timpson's was an extreme case, but even dwellings which were less inadequate than his usually added immeasurably to the burden of those who look after disabled persons.

The greater the degree of a person's incapacity, the greater were the difficulties presented by inadequate housing. More than half (28) of those who lived in dwellings which lacked more than one standard amenity were severely incapacitated. As many as three-quarters of those who did not have the sole use of piped water, piped hot water, a fixed bath or a flush W.C. were severely or very severely incapacitated.

Some of the persons interviewed lived in dwellings which were deficient in other ways too. The dwellings of seven people were clearly damp: the walls were marked, the wallpaper refused to stick, and the plaster flaked badly. That only four persons (two per cent compared with eight per cent in Greater London) lived in overcrowded dwellings[6] is largely due to the small proportion of young families in the sample, and the over representation of single and two-person households.[7]

2. *Unsuitable housing*

It is difficult to assess the extent to which a disabled person's activities are limited by unsuitable housing. The degree to which participation in household activities is restricted may depend upon the amount of help available to the disabled person. A few steps at the entrance to a kitchen may prevent a person in a wheelchair who has little or ro personal help using the kitchen. But if constant help is available to the same person, full use of the kitchen may be possible. Nevertheless, a few broad generalizations may be made about the unsuitability of the accommodation of the persons interviewed.

First, the general problems which face most disabled persons will be discussed. Later the particular problems of certain groups of the disabled will be considered. For all groups other than the bedfast, steps limited activities. This was true of some ambulatory persons whose upper limbs were affected by disability, particularly when they were dependent on trolleys for carrying things around the house. The ambulatory disabled whose upper and lower limbs were affected by disa-

6. See *Report of the Committee on Housing in Greater London*, Cmnd. 2605, H.M.S.O., 1965, p. 321. In the present study, dwellings were deemed to be overcrowded when there were more than one and a half persons per habitable room.

7. Of the persons interviewed, 26 per cent (54) lived alone and 38 per cent (81) lived in two-person households compared with 15 per cent and 29 per cent respectively in England and Wales. See statistics of General Register Office, *Sample Census 1966*, London, H.M.S.O.

bility found indoor steps dangerous especially when they were unable to make use of the handrails.

Chairbound persons were carried upstairs. In theory, ramps eliminate the difficulty of steps for the chairbound. But in only a few of the households in the sample, did the position of indoor steps allow for the construction of a ramp. In all but two cases, indoor ramps were too steep to be managed by the disabled person alone.

Outside ramps were often too steep because they were not allowed to project on to a public right of way. Only one chairbound person was able to use an outside ramp without help. Where a shallow moveable ramp was provided, it had to be taken up immediately after use. None of the chairbound persons interviewed were able to take up a moveable ramp.

More than half (113) of the persons in the sample had to climb stairs to the entrance of their dwelling because no lift was available. Of these, about one-seventh lived on the second floor or above. Furthermore, the policy of rehousing disabled persons on the higher floors of blocks of flats with single lift access appears to be unwise. Lifts were usually unreliable.

Over half of the people in the sample (120) had three or more steps to their front door. In more than one-third of these dwellings the steps were considered to be unsafe because they were steep, broken or lacked a handrail.

> Mrs. Johnson was about to be registered as partially sighted. 'I can't see well now at all. I don't go far—only round here for my shopping. I never cross the main road at the bottom there. But I have to go up the basement steps. The welfare lady was shocked when she came and saw them. They're going to do something about it. Those steps are so steep, and there's no rail or anything. There used to be a wooden one but it broke. I keep to the wall because the steps are so narrow where they turn. I have to count them carefully as I go up, because I know that the fourth step up is missing. And you have to be ever so careful because all the steps are uneven—there are great lumps out of them.'

About two-thirds of the people living in these dwellings were severely or very severely incapacitated. Altogether, two-thirds of the persons interviewed lived above the ground floor or had to climb unsafe steps to the front door. Four-fifths of privately rented dwellings in the sample were of this type, compared with three-fifths of the local authority and just under half of the owner occupied accommodation.

The significance of stairs within a dwelling varied according to the importance of the facilities to which they gave access. Altogether a little under half of the people in the sample had more than five continuous steps within their dwelling. Three-quarters of these (76)—

or about one-third of the total sample had upstairs bedrooms. But bedrooms were the least important of upstairs facilities. The majority of the ambulant disabled arranged their activities so that they went upstairs to the bedroom only to sleep. A further ten people had abandoned the room upstairs and slept in the living room.

More than half (38) of the dwellings in which bedrooms were upstairs had other facilities upstairs as well. A little more than one-fifth (46) of the persons in the sample had an upstairs bathroom. It was much more disturbing to find that one-seventh (32) of the people interviewed had an up- or downstairs lavatory. But to continue to use the lavatory, whatever the difficulty, was held to be an important test of independence. Only in the last resort were people prepared to use a commode. For those in wheelchairs there was no alternative to a commode when the lavatory was upstairs. People regarded their inability to use a lavatory as the greatest indignity which disability forced on them. One woman said: 'This is the part of it that I really hate. It's like being a child all over again.'

Ten disabled housewives had to go up or downstairs to the kitchen. All lived in privately rented accommodation. In each case they shared a kitchen on a landing with other households. Inevitably, such arrangements added enormously to the difficulties which faced a disabled housewife who attempted to fulfil her role within the home.

Mrs. Trenden, aged thirty-eight, had multiple sclerosis. She lived with her husband in one room above a cafe in the City of London. They ate all their meals in this one room. Most of the space was taken up by the bed, and there was room for only a small table. The kitchen was upstairs on the landing, and was shared by three other families in the house. Everything required for cooking or washing had to be taken up to the kitchen and brought down again. 'If we want water to wash or anything I have to go up there to get it. I'm always scared of falling because my legs go now and then. I walk funny anyway. I have to take it slowly. The trouble is that I can't hold the rail to steady myself when I'm carrying dishes and things.'

Analysis of accommodation by tenure shows that whereas seven-tenths of owner occupiers had at least one facility up or downstairs, this was true of little more than half of people in privately rented accommodation, and about one-third of local authority tenants. Altogether almost a quarter (48) of the persons interviewed had to go up or downstairs for more than one facility. Just over one-third of owner occupiers lived in such accommodation, compared with one-fifth of those in privately rented and local authority dwellings.

About one-tenth of the persons interviewed lived in dwellings which not only had more than three steps to the entrance or stairs inside, but also lacked two or more standard amenities. More than a quarter (16) of privately rented dwellings fell into this category, compared with only three owner occupied and one local authority dwelling. On the whole, therefore, council tenants were the most adequately and the most suitably housed.

So far the discussion has centred on general problems which faced most of the persons interviewed. There were additional problems which worried only certain groups of people. There are certain household facilities which people must be able to use if they are to participate fully in household activities. A short list of these was devised and the persons interviewed were asked if they were unable to use any of them—lavatory, taps, sink, cooker, cupboards, light switches, gas and electric meters, windows. As we shall see, it was seldom possible to specify standard installations which would facilitate their use by all disabled persons. The requirements of the disabled tended to vary widely, and in some cases they clashed with those of the non-disabled.

Five people were forced to use a commode solely because the lavatory was the wrong height.

> Mrs. Gipson said, 'I've got all I want here really. It's ever such a nice flat. The only thing is I can't use the lavatory. The welfare lady came to see it, and she said that she would get the seat highered for me. Some men came to have a look at it and measured it up, but they said nothing could be done about it. I didn't really understand why not. I have to use the commode. I don't like it. It seems a shame with the lavatory there, doesn't it?'

Where possible, local authorities and hospitals adjust the height of lavatories to suit the individual disabled person, and this had been done for almost a twentieth (10) of the persons in the sample. It is impossible to devise a standard height for a lavatory which would be suitable for all disabled persons, still less for the non-disabled as well. For example, a high lavatory is required for most arthritics, and a low one for many other disabled persons and all the non-disabled

One-fifth (46) of the persons interviewed were unable to reach the kitchen sink or taps. Of these, more than half were housewives. Even more serious, four of the people who were unable to reach the kitchen sink or taps lived alone. It seems unlikely that a standard kitchen sink could be designed which would be acceptable to everyone. Clearly, all chairbound people need a low sink. On the other hand, the arthritic housewife who cannot stand or bend, has to sit on a high stool to work in the kitchen, and therefore requires a high sink. Probably neither height would be suitable for non-disabled persons.

Over one-fifth of those in the sample (46) found that their cooker. were too high to be used without danger. Again, more than half were women whose role as housewives was thus severely restricted. A few

98

people had bought cooking rings which they fixed to a table of a suitable height.

A quarter (53) of the people in the sample were able to reach only some of their cupboards. In most cases there was sufficient accessible cupboard space to accommodate everyday necessities. But another fifth of the persons interviewed (46), most of whom were chairbound, were unable to reach any cupboards at all. Some people depended upon others to get whatever was needed from cupboards; others kept everything on accessible open shelves and other flat surfaces. Two-thirds of those to whom all cupboards were inaccessible were housewives. Of the people who were unable to reach any cupboards, a quarter lived alone.

Mrs. Rellen said: 'I spend all my days in this kitchen. I'm sorry it's so untidy. I have to keep all my food and stuff out on the draining board because I can't reach any of the cupboards. I don't like it like this. It means I haven't got room to prepare meals, and it all gets so dusty.'

Some household fixtures may be designed in such a way as to be accessible to all disabled persons, and the non-disabled as well.

Three people were unable to reach the light switch at all, and a large proportion of persons in the sample, in particular those in wheelchairs, found it difficult to do so. It is probable that if switches were placed so that they could be used without effort by the chairbound they would be easily accessible to most disabled and non-disabled persons. The same is true of money in the slot gas and electric meters. More than two-fifths (77) of those in the sample who had meters of this kind, were unable to reach them. Elderly or disabled couples, and those who lived on their own, feared the occasions on which they would be without gas or electricity.

The majority of persons in the sample (147) were unable to open the windows of their living room and kitchen. For those in wheelchairs, most windows were too high, and for others they were too stiff to be opened.

In addition, those in wheelchairs experienced special difficulties.[8] Two persons found it difficult to manoeuvre their wheelchair through the narrow doorways of their homes. Once in a room, some people found that they needed help to get out because there was insufficient space in which to swing the chair. Three housewives found that their household activities were restricted because space was too limited in some rooms.

Mrs. Guierson said: 'If the bedroom was a bit bigger I would not have to have the home help for so long each day. I could

---

8. For a full discussion of the problems involved in designing for the chairbound, see Goldsmith, P. S., *Designing for the Disabled*, Second Edition, Royal Institute of British Architects, 1967.

make the beds from my wheelchair for a start. And I could clean, like I do in the front room. But in the bedroom there's not the room to swing the wheelchair, and I can't get all round the bed, either.'

During the course of the interviews, problems relating to the use of three other facilities emerged. Electric points tended to be at or near floor level, and were inaccessible to many people. Disabled persons who lived alone or with an elderly or infirm relative, were sometimes terrified of finding themselves unable to change an electric lamp.

Some forms of heating raised problems. Almost half (101) of the persons in the sample relied on gas or electric fires. But six people were unable to reach switches which were at or near floor level. Many of the people who had coal fires depended upon help with at least part of the process of lighting a fire. Bringing fuel into the house and cleaning the fireplaces presented particularly difficult problems. As a consequence, some people were unable to have heating until late in the day when they were visited by a home help, relative, or neighbour.

3. *Adaptations*

Often much can be done to improve inadequate and unsuitable dwellings. Local authorities have permissive powers under Section 29 of the National Assistance Act, 1948, to provide the structural alterations and adaptations required by the disabled. The Ministry of Health reported in 1955 that 'the majority of local authorities were providing this service as such needs are brought to their notice'.[9] However, in the following year, the Piercy Committee stated that provision was made by 'some' local authorities and recommended its extension to all areas.[10] In 1962, the Ministry of Health[11] reported that local authorities were making wider use of their powers to adapt dwellings than had previously been the case, but the Blue Book on Community Care[12] made it clear that more could be done through adaptations to help the general classes of the disabled.

To what extent do local authorities adapt the homes of the disabled? What kind of adaptations are made, and how effective are they?

The homes of a little less than half the persons in the sample had been adapted in some way. Most of the adaptations were of a simple kind: rails were provided up stairs and steps, near the bed, and in the bathroom and lavatory; lavatory seats had been raised; and ramps were constructed. Only occasionally were more ambitious alterations, such as widening doors, attempted. By far the most common type of

9. *Report of the Ministry of Health for the year ending 31st December 1955.* Cmnd. 9857. p. 138, London, H.M.S.O.
10. *Report*, Cmnd. 9883, London, H.M.S.O., 1956, para. 135, p. 34.
11. *Report of the Ministry of Health for 1962.* Cmnd. 2062. p. 81, London, H.M.S.O.
12. *Health and Welfare. The Development of Community Care.* 1963. Cmnd. 1973, London, H.M.S.O.

adaptation was the provision of handrails. Handrails had been provided in the bathroom for about one-fifth (38), up stairs and steps for a little more than one-tenth (23), and at the side of the bed for six of the people in the sample. The height of the lavatory seats had been raised for nineteen people. Ramps had been provided in fifteen homes. In a few cases, the position of light switches had been lowered, and electric points raised. Four people had had doors widened. In only one case had more systematic adaptations been attempted.

Miss Jenkins said, 'Of course, I can't go upstairs to see how things are, because I am confined to my wheelchair. Until five years ago my parents looked after me. Then my father became ill and was taken into hospital permanently, and my mother died suddenly. I was immediately faced with the problem of having to look after myself. I did not even know how to get out of bed without help. I was glad to have the welfare officer to turn to, because they know about things. The welfare lady thought it all out and planned it. Here in the living room she had the electric points raised so that I can reach them easily from the wheelchair. And the kitchen was altered completely. They made the sink shallower, and put extended handles on the taps so that I can reach them.' The draining board was lowered at the same time, an old kitchen top was covered and gas rings were put on another old table. 'They moved the fridge to the opposite wall, and put in a point for it there, so that I've got room to swing my chair round now. And they've made a ramp for me at the threshold of the back door. It's rubber, so that I won't slip, but even so it isn't very successful. All I paid was a shilling for something they needed when the immersion switch was lowered.'

Local authorities were the main agencies through which adaptations were carried out: in two-thirds of the households which had been adapted, local authorities were responsible for alterations. But in more than a quarter of adapted homes, alterations had been carried out by the householders themselves. Hospitals had made adaptations in seven, and private charities in four households. Of course, a few households had been adapted by several agencies.

How do people enlist the help of local authorities and hospitals in the adaptation of their homes? There appeared to be no standard system but the welfare officer was by far the most common source of aid. Well over half (51) of the persons whose homes had been altered had obtained adaptations on the recommendation of the welfare officer. A further ninth had obtained alterations at the request of hospitals. On behalf of the remaining seven people, pleas for adaptations had been passed on to welfare departments by district nurses, a home help, friends and relatives.

Some welfare officers were disturbed by the major role which they played in advising on adaptations. They felt that the guidance of the hospital was essential to ensure that dwellings were correctly adapted to meet the needs of each disabled person. One welfare officer said: 'I'm offering to raise the level of the lavatory in Mrs. Russell's house because Mrs. Russell says that she finds it difficult to bend. But the hospital may *want* her to bend. It's the same with aids and gadgets.' Frequent criticisms were made about delays in even simple adaptations carried out by local authorities.

The adaptations service provided by local authorities was means tested. More than four-fifths of the people whose homes were adapted by local authorities or hospitals had not paid anything. Of the reminder, half had paid a proportion of the cost, and the rest had paid the whole cost of adaptation.

Financial aid for the payment of adaptations came from a number of sources, of which by far the most common was the local authority. Almost three-quarters of the people whose homes had been adapted, received financial assistance for alterations from the local authority, while a further eighth had been helped by hospitals. Charities had provided a part or the whole of the cost of adaptation for six people. All of the people who had paid for their adaptations, grumbled about the cost. One man said: 'The welfare officer persuaded me to have that rail put up the stairs. She said the estimate was for a few pounds. When the bill came in it was for £5. 16s. 0d. That's rather different. There's not all that much coming in here, and we have extra expenses anyway because of the disability.'

Eight people said that their adaptations were unsatisfactory. In a few instances handrails had been incorrectly placed. In most cases it was said that the inadequate structure of the dwelling made satisfactory small scale adaptations impossible. For example, sometimes insufficient room was available for steps to be satisfactorily ramped.

Almost twenty-five per cent (50) of the persons interviewed said that their homes still required adaptations. Some of them were waiting for alterations to be completed. But the majority lived in accommodation which had been declared unsuitable for satisfactory adaptation.

The adaptations discussed above were enormously helpful. But they were carried out on a small scale and were of a minor character. As such they failed to make a significant impression on the unsuitable and inadequate accommodation in which many of the disabled persons interviewed lived. It was striking that adaptations and alterations were concentrated in the local authority sector. More than half of council tenants (55) had had their accommodation adapted in some way, compared with two-fifths (21) of owner occupiers; and only a quarter (15) of those in privately rented dwellings. Yet, as we have seen, local authority housing in the sample tended to be the most, and privately rented dwellings the least, suitable.

In most cases adaptations were little more than a token in meeting need. No alterations could offset access problems caused by stairs. The real problem is one of moving disabled persons into one-floor modern housing.

4. *Rehousing*

How far did the persons interviewed benefit from new housing schemes? It was striking that for the persons interviewed to be housed by the local authority by no means guaranteed modern accommodation. As many as forty-three per cent (47) of the persons in local authority accommodation lived in dwellings built before the Second World War. Almost a third (29 per cent) of the persons in the sample had lived in their present dwellings for five years or less, the majority of whom had been rehoused by the local authority. Yet none lived in purpose-built accommodation. However, not everyone who had been rehoused by a local authority within the previous five years had obtained new accommodation: a minority had moved on to inter-war council estates. Most disabled persons cannot expect to benefit from this kind of modest housing provision. Almost half of the persons interviewed (49 per cent) had been housed in their present dwellings for more than fifteen years, and most of them for more than twenty years.

What chance has a disabled person of obtaining suitable accommodation? To what extent is the problem of housing the disabled treated as a matter of urgency?

The majority of the persons interviewed who were unsuitably or inadequately housed felt they had little hope of obtaining better accommodation. Some were dismayed by their surroundings, and others were resigned. Many people rationalized their position, like the man who said 'Well, I'm lucky. At least I've got a roof over my head.' Only a minority found sufficient strength and optimism to fight aggressively for a suitable dwelling and back their claims with letters from doctors and hospitals.

As we have seen, most of those who were inadequately or unsuitably housed lived in privately rented accommodation. All were realistic about the possibilities of obtaining more suitable accommodation in the private sector. They were aware of their weak financial position and none of them were able to buy a house. In the circumstances, the local authority was the only possible source of adequate accommodation. Yet only one-third of the people who were unsuitably or inadequately housed said that they had applied for a council house. After moving to a new area some people had failed to reapply for a dwelling with their new housing authority. A number of them saw no point in starting at the bottom of yet another housing list. Others felt that only those who were sufficiently strong physically to make a nuisance of themselves were likely to be helped by the local authority. One man said, 'It's no good getting yourself on the list if you can't get down to the housing to give them a good row now and again.' A number of people were confused about the process of applying for a local authority dwelling.

Of the people who had applied for a council house, more than half (18 out of 34) had been waiting for new accommodation for over two years, and three people for more than 15 years. In the circumstances it is hardly surprising that people were pessimistic about the possibility of being rehoused.

Three-tenths (63) of the persons in the sample had been rehoused by a local authority since 1955. However, only a little more than half of these thought they had been rehoused because they were disabled.

In some cases rehousing had been commendably swift. A third of those who were rehoused because of their disability obtained new accommodation within a year of their application. However, about half had to wait more than two years, and a quarter more than three years to be rehoused.

How successfully were the disabled persons interviewed rehoused? Almost half (30) of the people who had been rehoused said that the location of the new flat or house was unsatisfactory. Some people had been moved to hilly districts, while others were a long way from public transport, shops, and other facilities. Such criticisms were particularly frequent among disabled persons who had been moved to the larger inter-war local authority estates in north-west and south-east London.

Mrs. Dibson, aged seventy-four, had arthritis. She lived with her disabled husband at the top of a hill, on a large local authority estate in south-east London. 'When we had the old house down the bottom (of the hill) I could go out and do the shopping lovely. I could even take dad out in the chair. But the home help has to do my shopping now. It takes me twenty minutes to get to the shops, and about half an hour to come back because of the hill. Well I just couldn't do it. I used to have little rests, but it wasn't enough. And dad never goes out now because I can't control the chair down that hill. It's like that for everyone up here. We call this "Hospital Row" because we're all sick, or disabled, or something. None of us can get to the shops. And things aren't going to improve: none of us are getting any younger or better.'

Few people were rehoused in inadequate dwellings, but by no means everyone was suitably rehoused. Indeed, a little more than three-sevenths (28) of the people who had been rehoused, found

104

that their new accommodation was unsuitable, usually because of the presence of stairs.

People were realistic and knew that there was no easy solution to their housing problem, and therefore found it difficult to envisage the possibility of purpose-built dwellings. Nevertheless five-sixths of those who were unsuitably housed said that they would like to live in dwellings specially designed for the disabled, if they were available.

5. *Conclusion*

Much could have been done by means of a more ambitious programme of adaptation to make the lives of the persons interviewed more comfortable. But their main requirement appeared to be *local* rehousing to ensure that important contact with relatives and friends were maintained. To be effective, rehousing would have to take into account the accessibility of facilities such as shops and transport, as well as those within the home.

In 1956 the Piercy Committee pleaded that 'all those responsible for new local authority housing schemes should bear in mind the needs of the disabled. Some of the accommodation should be specially designed without steps and with wider doors to allow the passage of wheelchairs.'[13] In 1962, the interest of many local authorities and voluntary organizations was aroused by an exhibition of purpose-built accommodation for the disabled. The event was symptomatic of the growing awareness of the importance of suitable housing in the rehabilitation of the disabled. In 1963, the Ministry of Health reported that 'some additional housing designed for disabled people was provided by local authorities, but this remained on a small scale.'[14]

Purpose-built housing for the disabled is still confined to a relatively few small-scale schemes. As a consequence, none was represented in the sample. Yet the need for sheltered housing was clear from the experience of the persons interviewed. Severely disabled persons who lived alone, or with an elderly or infirm relative or friend clearly indicated that they would prefer such accommodation. Even so, the need for adaptations would remain: it seems unlikely that certain facilities, such as lavatories and sinks, could be produced to standard specifications which would be suitable for everyone.

6. *Summary*

The proportion of local authority tenants was twice as high in the sample as in the general population. Owner occupiers, though not those with private tenancies, were correspondingly under represented in the sample. Almost half (49 per cent) of the people inter-

---

13. *Report 1956*. Cmnd. 9883. Para. 50.
14. *Report of the Ministry of Health for the year 1963*. Cmnd. 2389. London, H.M.S.O., p. 24.

viewed had lived in their present dwellings for more than fifteen years.

Two related problems emerge from the study—inadequate dwellings and unsuitable dwellings.

The proportion of households without the standard facilities—sole use of indoor piped water, piped hot water, flush W.C., and a fixed bath, was higher in the sample of registered disabled persons than in the areas studied generally. As many as three-quarters of the people who were without all of these facilities were severely or very severely incapacitated. Of all dwellings, those which were privately rented were the most inadequate. Three-fifths of the persons who were inadequately housed had lived in their present dwellings for more than fifteen years.

About two-thirds of the persons interviewed lived in accommodation above ground floor level without a lift, or had to climb at least three unsafe steps to the front door. Adaptation could not overcome these obstacles. Almost half of the people in the sample had stairs within the household. Stairs were the only means of access to the W.C. in thirty-two cases, and to the kitchen in ten cases. In almost a quarter of the households, more than one facility was up or down stairs. All privately rented dwellings, over half of owner-occupied and two-thirds of local authority dwellings were unsuitable—altogether seventy-five per cent of the households in the sample. Owner occupied dwellings seemed to be the most unsuitable. A tenth of the households were unsuitable and lacked two or more standard amenities: on the whole local authority housing tended to be the most satisfactory.

In addition there were problems which worried only certain groups of the persons interviewed. Many disabled persons found that some facilities were unsuitably designed. Five people were unable to use the W.C. because it was too low. A fifth of the persons interviewed were unable to use the kitchen sink or taps; a fifth were unable to use the cooker; a quarter were able to use only some cupboards, while a further fifth were unable to use any cupboards, and more than half of these were housewives. Two-fifths of those with money in the slot gas and electric meters were unable to reach them, and the majority of persons in the sample were unable to open the living room and kitchen windows. People also found it difficult to change lamps, switch on gas and electric fires, and make coal fires. Thoughtful design could eliminate some of these problems. But there are facilities particularly W.C.'s and sinks, which have to be adapted to meet individual needs.

Most adaptations were of a simple kind. The majority involved the construction of handrails, the raising of lavatories, and the provision of ramps. Twenty-five per cent of adaptations were carried out by the disabled themselves, while another two-thirds were completed by local authorities and the remainder by a hospital or charities. Most applications for adaptations in the home were made through welfare officers. Delays in completion were reported to be usual. Local authority adaptations were a means tested service. As many as fifty households required alteration, but most of them were said to be unsuitable. The small scale service in the areas studied made little impact on the housing problems which affected many of the persons interviewed.

One-third of the people who were unsuitably housed had applied for local authority housing, half of them more than two years ago. Three-tenths of the persons in the sample had been rehoused by the local authority since 1955. Of these, half had waited more than two years, and a quarter more than three years, for new accommodation. Half of them found the location, and almost as many, the dwelling, unsuitable. In fact, by no means all of those who lived in local authority accommodation benefited from new housing schemes: almost half were housed in dwellings which had been built before 1939. It is clear that the long term housing needs of the majority of the disabled persons interviewed were more likely to be met through the local authority than the private sector: most of those interviewed belonged to the low income groups. The real need was for local rehousing to avoid removal from nearby relatives and friends. Moreover proximity to shops, public transport and other facilities was essential. Some of the persons interviewed, mainly those who were severely incapacitated and lived alone or with a frail or infirm person, required sheltered accommodation in their own locality.

7. DISABLED PERSONS AND THEIR FAMILIES

It is the purpose of this chapter to explore the changes brought about by disability in the expectation of family life over time. How far do these differ according to degree of incapacity and the variation of capacity over time? How did people feel that disability affected their relationship with members of the family, and in particular their attitudes towards marriage and children?

1. *Disabled persons living with their parents*

Although none of the persons interviewed were below the age of sixteen years, eleven per cent of them (25) still lived with at least one parent. All of these were below the age of sixty-five years, but less than half were aged forty-five years and under, and only three of them were below the age of twenty-five years. The majority of persons living with their parents—three-fifths—were slightly or moderately incapacitated.

Capacity for employment appeared to be a major factor in reducing the possibility of tension between parents and disabled adult children. The relative youth of persons living with their parents, together with their generally low degree of incapacity, determined that a comparatively high proportion of them were employed—almost half (11), compared with less than one-fifth of the sample as a whole. Where the disabled person went out to work, disability appeared to place little strain on relationships within the household. This was true even when the disabled person was severely incapacitated. Even among those who were unable to work, relatively young disabled persons and their middle aged parents usually accepted the necessity for even extensive help with little difficulty.

But there were cases, particularly when the disability was progressive, in which middle aged parents found the prospect of the continuing and probably increasing dependence of the child in their old age distressing. For them, nothing could compensate for the loss of the prospect of decreasing parental responsibility.

Mr. Duncan said, 'I can't do a lot of things, but I'll be all right. They've taught me how to make baskets at the hospital. I'm sure I can make a good living selling them round here. The hospital has promised to put customers on to me. And I'm friendly with two of the nurses. My parents don't do much for me. In fact, I get more help from friends than members of the family. They take me out in the car and so on.' His mother, aged forty-seven, said, 'It takes a lot of money to keep a man like that. Much more than the allowance. He wants to go out, have records, and clothes, and so on, the same as anyone else of his age. So I have to go out to work. I cook hospital meals. The trouble is that when I'm out there's often no one to look after him. I have to help him in all sorts of ways when I'm at home, and then there's the housework to do. I get to the end of my tether sometimes—I don't know how long I can keep it up for. The trouble is, he'll never work. He's going to get worse, not better. It's like having a young child all your life. You're so tied all the time.' His father was also upset. 'I'm a bus driver. That means I've got to work shifts, so I sometimes manage to get home while my wife is at work. I can get Gerald's dinner then, and make sure he's all right. It's a load off his mother's mind. I mean to say, it's not natural for a man of his age not to be working. I'm fifty-six now, so I haven't got much longer to go myself. How will we do for money when I retire?'
(Moderately incapacitated, but a progressive disability).

The likelihood of a disabled person expressing guilt about dependence on a parent increased with age. The strain on parents in households where the disabled persons were not employed increased with age, too. Altogether, of the parents with whom disabled persons lived, three-fifths were elderly and one-third were disabled. In such circumstances parents worried about the unreliability of the help they provided.

It was striking that none of the disabled persons interviewed, however great their dependence on a parent, articulated any fear for the future. In contrast, parents invariably expressed anxiety: what was to become of the disabled child when no parental home was available? Some parents had been forced to consider concrete proposals for alternative forms of care. All were profoundly uneasy.

Mr. Sampson, aged forty-eight, was a spastic. He lived with his mother, aged eighty-one, and his forty-six years old sister who was an epileptic, in their own house in Middlesex. His movements were erratic, and he could move only when supported on both sides. His mother said 'His hands are affected and all down his left side. He can't even feed himself. He can't speak much. They reckon he's mental but I don't believe it. It's just that he's never been taught. I've got to run round after him all day long. It's like having a baby, except that he's so heavy and strong.' (At this point she bundled him into a cap, muffler and coat, and pushed him to a chair beside a table in the small back yard, where he had an enamel bowl full of tape measures. He proceeded to roll the tape measures slowly one by one and put them carefully into the enamel bowl). 'I undo the tapes every evening ready for the next day I feel like a murderer. He's so pleased when he's finished them. And it takes him ages to do them up. We can't go on much longer I'm getting old, and Rita's bad. We told them, so the rehabilitation people sent him to a mental hospital. But they showed me where they put the patients when they're ill. It was a huge long room with a window at one end. All down the side of the walls there were beds close together. There was a young chap sitting at a desk in the middle of the room. The men in the beds were just lying still staring up at the ceiling. It looked like the poor house. I didn't like the thought of my son having to go there. You want a bit of home comfort when you're ill. That would just put him back, wouldn't it? We're good class, we are, above that sort of thing. I don't know what to do. They might even cure him. But he'd miss all his home comforts like his electric blanket. That doctor was very good though. He said he'd look after him personally. But I can't get over the sight of those men lying there doing nothing—just like animals And that chap writing at the desk and taking no notice of them. It breaks my heart to think my son might be put there. I'm afraid of what will happen when I'm dead. I want to get him into a nice home before then. Somewhere by the sea. I've devoted my life to that poor afflicted boy.'

(Mr. Sampson was very severely incapacitated).

2. Single persons and marriage

How far did younger persons feel that disability had affected their opportunities or wish for marriage? Did they feel that they were likely to be able to bring up children?

Altogether, twenty-nine of the younger persons interviewed were single. Of these, two-thirds stated that they thought disability had made no difference to their chances of getting married. All but one of the single persons below the age of forty said that they intended to get married. They expressed their intention with calm confidence Two people were busily planning for weddings and new homes But certain conditions, particularly epilepsy, may produce more difficulties for marriage than others. Most of the epileptics interviewed were divorced, separated or single.

One third of younger single disabled persons felt that a marriage partner could not be expected to look after someone disabled from the outset of marriage. A distinction was drawn between disability which occurred in the course of married life, and that which occurred beforehand. In the case of the former, it was held to be perfectly justifiable to expect a spouse to provide all the help and support required by the disabled person. On the whole, interest in the possibility of marriage declined with capacity.

3. *Bringing up a family*

What difficulties did disabled persons experience in marriage and family life? Only a little more than one-third (23) of married persons below pensionable age had dependent children. Most of the disabled parents with children were women. The effect of disability on disabled parents differed enormously as between men and women. As might be expected, disabled fathers with dependent children were of all the younger men interviewed, those most acutely aware of their loss of role if they were unable to find employment. The two employed fathers with dependent children in the sample experienced constant anxiety about their ability to maintain their jobs until their children were at work. Both were determined that their own disability should not limit the opportunities available to their children. The non-employed fathers were deeply concerned about the economic effects of their disability on their families. They were aware that their families were missing commonly accepted activities.

Mr. Franklin, aged fifty-two, lived with his wife, son aged sixteen, and daughter aged thirteen, in a council flat in an industrial area of Middlesex. 'I'm paralysed down my right side. I had a stroke two years ago, so I had to give up work. It's affected the kids in lots of ways because I can't go to work. I just sit and sleep and smoke alone all day. We haven't had a holiday in three years, not since the stroke. We can't afford it. But we're going to Lourdes this year through the Church. You pay so much and the Society helps with the rest. They organize it. It's the Society of Our Lady of Lourdes. We're going with all the other invalids.'
(Severely incapacitated).

Non-employed men with dependent children appeared to become more anxious than others about the loss of their role as breadwinners. It was not merely that their families suffered economically. They themselves often felt purposeless, and expressed resentment at the family's economic dependence on the wife. Moreover they were conscious that as a result their relationship with their wives and children was frequently strained.

None of the fathers interviewed felt that their disability had interfered with their capacity to play their part in bringing up the children. Only one man admitted that his children were conscious of his

111

disability, and he was himself acutely aware of his physical appearance. However, the others felt that their children accepted their disability completely.

All but three of the women with dependent children had the support of their husbands. Disabled mothers of dependent children were conscious of the economic loss suffered by their families as a result of their disability, but for most this was a peripheral problem compared with the practical difficulties which faced an incapacitated mother who attempted to bring up young children. Where the mother was severely incapacitated, her husband tended to take over many of her responsibilities. Wherever this situation arose, women expressed disquiet about the resulting strain on their husbands. Moreover, they tended to feel some resentment when much of the attention of the children, which they knew in other circumstances would be attracted by them as mothers, was inevitably diverted to the fathers.

Mrs. Guierson said, 'When I was first really bad two years ago I had terrible back aches after the baby. I did nothing but cry, I was very depressed. My husband is placid, he can't row. I was a bit dogmatic. I cried if someone asked me how I was. My husband used to do everything for me. But I've been more independent since I've had the chair. I get frustrated now because of the baby. It's always watching and not being able to get up and do what he wants yourself. I give him a blanket bath in his pram. I kept him with me till he was eighteen months old. They wanted me to put him in a nursery but I refused. The baby has turned into a real daddy's boy. He washes him and dresses him. His father's had more to do with him than me. But you can't really say that it's made any difference because no two babies are the same. He still wears nappies at night because I don't like to wake up my husband to ask him to put the baby on the pot, and I know I can't get there. He's at nursery all day now. And when he comes home he's a little rebel. He shows off because he's away from discipline. My husband is the only one who can do anything with him. He takes no notice of me, and he goes to his dad for everything. I get very depressed if I feel bad, or I can't manage the baby, you know, when I see the baby getting my husband down. The tears just fall.'
(Very severely incapacitated).

Others regretted being deprived by disability of some of the ordinary pleasures of motherhood, such as helping to teach young children to walk. Most mothers felt that their disability had made little difference to their children. Children usually appeared to have accepted their mothers' disability easily, though the majority were said to have matured earlier than other children because their mothers de pended upon their help. Five mothers reported that their children had become disturbed as a result of their disability. It was striking that all these children had been taken into care. Two mothers found that serious disciplinary problems arose when their children came home.

Mrs. Warner, aged forty, lived with her husband and two dependent children in a council prefab in Middlesex. 'I was taken to hospital with pneumonia four years ago. I had a stroke while I was in there, and I couldn't move my right arm and leg. The leg went gangrene and I had to have it amputated. I was in hospital about a year altogether. My arm still doesn't work. It's very weak. I went into hospital again last year. I feel that the children play me up too much. They were with a foster mother the first time I went to hospital. Last time they went to a children's residential nursery. They were not like that before.'
(Moderately incapacitated).

In one of the families interviewed, the five dependent children were taken into care while their very severely incapacitated mother was in hospital. But their father became so anxious about their apparently disturbed state, that he felt there was no alternative to having his wife and children at home. Therefore, he gave up work, accepted national assistance, and stayed at home to look after his family. Another woman blamed the apparent instability of her children on her condition.

In two households, both mother and father were disabled. Both sets of parents felt that the children had adapted to the situation. They themselves, however, felt considerable guilt, and missed some of the pleasures usually involved in having young children. Nevertheless it was clear that there were additional problems involved in bringing up children when both parents are incapacitated. For example, role sharing was far more difficult. Moreover, acute practical problems arose at times of emergency, such as illness. In both cases parents were anxious because they were sometimes too exhausted to give attention to their children. The additional strains arising from the determined attempts of disabled fathers to maintain a job imposed further stress on their respective marriages. In both cases, the father had moved from job to job. In an attempt to share roles more effectively, one couple had become joint wardens of business premises.

Even when children were independent, the disabled parent still faced problems. Of course, the difficulties of younger parents were different from those of the elderly. Of the forty persons in the sample who lived with older children, more than half (26) were below pensionable age. In households where children had recently become employed (20) the majority (13) included a disabled man. Disabled fathers in such households found that they were still required to make the major contribution to their families' income. Their employment difficulties continued to produce personal frustration, and economic problems for the household.

As many as thirty-seven per cent (78) of the persons interviewed had considered seriously before having a family, whether disability was likely to deny their children any crucial opportunities. Only nine people (six per cent of the sample) had decided that they would have no children. In most cases they said that their decision had been made for financial reasons. However, there were a few people who had been advised against having families for medical reasons. Those who accepted such advice later regretted having done so.

Mrs. Elson, aged fifty-one, lived with her husband in a new council flat in Hackney. She was confined to a wheel chair. 'I've got multiple sclerosis. I've had it for twenty-five years. I found out just before I got married. For about a year before that, my leg used to drag occasionally. I went to see about it because I was going to get married. They told me to give up work, and that I was not to have children. I'm sorry I took any notice of the advice about children. I should have just had them. Plenty of people manage. But I didn't know other people with it then. We didn't adopt any because we didn't think it fair on the child.'

Others ignored advice against having children, and did not regret their decision.

Mrs. English, aged fifty, lived with her son in a council flat in South London. She had a magnificent corgi. 'My husband was killed in the war just after my son was born. I was advised not to have children. I didn't tell my husband, because he'd never have agreed if he'd known. I don't regret it at all. But he never saw the baby. Seven years of my life was gone, spent in hospitals. All that time I was away from my son. He had foster parents, and my sister used to bring him to see me every Sunday. That was the greatest thing—I missed his childhood. He was a very quiet, placid boy. He never said very much. My sister was very good to him and so were the other children. But he worried because he never had a sister or a brother like his cousin. He never knew his father so we don't talk about it. I feel I miss something even now. He was a very good husband. It's a long while ago, but the feeling is still there.'

More than two-thirds (43) of those who had families said that their disability had made a substantial difference to the way in which the children had been brought up. Disabled mothers tended to emphasize

114

the difficulties caused by inevitable periods of fostering, and an early acceptance by the children of responsibilities within the home. Disabled fathers, on the other hand, were anxious because their unemployment, long periods of sickness, or low wages had restricted their children's opportunities for staying at school, going on holidays, having a nice home, and enough pocket money. Although most parents candidly admitted the difficulties involved in caring for their children, only a few regretted their decision to have a family.

Some disabled parents found that the practical difficulties of bringing up children were more easily overcome than the prejudice of persons outside the home. Mothers sometimes found that neighbourhood opinion reacted strongly against the disabled mother and her child.

> Mrs. Edmonds, aged twenty-seven, lived with her husband and young baby in a house on a large inter-war council estate in South East London. 'I had polio in 1945. People think I'm mentally retarded because I've got something wrong with my legs. I don't get much time to go out with the baby, but when I do I get stared at. It makes you feel embarrassed. Friends who are all right don't come round any more. They say you shouldn't get married and have children because you're not capable. I've learnt new ways of doing things since I've had the baby home. I've learnt how to bath the baby on the table from my handicapped friend. In the hospital they told me to bath her on my knee, but I've got no lap. I don't really think the disability will affect her. She's born with this, so it doesn't matter.'

4. *Younger married couples*

For those below pensionable age whose children had left home, the problems created by disability had become simplified to some extent. In particular, the economic pressure on fathers was eased, while mothers were relieved of many of the duties which they felt obliged to carry out even for independent children who remained at home. But the desire to maintain traditional roles within the household remained strong. However, the ability to do so was often less assured than in the earlier years of marriage: degree of incapacity tended to increase with age. Altogether, a little more than one-fifth (23) of persons below pensionable age lived with a spouse alone. Of these, only three were slightly incapacitated. Thus, with only one person available at home to provide help, the strain on a marriage usually remained considerable and sometimes increased, when children left home.

Heads of households often found that the maintenance of their role involved a change of job and a consequent loss of prospects. Moreover, age as well as disability restricted choice of employment.

Housewives found their environment more flexible than did men in employment. Most reported that in spite of severe incapacity they were able to adapt their methods to enable them to carry out most of the tasks required of them in the home. Housework, particularly cooking and cleaning floors, presented great difficulties to those who were unable to stand or bend. Several housewives used long benches in the kitchen from which they managed to reach all their flat working surfaces as well as the stove and sink. Two women found that they were able to clean floors with mops and buckets of water from long benches. A number of housewives had produced a variety of methods for carrying things about the house because they were unable to walk without support. Some used specially made trolleys, while others sewed pockets to walking frames, or used push chairs. Women with the use of only one hand found certain aspects of cooking particularly difficult.

Mrs. Lennox, aged fifty-six, lived with her husband in a terraced house in West London. She had a stroke five years ago, and as a result, was unable to use her right arm. 'I just couldn't manage the potatoes, and I felt it was all wrong for my husband to come home and do housework after a day at work, when I was at home all day. So I found that if I got a nail screwed to the draining board, I could push the potato onto that and peel round it. Then there were tins. I couldn't open tins with one hand. I've taught myself to use my left hand, but I've got nothing to hold with. Well, now I take my shoes off and hold the tin with my feet.' (Moderately incapacitated.)

Of course, to restrict analysis to the performance of traditional roles is to simplify enormously. In most households men wanted to help with the housework, while women were keen to find employment outside the home. Some people went to considerable lengths to ensure that they would continue to engage in these activities. A few men found that housework provided a useful opportunity to develop manual dexterity which was often important in finding a job later.

Married women who were used to employment outside the home, felt that they were missing a great deal by being forced to stay at home, particularly once they were freed from the care of children.

In the case of disabled women, it often happened that the husband took over part of his wife's role within the household. Such arrangements sometimes gave rise to considerable difficulties.

Mrs. Masterton's husband said, 'She's very up and down. You've caught her in one of her bad patches. When she's like this I have to do most of the housework. She'll have spent all afternoon doing my dinner. I have to leave early to come home and see that she's

116

all right. And I have to get the breakfast and put her to rights before I leave in the morning. I do the shopping in the dinner hour and bring it home. It breaks up the day for her and I can make sure nothing terrible has happened. But I'm losing a lot of overtime. I'm a fitter. We need all the money we can get, too. We're up to our eyes in debt because we bought all new furniture when we moved in here last year. It's a terrible headache. And I never seem to stop.'
(Very severely incapacitated).

Most of the women whose husbands provided extensive help within the home expressed guilt at their failure to fulfil all their duties.

Mrs. Messingham, aged thirty-seven, lived with her husband in a new council flat in South East London. She had Parkinson's disease. 'You must get sick of hearing me say that Jack does all these things. I feel terrible about it. It seems ever so bad that a man comes home from work, and then has to turn round and do all these things. But it's true, and I can't help it. It must sound dreadful to other people.'
(Severely incapacitated).

In some cases roles had become reversed: the disabled husband stayed at home to look after the house, while the wife went out to work. But none of the men involved felt at ease with the situation. Most of them talked about 'being on the scrap heap'.

There were a few households in the group in which the disabled person was so severely incapacitated as to depend entirely upon the spouse. Most of these cases involved very severely incapacitated men. In some ways the stress arising from this situation was greater for younger couples than those in retirement. Younger non-disabled wives usually felt impelled to engage in full time employment to support themselves and their disabled husbands. Usually they were only marginally better off than they would have been had they depended entirely on state benefits. Most were unsure whether it was worth the effort involved. There were men entirely dependent on their wives, whose capacity varied from time to time. At certain periods of the year they required the constant attendance of their wives. As a result, the wives' employment tended to be intermittent, and difficult to obtain.

Mr. Thomas, aged fifty-six, lived with his fifty-four years old wife in a council house in South East London. He had bronchitis. 'I'm not too bad now. I can sit in the chair, but I can't do anything. Come November time though, and regular as clockwork I take to my bed. My wife didn't think I'd get over the last lot. I was upstairs for three months. She works in the cleaners normally, but when I'm like that she has to stay home. And then we're back on the old assistance. The time before last she lost her job. They kept it open for three weeks, and that was it. Mind you, I can see their point of view. I don't blame them. It was a better paid job than this one. They were very good in this job last year. But you can't tell how long they'll let it go on for. They'll probably get fed up too.'

(Very severly incapicitated).

In a number of cases the demands of a severely incapacitated man on the wife had become overwhelming, and the marriage was under a great strain.

Mr. Beck, aged fifty-six, had a stroke five years ago, and was unable to work. He lived with his wife in a crowded and poor area of North London. Mrs. Beck said, 'He won't do anything. He just sits in that chair watching me. He says he can't do things, but how does he know if he never tries? He won't go as far as the garden because he says he can't walk. He does nothing but sit in that chair and smoke. I have to do everything for him—wash him, dress him, he won't try nothing.' (She burst into tears). 'But it's the money that's the worst. He smokes all day and the assistance won't run to it. I keep telling him that. But since that stroke he doesn't seem to understand some things. Look at him. He just sits there grinning. He doesn't understand. It's got me down so much lately that I'm under the doctor. These are the pills he's given me to take. He says it's my nerves. I don't know how much longer I can stand it.'

(Very severely incapacitated).

In fact, surprisingly few of the very severely incapacitated men who were entirely dependent on their wives were prepared to express concern for the strain which their disability placed on their wives. This may have been due to a refusal to acknowledge utter dependence or it may reflect the expectations of submissiveness in a wife on the part of a husband in our culture. Doubtless, some men preferred not to face the possibility of a relationship on which they were dependent being destroyed. To others there probably appeared to be no point in expressing concern about a situation over which they had little control. Moreover, some people were understandably resentful at being forced to make demands on their wives against their own wishes.

It seemed clear that a few men were willing to exaggerate their incapacity in an effort to tie their wives more closely to them. But there were others who felt that disabled persons should not be expected to attempt to extend their capacity. One man said, 'It's bad enough being disabled without having to try to do difficult things'.

In spite of the difficulties, most people reported warm and loving relationships. Indeed, some people felt that disability had brought them closer together. But a minority of marriages—about ten per cent —were reported to be under great strain. In particular, stress seemed to arise where both partners in the marriage were substantially incapacitated, or where one was very severely incapacitated and largely dependent upon the help of a non-disabled husband or wife.

Whereas men tended to expect to be cared for by their wives, women did not feel that husbands had the same obligation. The distress felt by some wives at the stress placed by disability on their marriages added immeasurably to the difficulties presented by their condition.

Mrs. Atkins said, 'I've got rheumatoid arthritis. Nothing seems to come of my prayers. I've got used to the chair now. It's better than staying in. My daughter takes me out. But I'm worried about her. She's thirty-two. She should be out meeting people, not looking after me. My husband won't do anything to help. I don't even know how much money he gets now. He just gives me £6 a week for the house and I have to pay £2 11s. 0d. out of that for rent. He never used to be like this. I know it's no good for him any more. I get very depressed. He won't speak to me. He hasn't spoken to me for six months.'

Altogether, eleven of the persons interviewed (five per cent) were divorced or separated. It appeared that marriages were more likely to break up if it was the wife rather than the husband who became disabled. Moreover, marriages tended to break up soon after the onset of a condition rather than after a long period of strain induced by disability.

Of course, those who faced the greatest difficulties on the breakup of a marriage were women who retained the care of dependent children. There were three divorced or separated mothers in the sample who were bringing up dependent children without the help of a husband.

Mrs. Fulmer said, 'I've got rheumatoid arthritis. It began in 1961. My husband left me for another woman in 1961 as soon as I knew I was like this. I haven't seen him for four years. I've got a separation for adultery. I don't think I'll improve now. I was marvellous after Camden Road. The children came back and I took them every day to the nursery. But my legs got too bad, so I had to send them back to care. My little girl of eight lives with me. She does most of the housework. The two youngest come home now for week-ends, and holidays because they're old enough to see to themselves a bit now. They like being home. My eldest daughter has been back home for five months. The other two cry when they

have to go back. It hurts me, especially when the youngest wants to know why she has to go when the eldest can stay. I feel bad about putting on the eldest. But she's got her friends and she goes to Brownies and that. Still, it is difficult to manage without a man. But they are my three children and I can't forget them. And they're not bad children.'
(Very severely incapacitated).

Yet even experience of upheavals which result from divorce in households where there are young children and a disabled mother, did not necessarily destroy faith in the institution of marriage. One divorced woman had remarried, while another was planning to do so.

5. *Older married couples*

Even among the younger persons interviewed there were some who lived with a disabled spouse. For them, the help which each partner in the marriage could provide for each other was often uncertain. But in general such problems became pressing among disabled persons of pensionable age. Altogether, a little more than two-fifths of the persons interviewed lived with an elderly spouse. Yet with age and increasing incapacity the burden of help required of a spouse was often immense.

Mr. Gordon, aged eighty-two, had his right leg amputated from below the knee. In addition, he had gangrene in a toe on his left foot. He lived with his wife in one room at the top of a tall terraced house in North London. He was in bed fully clothed, trying to keep warm in bitter weather. In spite of the small electric fire on a chair, the room was very cold. A black cat was curled up in front of the fire on the chair. Most of the room was taken up by the bed, the small kitchen table which was littered with food spread out on newspaper, and a small gas stove and sink. There was only one small cupboard, so that most of their belongings were arranged in neat piles on the floor. His wife said, 'I have to do all for him now, girlie. Wash him, dress him, and all. He's somehow lost heart. And he can't hear at all. I might as well talk to myself. It's very wearing having to shout everything, if you know what I mean. Of course, I do all the housework. It's what you'd expect. But I can't heave him in and out of bed like I used to. It's a terrible struggle and I've strained myself a couple of times already. My sons clubbed together and bought him a nice new wheel chair but I've got to get him into it. It's too much at my age, you know. And since he's had that toe it's been murder. The lavatory is right at the bottom, you see. Well, I mean, he can't get down there. So we have a pail up here. And there's only one person who can take it downstairs to empty it. It's coming up that nearly kills me. The nurse comes in

to do his toe, and that's all the help we get. I don't know how much longer I can go on like this, I'm sure.'
(Mr. Gordon was very severely incapacitated).

. *Living without a spouse*
More than two-fifths of widowed, divorced or separated persons ved with their children. In all but three cases, such persons were middle-aged or elderly, and the children with whom they lived were independent.

Men living with older children at the height of their earning ower found their sense of inferiority accentuated. In financial terms, he disabled person compared unfavourably with the child. The economic disadvantage of the disabled parent compared with the working hild was clearly reflected in the contraction of the parent's recreational and social activities.

Most of the disabled persons who lived with single children expressed anxiety about their own future once the child married. ven those who lived with adult married children and their families elt insecure lest the whim of the child or in-laws should leave hem without home or help. In reaction, the disabled person ended to claim complete independence from the family, and only fter probing, grudgingly acknowledged a wide range of family help. Disabled parents were often willing to express openly their anxiety bout their relationship with their family. But in some cases the nxiety emerged only after detailed descriptions of the lengths) which the disabled person went to avoid conflict with children nd their families. One woman said that she did not use the oven ecause she was unable to clean it to her daughter's satisfaction. nother remained in her bedroom throughout the day to avoid nnoying her family. Most people said that they were careful not to nterfere in the way in which grandchildren were brought up. Open fts were rare. Where they occurred, additional factors, such as inadequate housing, were present.

In middle or old age, some single, seperated or divorced persons ithout children lived with siblings, usually unmarried sisters. Most eople remarked that they were grateful that an unmarried sister was vailable to provide security for them. In such cases, it was usual for ne disabled person to adopt the role of housewife, while the non-isabled sister went out to work. However, their financial independnce of each other was invariably emphasized. But it was clear that ne disabled person benefited incidentally from the household pos-ssions which the working sister was able to provide, even though ousekeeping and rent were contributed equally. However, a sister's ome did not necessarily guarantee security for the disabled person.

121

Miss Dawson, aged sixty, lived with her sister in a new council house in North London. 'I had infantile paralysis when I was four years old. I can't do the housework like I used to. I've always done the housework and cooking because my mother died when I was ten. Things take such a long time now. But I can do most things for myself. I felt very badly about it when my sister had to start doing some of the housework. She's never had to bother before, you see. And she goes out to work all day. The flat's no good for me. I've got to go upstairs to bed, and I can't really manage the stairs. So once I'm down I have to stay down for the day. We've been living here for six years. I don't feel I can ask to move from here because my sister has just spent so much money on doing it up. Apart from that, she hasn't been widowed long. She'll probably meet someone and get married again. I couldn't intrude on that sort of thing. Anyway, I don't altogether see eye to eye with my sister. If I had the choice I'd live on my own. Why don't they build special little flats for us disabled? I'd love that. I hope you don't mind talking here in the kitchen like this. You see, my nephew has come here for the day. He's in the front room, and I don't like to disturb him. He'll be going out soon, and then we can go in there.'
(Severely incapacitated).

7. Living alone

With age it became more likely for people to suffer bereavement and to live alone. Almost a quarter (50) of the persons interviewed lived alone,[1] and of these only one was below forty-five years, while three-fifths were above pensionable age. More than three-quarters of those who lived alone were widowed.

For such persons, the effects of disability were in some respects simplified. The impact of disability was concentrated on them alone. There were no complex relationships within the household to be affected nor were there family roles to be modified. The major preoccupation of persons living alone was to maintain themselves, to survive physically, not to play roles within the family.

The difficulties involved in surviving were often immense. As many as half of the persons interviewed who lived alone were severely or very severely incapacitated, whereas only three were slightly incapacitated.

Mrs. Adams said, 'I can't walk at all without the boot and iron. I've got duodenal ulcers, and I've had three haemorrhages. I have to have a walking frame now, so I can't carry anything. That's why

---

1. The proportion of single person households in England and Wales was 15 per cent. See statistics of the General Register Office, *Sample Census 1966*, H.M.S.O., London. The large proportion of single person households in the sample is probably a function of the registers. It is reasonable to assume that persons living alone are likely to create a large proportion of the demand for local authority services.

I've made these pockets to go on the frame. I carry everything in these. There's always a way. I'm a living wonder really, I shouldn't be here at all. I haven't been out except in the garden for over a year now. The home help has to do the shopping and the cleaning, but I manage the rest on my own. It's very slow, though. I managed to do some ironing last week. But I'll never get upstairs again, I know that. For the sake of other people I stay downstairs. Accidents cause such a lot of trouble for other people. I'm on my own all the time now, of course. I worry a lot in case I have an accident. No one will find me until the next day. I was on my own here for four years before the welfare knew about me. But they've done a good job.'
(Severely incapacitated).

Most of the elderly persons interviewed seemed to find it easier to accept dependence on outside help and the enormous contraction of social contacts than was true of younger persons. Their expectations of a social and family role were lower. Younger persons usually found the frustrations of being housebound and largely dependent on others far greater.

However, the problems arising from incapacity were most acute for persons who had been deprived of companionship and help within the home after the onset of disability. For them, the transfer of dependence from the flexible and constant care of a relative, usually a spouse, to the rigid support provided by the statutory services, and the sporadic and less reliable help of neighbours or relatives beyond the household initially created a large measure of insecurity. Moreover, in some instances people suddenly lost the help which enabled them to participate to some extent in household activities.

Mrs. Jones, aged sixty-five, had rheumatoid arthritis. She lived alone in a new council flat in South London. She walked slowly with the help of crutches. 'It all began eight years ago. My husband had to do everything for me. He stayed home from work. It was he that got me to walk, then I gradually began to get about the house with his help, and do a bit of housework. But I couldn't have done without him. You know, he helped me to do things. He helped me to a kitchen chair to get the dinner. Then one day—it was just over five years ago—he had a heart attack. And that was it—dead. I didn't know what to do. We had been together for so long, and he was ever such a good man. Well, I just went back. I couldn't do anything. They took me into hospital again for a few weeks, and when I was due to come home I went to see the almoner about some help because I knew I couldn't manage on my own. I was ever so worried. So she put me in touch with the welfare and got the home help and that. They had to come and raise the lavatory

seat for me before I could come home, you see. But it's not th
same at all. I can't do so much myself, and it takes a long time.
(Severely incapacitated).

8. Summary

Where younger single persons still lived in the parental home, th
difficulties arising from disability were mainly those which resulte
from anxiety about the future rather than the problem of providin
help in the home. Both the disabled persons concerned and their mid
dle aged parents readily accepted the necessity for the provision eve
of extensive help where it was required. But some parents were ap
palled at the prospect of the continuing and, where the disability wa
progressive, increasing dependence of the child. Elderly parents wer
fearful for the future of the disabled person: what would happe
when they were too frail to provide the help required? Some parent
had already been forced to explore the possibility of alternative, in
stitutional forms of care, and were discouraged by what they ha
found.

Most younger single persons felt that their attitudes towards mar
riage remained unchanged by disability; indeed, some were plannin
to get married in the near future. But attitude towards marriag
appeared to be affected by degree of incapacity. In general, those wh
were severely or very severely incapacitated felt that they were un
likely to get married. They tended to rationalize their disappointmen
by distinguishing the care required of a spouse from the outset o
marriage from that necessitated by the onset of disability in the cours
of marriage: the latter, but not the former, was considered to b
acceptable. Altogether, two-thirds of younger single persons felt tha
they would get married.

Most people thought it worthwhile to accept the difficulties invol
ved for a disabled person in marriage. Most of the married peopl
interviewed reported warm and satisfactory marriages. Thirty-seve
per cent of the persons interviewed had been disabled when faced wit
the decision of whether to have a family. But only six per cent ha
decided against having children. Most people with families admitte
that there had been problems: for disabled mothers, there were th
difficulties of caring for children; for disabled fathers there wer
problems arising from the consequences of a low income. All but a fe
people felt that they had been right to have children. The parents
main preoccupation was to maintain the role of breadwinner or house
wife. People tended to express guilt whenever they were forced b
incapacity to share roles or abandon them altogether to the spouse
In addition, of course, there emerged the practical problems involve
in one spouse adopting part or all of a second major family role. I

was felt that the role of the disabled mother was most important for younger children, whereas the father's role became important later as his income was required to buy opportunities and a satisfactory environment for the children. But the problems remained, though they were less acute, even when children became independent. Some marriages were reported to be under strain, particularly those where one person was severely or very severely incapacitated. About five per cent of the persons interviewed were divorced or separated. In most cases, marriages had broken up soon after the onset of disability. Almost all involved disabled wives. But two of those who had experienced broken marriages were prepared to embark upon a new marriage.

Later in married life, when the children had left home, the contraction in the sources of help available in the home presented considerable difficulties. Almost a quarter of the persons interviewed lived with a spouse alone. The preservation of the disabled person's role as breadwinner or housewife continued to be a major preoccupation.

In old age, expectations changed. Those who lived with a wife or husband found that the help of an elderly or frail person was not always reliable. On the other hand, elderly persons in the care of their children were usually anxious lest conflict within the household should deprive them of a home. As might be expected, with age the proportion of persons living alone increased. For persons living alone (about a quarter of the sample), the main problem was to survive, if necessary by enlisting the help of relatives, and, where these failed, the local welfare services. On the whole, elderly persons found dependence on others easier to accept than the younger persons interviewed.

The purpose of this chapter is threefold. First, the kind and extent of help required by the persons interviewed to maintain themselves in their own homes will be described. Second, the sources of help used by the disabled persons interviewed will be discussed. Finally, the use and availability of local authority services will be considered: what role did they play in enabling persons to remain in their own homes? How far did the help available meet the needs of disabled persons? Were there particular needs which were not met?

In recent years attention has been increasingly focussed on the importance of domicilary services as the emphasis on the goals of social policy has shifted from institutional to community care for incapacitated persons. In spite of the publication of ministerial guidance there are enormous regional variations in the provision of domicilary services.[1] For example, in 1963, it was found that some local authorities provided three and four times more district nurses and home helps per thousand persons aged sixty-five years and above, than others.[2] More recent attempts to compare local authority provisions show similar variations.[3] Local authorities even vary in the methods they adopt to administer services: some local authorities administer, say, their own meals service directly, while others may do so through any one of a number of voluntary bodies such as the W.R.V.S. and the Red Cross.[4]

Most of the studies which have attempted to compare need with the provision of aid have concentrated largely on the requirements of elderly persons.[5] Little attempt has been made so far to describe and assess the needs of incapacitated persons generally. The present study can make only a modest contribution to this end: persons registered

1. *Health and Welfare: the development of community care*, Cmnd. 1973, London, H.M.S.O.
2. Townsend, P., 'The Timid and the Bold', *New Society*, May 23, 1963.
3. Davies, B., *Social Needs and Resources in Local Services*, Michael Joseph, 1968.
4. Harris, A., *Meals-on-Wheels for Old People*, National Corporation for the Care of Old People, 1961.
5. For example, Tunstall, J., *Old and Alone*, Routledge, 1966; Townsend, P., and Wedderburn, D., *The Aged in the Welfare State*, Occasional Papers on Social Administration, Welwyn, 1965.

with their local authority may be expected to be those disabled persons most likely to be in receipt of welfare services.

1. *The need for help*

A list of personal and household tasks was devised according to which persons in the sample assessed the kind and extent of help they required to enable them to remain in their own homes.[6] (See Figure 2.) The degree of physical capacity which each of the tasks needed varied considerably. On the whole, people found that the household tasks required greater physical capacity, particularly for mobility, than the personal tasks. Moreover, some were performed more frequently than others by the persons interviewed. Broadly speaking, then, the activities in question were a selection of those which to some extent reflected levels of independence: incapacity for any one of them challenged the disabled person's ability to remain at home.

FIGURE 2

Personal and household tasks on which capacity for self-care was assessed

1. *Personal tasks performed*
   at least daily
   washing
   dressing and putting on shoes
   getting in and out of bed
   feeding self
   going to W.C.
   shaving (men)

   less than daily
   all over wash or bath
   cutting toenails
   washing and setting hair (women)

2. *Household tasks performed*
   at least daily
   washing up
   making a cup of tea
   cooking a hot meal

   less than daily
   dusting
   cleaning floors
   cleaning windows
   shopping
   washing

All but five (97 per cent) of the persons interviewed required help with at least one of the tasks. The proportion of persons living alone who were unable to do at least one of the tasks was as high as that of other persons. Although the majority of persons interviewed—149 —required help with between one and eight tasks, more than a quarter (57) required help with between nine and seventeen of them, and almost a tenth (19) with thirteen or more. The proportion of persons living alone who were unable to do more than eight of the tasks was only slightly less than that in other households—twenty-two per cent (12) compared with twenty-eight per cent (45). Indeed, a higher proportion of persons living alone (63 per cent) than others in the sample (57 per cent) required help with daily tasks. However, persons living

6. The tasks were based on the Index of Self-Care in Townsend, P., *The Last Refuge*, Routledge, 1962, p. 259.

alone were less likely than others to require help with a large number of daily tasks: eleven per cent (7) of persons living alone, but fifteen per cent (25) of those in other households required help with five or more.

2. *Sources of help*

Clearly, the disabled persons for whom capacity to perform the tasks was crucial were those who lived alone. But, as was indicated in the previous chapter, many of those living in two person households were vulnerable, too. The proportions of persons who required help with tasks in single-person, two-person and three- or more person households were strikingly similar. (See Table 16.) Altogether ninety-six per cent (207) of the persons interviewed received help with at least one of the listed tasks. In the sample as a whole, relatives were the most important source of help: almost three-quarters (152) of the persons interviewed received help from relatives. But the persons in the three types of households differed widely in their use of sources of help—relatives, neighbours and friends, statutory services

a) *Relatives*

A quarter (14) of the persons living alone had a relative who lived within a half hour's journey or less of their home. And only half of these were visited by a relative at least once a week. It is not surprising, therefore, that only a fifth (11) of persons living alone received help from a relative. As might be expected, such help was usually given by a daughter.[7] Of the persons who received help from relatives, half obtained no help from other sources. Where a number of relatives lived in the neighbourhood, help was usually provided by more than one of them. But in most cases people were dependent upon the help of a single relative.

In contrast, relatives were the most important source of help for those living with one other person. About four-fifths (62) received help from this source, but more than half (34) of these lived with relatives who were themselves elderly or incapacitated. More than half (45) of the people in two-person households depended solely upon the help available within the household. One-third (15) of these required help with only a few tasks, but another third depended on the second person in the household for help with most of the listed tasks. Almost three-fifths of those who depended upon help available within the household lived with an incapacitated or elderly person.

It was striking that in some households men gave considerable help with household tasks.

---

7. For the relative importance of daughters and sons in providing help for elderly persons, see Townsend P., *The Family Life of Old People*, Routledge and Kegan Paul, 1957.

Mrs. Swinton, aged sixty-five, lived with her sixty-nine year old husband in a privately rented house in Chelmsford. She had an artificial left leg, and arthritis in her right leg. She needed help getting in and out of a chair—this was painful and slow. Her husband took her out in a wheelchair. The only household tasks she could do were very light washing up and dusting and some of the cooking. Her husband did the rest—cleaning, most cooking, shopping and washing. 'It's difficult, but we don't want the meals and a home help while my husband is alive.'

But in no case was a disabled person entirely dependent on a man for all household tasks. Unlike most women, men called on the help of local authority services and neighbours before the disabled person was entirely dependent upon them. Disabled persons who lived with employed persons usually found themselves alone during most weekdays. To some extent this factor explained the low proportion of men giving substantial aid to disabled women. As many as fourteen (about three-fifths) of those dependent upon help within the household lived with employed persons, most of whom were men.

Only four of those living with one other person were helped by relatives outside the household, yet more than half of such persons (24) received at least a weekly visit from a relative who lived nearby. In some cases the relatives who visited were considered to be inappropriate to offer help. Others were siblings who were themselves too frail to do more than visit.

All but two of those living in three- or more person households received help with at least one of the listed tasks. As might be expected a higher proportion of those living with two or more persons than those in other households depended upon help from relatives. Most people received all their help from relatives with whom they lived. Although most of the persons who required substantial help were men who were looked after by their wives or other female relatives, there were some severely incapacitated women who were dependent upon male relatives. Indeed, almost two-fifths (28) of those who received help with household tasks were women who would have had the complete care of the house. More than one-third (11) of these received substantial help in the house from the male relatives with whom they lived. Even so, more than one fifth of those who were helped by the relatives with whom they lived required help from other members of the family as well. There are two possible explanatory factors. First, a seventh of all the persons in these households (11) lived with a spouse and at least one young child only. In cases where the mother was disabled, the difficulties of looking after a child were added to those of performing the necessary household and personal tasks. Outside help was therefore a welcome supplement to the help available within the home. Second, more than a quarter (21) of the persons in the group were alone for most of the day during the week. A number of these required help at a time when it was not available within the household. Indeed, this was true of half of those who required substantial help. Yet the absence of help from relatives outside the home was striking. More than seven-tenths (53) of the persons in the group had relatives living in the vicinity, and two-thirds of these were visited at least weekly by a relative. Thus in spite of the availability of other relatives in the neighbourhood, where a disabled person required considerable help during the day, the burden of care was usually undertaken by one relative within the household who in many cases went out to work as well.

b) *Neighbours*

The majority of persons living alone—forty-three (79 per cent)—depended to some extent on help available outside the family. For them, even neighbours were a more important source of help than relatives. Almost two-fifths of those living alone who required help, obtained some aid from a neighbour.

For most people, neighbourly help was restricted to collecting the pension and doing shopping. But there were cases in which more extensive help was given.

> Mrs. Rochford, who had multiple sclerosis, was aged sixty-two, and had been widowed for eighteen months. She lived in a new first floor council flat in Lambeth. 'I depend on the neighbours a lot. I didn't realize people were so helpful until I got bad. There have been no cold shoulders. My neighbour comes in to do the floors and the windows. I can do a little shopping myself when the weather is good, but I really depend on my neighbour. I can't carry much. But I can get my pension on a dry day, otherwise my neighbour gets it. Then another neighbour has got a washing machine, and she does some of my stuff for me. She takes the rest to the laundry.'

But for the majority of people, neighbourly help was limited to one or two tasks, though in some cases it was given regularly every day: two people were washed and bathed by neighbours, while five people depended upon neighbours to get them in and out of bed. Only a little more than a fifth (9) of those living alone obtained all the help they required from neighbours: usually a neighbour's help supplemented that provided by relatives or the welfare services.

Only eleven per cent (9) of those living in two-person households received help from neighbours. Even so, they were a more important source of outside help than relatives: one-third of persons receiving help from outside the home were helped with household tasks by neighbours. Only four of those living with more than one other person received help from neighbours.

c) *Statutory services*

Altogether, a little more than two-fifths of the persons interviewed received help from statutory services. Not surprisingly, the consumption of these services reflected household composition. For those living alone, statutory services were the most important sources of help: more than three-quarters of them received help from this source. In most cases such aid with personal tasks was restricted to the provision of qualified help with cutting toenails and bathing. But sources of help varied widely. Of the thirty-two persons living alone who received help with cutting their toenails, all but two received expert help. More than a third (13) were visited in their own homes by a chiropodist working as part of the local authority health service. About another fifth (6) visited their own chiropodist privately. The same proportion received free expert attention at hospitals, clinics, and clubs for the disabled. Finally, about a sixth (5) had their toenails cut by the district nurse. But in addition there were two people who received unqualified help through the statutory service: they depended upon their home help to cut their toenails.

Almost two-fifths of the persons living alone required help with washing or bathing. Of these, more than half (9) had the help of a local authority service. Six people were bathed by district nurses, who were thus more important as a source of help than the borough bathing service, of which there was only one recipient in the sample. Two people were bathed, dressed, and had their hair cared for by home helps.

Most of the aid given to persons living alone by statutory services with household tasks was provided by the home help and home meals services. As many as half (5) of those who received help from relatives, were also helped by statutory services. These supplemented help provided by neighbours, too. More than half of those (11) who were helped by neighbours, were helped by statutory services as well. Most people were dependent upon neighbours and the home help for a few tasks. But others depended upon help in the household from a number of sources for a wide range of tasks.

As many as one-third (16) of those living alone requiring help with household tasks were entirely dependent upon the statutory services for help. Most of the aid received was provided by home helps. The help given was usually substantial: most people received help with four household tasks. But a few people received even more extensive help.

Mrs. Grace, aged seventy-two, lived in a council house near

Chelmsford. Her husband had spent the last twenty years in a near by hospital occasionally coming home for weekends. She had arth ritis which was aggravated by a broken thigh two years ago. He eldest son lived in Somerset, and visited her every year at Christ mas. The other son lived in the Chelmsford area and 'popped i now and again'. She had two elderly sisters living in Chelmsford both of whom were ill and bedfast. She was unable to do an household tasks, even washing up. Everything in the house wa done by the home help, who arrived every day except Sunday, a 7.45 a.m. to get Mrs. Grace up, get the breakfast and light the fire The home help stayed until 9.00 a.m. and sometimes returned i the afternoon. She also came between 1.00 and 2.00 p.m. to ge Mrs. Grace some dinner. Mrs. Grace even depended upon the hom help to get her a cup of tea.

Statutory services were an important source of help for those livin in two-person households; altogether more than two-fifths (36) recei ved help from this source. Almost a third (13) of those who receive help with personal tasks from a second person in the household wer also helped by local authority services. In most cases this comprise qualified help with bathing and chiropody. Three people receive qualified help with washing and bathing, while another ten person received chiropody. The pattern of help which emerged, then, wa of substantial aid received within the household supplemented by hel from a specialist health service, usually with a single task.

Almost one-third (19) of the persons who received help with per sonal tasks relied on help from outside the home. It was among thi group that the proportion of persons living with an elderly or in capacitated person was highest—more than three-fifths (13). For al most a third (6) of the people who depended on help from outside th home, the help of neighbours and relatives was supplemented by tha of statutory services. In each case the second person in the home wa frail or incapacitated. The remainder (9) depended entirely on loca authority health and welfare services for aid with personal tasks.

Almost a quarter of those in two-person households received as sistance with household tasks from statutory services. In most case help was given by home helps, though two people received meals on-wheels, and another sent washing to the borough laundry. Thos who received help from statutory services were either alone for mos of the day, or lived with a frail or elderly person. Where the dis abled person lived with someone who was employed, the home hel tended to be responsible for only one or two household tasks, such a cleaning floors, and perhaps doing some shopping. But where the sec ond person in the household was elderly or incapacitated, the rang of tasks undertaken by the home help was understandably wider.

132

Almost a quarter (18) of those in two-person households depended entirely on help from outside the home with household tasks. Although two-thirds of them (12) were visited at least weekly by relatives living nearby, statutory services were their single most important source of help: half of them had a home help or meals-on-wheels. Generally, statutory services provided the only help with household tasks received by such persons.

Mrs. Lanchester, aged seventy-four, lived with her forty-two year old son who was going blind, in her own house in Middlesex. 'I manage to keep myself clean down to my knees, but the home help has to wash my feet. The chiropodist comes to do my toenails. I can manage the commode, but it hurts sitting down and getting up. Dressing is difficult: I've got a stick for my knickers. In the end it got so bad I asked the doctor for a home help. She comes for two hours on Tuesdays and Fridays. She does the washing, shopping and cleaning. I can just about manage the cooking and washing up myself.'

Only one-fifth (15) of those in three- or more person households received help from statutory services. As for other groups, statutory services provided the bulk of help obtained from outside the home.

As many as three-quarters (15) of those who required such help obtained it from local authority health and welfare services, compared with only one-fifth receiving help from relatives and the same proportion from neighbours. Altogether, more than two-thirds of those living in households containing three or more persons required help with personal tasks. Of these, two-fifths were alone for much of the day. It is not surprising, therefore, that almost three-tenths (14) obtained help with personal tasks from outside the household. In most cases (10) help was obtained from local authority health services: four persons were bathed and had their toenails cut by the district nurse, while six persons received the chiropody service. For the most part, then, help from outside the home was obtained for the less frequently performed rather than daily personal tasks.

Only a little more than one-seventh (11) of those living with two or more persons obtained help with household tasks from outside the family. Of these, the majority—eight—had home helps. In most cases the home help's duties were restricted to cleaning floors.

) A summary of sources of help in the home

Only two per cent (four) of the persons interviewed required no help with personal or household tasks. (See Table 16.) There was great variation in the proportion of persons in the three types of household who received help from each source. The proportion of persons living alone who received help from statutory sources was three times greater than the proportion helped by relatives. Among those in two-person households, almost twice as many, and among those living with two or more persons more than four times as many people were helped by relatives as by the statutory services. The proportion of persons living alone who depended upon neighbours for help with

TABLE 16

The number of persons who received help from relatives, neighbours and statutory services

Source of help	Persons living alone		Persons in two person households		Persons in three or more person households		All	
	No.	%	No.	%	No.	%	No.	%
Relatives	14	(26)	68	(84)	70	(92)	152	72
Neighbours	22	(41)	9	(11)	4	(5)	35	16
Statutory Services	41	(76)	36	(44)	15	(20)	92	43
Total requiring help	53	(98)	79	(97)	75	(98)	207	98
N =	54	(100)	81	(100)	76	(100)	211	100

some tasks was almost four times greater than the proportion of those living in two-person households, and more than eight times greater than the proportion of people who lived with two or more persons. Despite the variation in the use of the different sources of help in each of the types of households, it is noteworthy that even among disabled persons who lived with relatives, the contribution made by the statutory services was important.

Broadly speaking, the statutory services available to disabled persons for help with personal tasks were different in kind from those intended to provide help with household tasks. Help with household tasks was found to be provided largely through the home help and domiciliary meals services. The majority of those who depended upon statutory services for help with personal tasks, found that help was limited to that given by health oriented services, that is, those providing the chiropody and bathing services—district nurses, local authority bathing attendants, domiciliary chiropody services and chiropody provided through clinics and hospitals. Therefore, the comparative use made of these and other sources of help with personal and household tasks are first analysed separately here.

3. *How far were needs met?*

a) *Family help*

That family help was crucial to the disabled persons interviewed i illustrated by an analysis of the source of the care which they re ceived during their last illness. As many as two-thirds were cared for by relatives, the majority (61 per cent) in their own homes. Of the remainder, a fifth looked after themselves, one tenth were taken into hospital, while three per cent were cared for by neighbours.

Most of the people for whom no help from relatives was available, recognized their disadvantage. People who had been deprived of the help of relatives sometimes found it difficult to accept the available alternatives. Yet the help provided by relatives was by no means invariably reliable. The periodic illness or incapacity of a relative may deprive the disabled person of crucial help : nine per cent (14) of the persons who received help from relatives said that there were occasions when this help was unreliable.

Most of the persons interviewed were defensive about the scope of help provided by relatives living beyond the household. People tended to emphasize their distance from relatives who were not living in the neighbourhood, and the family committments of those relatives who lived nearby. In both cases, they were at pains to justify the lack of help, or their reliance on help outside the family. Only about a seventh of the persons interviewed felt that disability itself had determined the attitude of relatives towards them, and the amount of help relatives were willing to provide. Of these, half reported that their relatives' attitude towards them had become more generous after the onset of disability, while the remainder felt that disability had limited their family contacts because relatives feared that they would be expected to offer help.

b) *Help from neighbours*

Although only a small proportion (three per cent) of the persons interviewed were cared for in their last illness largely by neighbours, almost a sixth (16) received some regular help from neighbours. As we have seen, in some cases such help was extensive, as a substitute for family care. However, it was generally found that help provided by neighbours was not always reliable.

> Mrs. Gansom, aged seventy-one, had arthritis. She lived alone in a new council house in North West London. 'I can't get out at all now. I've got a friend just along the row here. She gets all my shopping. But she's getting on herself. Last winter when she had 'flu, and we had all that snow, I went without bread for a couple of days.'

About fourteen per cent (30) of the persons interviewed reported that neighbours reacted against their disability. Many people, particularly the elderly, firmly declared their independence of neighbours. Although most people were reluctant to admit that they had received help from neighbours, they were equally reluctant to criticize the scope or kind of help provided by neighbours. As many as ninety-one per cent of the persons interviewed felt that neighbours gave them enough help, or as much as could be expected. They emphasized that most of the neighbours were at work during the day, or had extensive family commitments.

c) *Help from domiciliary services*

Domiciliary services were used as a substitute for family help rather than as a means of supplementing it.

(1) *Home helps*

Of all statutory services, the home help service made the most important contribution to enabling people with little or no family help to remain in their own homes. Even so, only a quarter of the persons in the sample (57) had a home help.

What did the help given generally amount to? Cleaning and shopping were the tasks which were most commonly undertaken by home helps. All recipients had the rooms they used cleaned by the home help, and for three-quarters of them she scrubbed kitchen and bathroom floors. In addition, home helps did shopping for more than half the recipients interviewed. Some people received more extensive support, though they were only a small minority of the total sample: only ten per cent of those interviewed had their washing done, either at home or at a launderette, by a home help; nine per cent had their windows cleaned (against the regulations governing the service); four per cent had fires lit, and three per cent had some cooking done by home helps.

Most people expressed satisfaction with the way in which home helps carried out their tasks.

> Mrs. Norris, aged eighty-two, lived alone in a large detached house in a residential area of London. 'The hospital got me a home help many years ago. She comes Mondays to Fridays for one one and a half hours. It helps. She's good in the house, very good. And she's very good at shopping. You wouldn't think it by looking at her. She's Irish but she does everything you could want. She really is wonderful, and willing, that's the main thing. She would do anything.'

While recognizing that the service which they received was good, some people expressed anxiety about the high turnover in staff. Continuity was important to the disabled person interviewed. For them it represented security and ensured a stable friendship. A few people reported that home helps were inefficient and unpunctual. But the majority of disabled persons stressed that standards varied widely. Most people readily accepted that their own standards would not necessarily be those of the home help.

The unreliability of home helps worried a number of people. About a tenth of those in receipt of the service said that they had been without help on a number of occasions and in some cases this understandably increased their feeling of insecurity.

Mrs. Andrews, who was chairbound, was aged eighty-three, and lived with her husband aged eighty-four, in a small terraced house in North London. 'We've had a home help for two years. The lady almoner at the hospital got her for us. She comes twice a week for two hours. She just does the cleaning. Dad used to manage himself before. She comes on time and she does it nice. We've asked for her to come more often several times. They would if they could, but they can't. We've had a lot. Oh blimey, I couldn't tell you how many mate. We have a man for the windows, and Dad gets up early to light the fires. It's not hard work here. But she hasn't been for a week. I think them black ones get tired of their jobs.' (I went to the home help organizer to report that Mrs. Andrews had been without help for a week. She said, 'Oh, that's Mrs. Jones. She's very naughty. I've told her before she must report it if she's ill. Well, there's nothing I can do about it. My last home help has just been taken up by a maternity case. They're lucky to have one at all.')

The rigidity of the service troubled most people. The service was not sufficiently flexible to distribute the help provided throughout the week, to ensure that people had some social contact most days. Generally, help was given on two or three days.

The period of help given to recipients varied from one to ten hours each week. But almost half of the recipients interviewed were helped for only four hours or less each week, and about one-third of them for between five and seven hours. Less than a quarter (13) of those who received home help (about seven per cent of the total sample) were helped for eight or more hours. Clearly, the period for which help was given indicated the scope of help provided.

What were the principles governing the amount of help provided by the service? An analysis of the characterisitics of the recipients interviewed suggests that the service is primarily intended as a substitute for help normally provided by relatives, rather than a means of supplementing aid provided by hard-pressed relatives. Two-thirds of recipients had no relatives living nearby, and all but two of them lived alone or were alone for most of the day during the week, or lived with elderly or incapacitated persons. But it was difficult to establish the criteria by which the *amount* of help given was determined. Although most of those receiving help for eight or more hours each week were either severely disabled, or lived alone with an elderly or incapacitated person, this was not true of all of them. Furthermore, there were persons in these categories who received much shorter periods of help. The concept of functional capacity provides a useful basis for comparison and assessment of need for and provision of help across clinical conditions. The following persons were severely disabled. Although they were able to get around the house, wash up and make a cup of tea with difficulty, none of them could go out alone, clean, do the shopping or the household washing. Yet the help they received varied from three to ten hours a week.

1. *Help for three hours*

Miss Antrim, aged fifty-nine, lived alone in her own house in Bethnal Green. 'I've got a kind of paralysis from the waist down, and my hands shake a lot. I can't walk at all. I'm confined to the wheelchair. I can wash up and make a cup of tea, but it's very difficult. The home help does the cleaning and shopping but a friend helps with the shopping too. The home help takes the washing to the bagwash. I have meals-on-wheels during the week. I haven't got any relatives living round here to help me. The home help comes twice a week, on Wednesdays and Thursdays. Wednesdays she stays for two hours, and Thursdays for one hour.'

2. *Help for four hours*

Mrs. Holland, aged sixty-four, lived alone in a flat in a block of nineteenth century artisans' dwellings in Holborn. She had chronic bronchitis, and had recently fractured a femur. She was able to wash up and make a cup of tea with difficulty. But for other tasks she depended upon other people. Her only surviving relative was a nephew who lived a four hour journey away, and visited once a year. The home help did the cleaning and shopping, collected her pension, and took the washing to the laundry. Meals-on-wheels were delivered twice a week. The home help came twice a week and stayed for two hours on each occasion.

3. *Help for six hours*

Mr. Blackston, aged seventy-three, lived alone in a council flat in Stepney. He had had a stroke which affected his left side. He had two daughters living nearby who rarely came to see him. He was able to wash up and make a cup of tea with difficulty. A friend came in to do some of the shopping and collect his pension. Meals-on-wheels were delivered on five days a week. The home help came in to do the cleaning, some of the shopping, and some ironing. She also sent the washing to the laundry. The home help came three times a week, staying two hours on each occasion.

4. *Help for ten hours*

Mrs. Alexander, aged seventy, lived alone in a council house in Lewisham. She said that she had had rheumatism for forty years. She was confined to a wheelchair. The only family contact she had was with her foster son who was a merchant seaman, and visited her about once every three months. She could make a cup of tea and wash up with difficulty, leaning on her stick or using the floor from her chair. The home help did the shopping and cleaning, and on three days a week prepared a meal. Meals-on-wheels were delivered twice a week. A neighbour collected Mrs. Alexander's pension and took the washing to the laundry. The home help came five days a week, and stayed two hours on each occasion. In addition, she popped in on Saturday as well, when her family commitments allowed her to do so.

Thus the principles which determined the amount of help provided were far less consistently applied than those which governed eligibility for help. Consequently, the needs of some recipients of the service were less well met than those of others. It is not surprising, therefore, that almost two-thirds of recipients (35) said that they would like the home help to stay longer hours. The rigidity of the service prevented some needs being met. For example, almost one-third of recipients of the service said that they would like the home help to undertake additional tasks sometimes, usually spring cleaning and turning out cupboards. However, everyone appreciated the staffing problem of the service, and repeatedly emphasized it during the interviews.

In addition to the need for extra help among recipients there was considerable unmet demand for home helps among other persons in the sample. A further ten per cent (22) said that they required help in the home. All were careful to estimate their need according to the assumed limitations of the service. More than half (13) said that they required help only once a week, and the remainder twice a week. Nor were long hours demanded: most people (17) said that they needed only two hours, and the remainder (5) four hours help each week. A few people required help only periodically: because the service was inflexible, no provision could be made easily for them.

Requests for help were not made lightly. More than half (12) of the people who wanted help in the home were severely or very severely incapacitated, and almost three-quarters (16) lived alone or were alone for most weekdays. On the whole, people were proud to be able to look after themselves in spite of their difficulties.

2. The meals service

As many as thirty-eight per cent (81) of the persons interviewed were unable to cook their own meals. More than three-quarters of these (63) depended upon relatives for hot meals. Among the remainder, local authority meals services were the most important source of help, but recipients amounted to only one-tenth (8) of the persons who were unable to cook for themselves, and about four per cent of the total sample. Of those who received neither the local authority meals service nor help from relatives (10), half had their meals cooked by home helps, and the rest by neighbours.

The number of recipients interviewed was too small for a realistic assessment of the meals service to be possible. Nevertheless, the small numbers themselves were indicative of the comparative unimportance of the service for the registered disabled persons interviewed. In some cases, the delivery of meals was not well timed, nor were meals always attractively presented: in three cases meals arrived before 11.00 a.m.; six people complained that meals needed to be warmed up on arrival, and of these three, who were unable to use a cooker, ate their dinners cold. Most people were unenthusiastic about the meals. One man expressed most people's opinion of them when he described them as being 'very general'.

Even among recipients of the service, the need for meals was not fully met. In no case was a comprehensive weekly service received: everyone in receipt of the service had to make other arrangements for meals at weekends. In addition, two persons were forced to seek meals from other sources on two weekdays, and four persons on three weekdays as well. In fact, on days when it did not operate, half of the recipients of the service went without a hot meal.

All of the persons who received local authority meals were severely or very severely incapacitated, and either lived alone, or were alone most weekdays. Nevertheless, recipients were only a small minority of the total number of persons in these categories, most of whom experienced great difficulty in cooking meals. Yet only another six persons said that they would like meals-on-wheels.[8] In terms of the current availability of the service, this figure is high, but it did not reflect the extent of need. Most people were determined to continue to try to cook for themselves.

Mrs. Lomax, aged fifty-four, lived alone in a new council flat in Lambeth. She had rheumatoid arthritis. 'I can't do much in the house now. I can do the washing up slowly at the high sink they put

---

8. It must be remembered that the present study was confined to persons registered as physically handicapped with the local authority. The need for meals services among elderly and disabled person generally is likely to be very much higher. In 1965 it was estimated that a five-fold increase in the meals service was required for the elderly. See. Townsend, P. and Wedderburn, D., *The Aged in the Welfare State*, Occasional Papers in Social Administration, Welwyn 1965, p. 50.

in for me. But the home help does all the cleaning. I can usually make tea, but it depends on my hands. Sometimes I can't. The home help will make me a cup. She comes every day in the week. I can cook a little bit. But during the week I make do with a cup of something, and a sandwich. I cook a dinner on Sunday, though, with my grandson's help. He comes every weekend.'

A number of other people had previously received the meals, and this, together with the reputation of the service, appeared to limit demand.

Miss Etienne, aged seventy-seven, lived in two rooms at the top of a tall narrow house in Hornsey. She had had arthritis for twenty years and walked slowly, with the aid of a stick. 'When I've had meat and vegetables and fruit and custard I feel satisfied. I had meals-on-wheels for a little while. The doctor got them for me when I had a fractured leg. They gave you lots of potatoes and carrots, and there wasn't much meat. I like meat. They came twice a week. Other days my neighbour used to try and come in and help me, and the home help got in lots of tinned stuff. They used to bring the meals round about eleven—when it suited them. You had to warm them up. I don't know what the meat was—the cheapest they could get anyway. The puddings were just one mass of grease. Still, I was glad of them at the time.'

(3) The laundry service

The weekly wash presented great difficulties for most of the persons interviewed. Only ten per cent (20) were able to do their own washing at home, in most cases with the aid of a machine. The difficulties were often immense.

Mrs. Grantham, aged sixty, lived with her husband and nephew in a new semi-detached house in Middlesex. She had arthritis. She carried on washing throughout the interview. 'My hands are getting very painful now. My husband bought me the washing machine a few years ago when my hands first started to go. But I don't think I shall be able to go on doing the washing much longer. My hands are all bent up. It's lifting things up that's the trouble. It's so painful. I feel like crying by the time I get to the end.'

Of the persons who had their washing done at laundries or launderettes (49), a quarter (12) found that they still needed help. Mobility and other problems prevented some people from taking washing to laundries and launderettes. Everyone complained of the cost of using laundries. Therefore, where possible, people tried to obtain help elsewhere. A small proportion (four per cent) depended upon neighbours to do their washing. Home helps were a more important source of aid: ten per cent (21) of the persons in the sample had some washing done by home helps. But relatives were the most common source of help. Altogether, more than half (110) of the persons interviewed had their washing done by relatives, but of these one-fifth (25) relied on frail or incapacitated relatives. In addition, there were five women with dependent children who relied entirely upon their husbands for help in the home. Finally, ten people depended on relatives outside the home, most of whom lived beyond the disabled person's neighbourhood, a factor which sometimes affected the reliability of the service. Although so many people experienced difficulties with washing, only three people used the local authority laundry service: all three praised it highly. Yet there is clearly scope for the service to develop. Another twenty-seven per cent of the persons interviewed said that they would use a local authority laundry if the service was available to them. The majority of those who required the service lived alone, or with a frail or incapacitated relative, or were severely or very severely incapacitated.

(4) *The home bathing service*

More than a quarter (55) of the persons interviewed were unable to bath or have an over-all wash without help. Relatives were the most important single source of aid—more than half (27) were helped to bath by relatives. Almost one-fifth (12) were bathed or washed by district nurses. Only one person received the local authority bathing service. In terms of unmet need, the local authority bathing service was important. A further ten per cent of the persons interviewed (22) said that they would like a bathing attendant. The majority of these people lived alone or with an elderly or incapacitated relative. More than three-quarters of them (17) were severely or very severely incapacitated. Others who required help felt too shy to be bathed by an attendant.

(5) *District nurses*

Only fourteen per cent (29) of those interviewed received the nursing service. The allocation of district nurses to disabled persons is governed ostensibly by medical criteria. Yet more than one-third of the persons who were visited by the district nurse received no specifically medical treatment. All of them were bathed or washed and half were dressed as well by the nurse.[9] A number of those who received injections or had dressings changed were helped by the district nurse

---

9. District nurses tend to distinguish clearly between such tasks and their strictly medical duties, and to consider the former to be beyond the scope of their conception of their role. See, Sainsbury, S., *Home Services for the Aged*, *New Society*, April 2, 1964, p. 11.

with personal tasks as well. But it was difficult to establish standard criteria by which need for such help was determined. Although most of the persons who received help with personal tasks from district nurses were severely or very severely incapacitated, and lived alone or with a frail or incapacitated person, not all fell into these categories. Because it was generally assumed that need for the district nursing services was medically determined, the demand for it was lower than for other domiciliary services. Only five people said that they would like the district nurse to visit them. One person who depended upon an elderly relative with failing eyesight to change a dressing felt that a district nurse would be more appropriate for this task. The others required help with bathing and cutting toenails and preferred the help of a district nurse to that of a local authority bathing attendant. It may be that a 'day attendance' service is required to supplement the district nursing service to undertake those duties such as help with bathing and dressing which are not so specifically medical.

(6) Home chiropody service

As many as sixty-two per cent (130) of the persons interviewed depended upon others to cut their toenails. Almost half (58) of these received unqualified help, mainly from relatives, but in a few cases from neighbours and home helps. More than two-thirds (52) of those who received qualified help, had their toenails cut at clinics, hospitals, centres and clubs for the aged and disabled, or by the private chiropody service or district nurses. Only fifteen per cent (20) of those receiving help (nine per cent of the sample) benefitted from the home chiropody service. Most recipients had experience of other services, usually private chiropody or that provided by hospitals. It was generally considered that the home service compared favourably with these. Most (17) recipients of the home service were attended by the chiropodist four times a year.

The source of qualified help other than the home chiropody service, often appeared to be determined by the use of certain health services for other purposes. Thus persons who attended outpatient departments regularly tended to have their toenails cut at hospital; where people attended centres and clubs which provided chiropody, they often made use of this facility; most of those who were attended by the district nurse for injections or the application of dressings, had their toenails cut by her as well. But there were exceptions. And when, for some reason, one of these sources of help was no longer available to the disabled person—for example, when people no longer attended centres or outpatient departments—there was no guarantee that a substitute source of help could be found. Moreover, it was not always clear why some persons received qualified help, while others who were similarly incapacitated and equally isolated received no such help. In fact, another twenty-one per cent (45) of the persons in the sample said that they required home chiropody. All were severely or very severely incapacitated persons who lived alone or who depended upon relatives with failing sight or other physical impairments.

(7) Other domiciliary services

A little less than one-tenth (20) of the persons interviewed received other domiciliary services. In most cases there were visits from opticians and dentists. Most recipients reported that opticians and dentists considered home visits unsatisfactory, and where possible arranged for housebound persons to be brought to them by car.

(8) Payment for services

Only one of the domiciliary services discussed here—the district nursing service—was invariably provided entirely without charge. Charges were made according to a means test for most of the other services—home helps, borough laundries, home bathing, and home chiropody. Flat rates were charged for meals-on-wheels. Unfortunately, the number of recipients of each of the services were too small to allow for any assessment of variations in charges between local authorities.

4. People without help

In spite of the high proportion of persons who received help, often from a wide variety of sources, as many as seventeen (eight per cent) of the persons interviewed received no help with at least one personal task which they were unable to do themselves. Only one person was without the help required to perform a *daily* personal task.

> Mrs. Gipson, said, 'There's my in-laws' children. There's a nephew in Bethnal Green. He's a gas man. He drops in once a week on his way round. He can't do much, though. His wife is in hospital and he's got to look after his two little girls. But when he comes he puts money in the gas and light for me, and he does my toenails. I can't put shoes or stockings on myself even with an aid. So he does it when he comes. He puts on my stockings and my slippers, then I have to leave them on until he comes next time. I have to go to bed in them.'

Lack of help prevented other people from carrying out some of the less frequently performed personal tasks: 11 people never had a complete overall wash or bath and seven never had their toenails cut. One woman said that she had never had her hair washed since the onset of her disability. There were three people who lacked help for more than

144

one of the personal tasks which they were unable to undertake themselves.

In addition, many people remained at risk to accidents during periods when no help was available. In the previous twelve months, as many as sixty-one of the persons interviewed (29 per cent) had had an accident, and had been without help for many hours. In most cases they had waited until relatives arrived home in the evening. But five people lived alone, and had waited until the home help arrived on the following morning.

5. *Referral to services*

To some extent the disparity between need for and allocation of domiciliary services is explained by variations in the provisions made by different local authorities. But it is likely that other important factors were the disabled persons' lack of knowledge of the services available, and the absence of a central referral agency. The only services of which people were generally aware were the home help, district nursing, and meals services. But even these were not usually applied for directly. In most cases the people interviewed said that they happened to mention their difficulties and were thereafter referred to services. They were put in touch with services by friends, relatives, neighbours, the church, clubs, centres, welfare officers, or the personnel of other local authority services. But the main referral agencies were doctors and medical social workers.

To some extent, therefore, referral depended upon close contact with the medical profession. But only fourteen per cent (30) of the persons interviewed had regular contact with hospitals through out-patient departments. However, eighty-one per cent (172) had seen their doctor at least once in the previous twelve months and fifty-four per cent (114) within the previous month. Furthermore, almost a quarter (51) of the persons in the sample were visited regularly in their own homes by their doctors. Therefore, unmet need for domiciliary services may reflect limited knowledge of available provisions among some doctors, or their limited awareness of social needs.

5. *Summary*

The purpose of the chapter is to demonstrate the kind and extent of help required by persons in the sample, to evaluate the various sources of help, and to assess how far needs were met.

The majority of persons interviewed required help with both personal and household tasks. The source of help in the home depended largely on the type of household to which the disabled person belonged. Persons who lived alone depended predominantly upon local authority welfare services. Those living in two-person households depended mainly on relatives for help, but received a considerable amount of help from welfare services as well. Few persons in other types of household received help from welfare services: they depended almost entirely on the family for help. For the sample as a whole, relatives were by far the most important source of help. But for those living alone, neighbours and welfare services were both more important than relatives. Broadly speaking, local authority services were substitutes for family help. Domiciliary services were not sufficiently developed to play a well defined supporting role where disabled persons lived with their families.

Recipients of statutory services discussed tended to be persons living alone, or with a frail or incapacitated person, and were usually severely or very severely incapacitated. But this was not invariably the case. Not only was there no guarantee that domiciliary services would be available as a substitute for help normally available from the family; there appeared to be no standard criteria by which services were allocated to play a supportive role in situations where limited family help was available. Furthermore, the extent of help provided by domiciliary services for the disabled persons interviewed appeared to be governed by no objective assessment of need.

The most significant contribution to help in the home was made by the home help service. However, only a little more than a quarter (57) of the persons in the sample received the service. In the majority of cases, the home helps' activities were restricted to cleaning and shopping. But a small minority of the persons interviewed received extensive help. Although thirty-eight per cent of the persons interviewed were unable to cook, only four per cent received meals-on-wheels. In only two cases did a five day service operate, and no provision was made by local authorities for meals to be delivered at weekends. More than a quarter (55) of the persons interviewed required help with bathing, but only one person was helped by a bathing attendant. The majority (90 per cent) of people were unable to do their own washing at home, but only three of them benefitted from a local authority laundry service. As many as fourteen per cent of the persons interviewed were visited by the district nurse: for about one third of recipients of the service, nurses undertook tasks which were not strictly medical. Almost two-thirds of the persons interviewed were unable to cut their own toenails, yet only ten per cent were in receipt of the home chiropody service.

In spite of the wide variety of sources of help available to most of the people interviewed, as many as seventeen (eight per cent) received no help with at least one personal task which they were unable to do themselves. In fact, there was considerable unmet demand for statutory services. A further ten per cent of the persons interviewed said that they required help in the home. Demand for home helps was

146

consciously limited by the known staffing problems of the service. Only a further six persons said that they would like meals-on-wheels. Most people were anxious to continue to cook for themselves however great the difficulties. To some extent demand for the service appeared to be limited by the reputation of the meals. Only a further five people said that they required a district nurse: demand was limited because it was generally assumed that nurses were restricted to medical duties. Most people were unaware of the existence of other services, and, of course, not all local authorities provided them. Thus demand for them did not reflect need. In fact, there was considerable demand for other services once they were made known. Another twenty per cent of the persons interviewed required home chiropody; a further ten per cent said that they would like a bathing attendant; and as many as twenty-seven per cent required the borough laundry service.

Some of the disparity between the need for and allocation of services may be due to variation between local authorities in their provision of services. But there are other important explanatory factors. Few people seem to know of the existence of some services. Most people did not apply directly for a specific service: the effect of their condition on their capacity for self care became known to other persons, usually doctors or medical social workers, who referred them to services. But generally little attempt seemed to be made to assess needs thoroughly and refer people to all the services required. There appeared to be a need for a single referral agency within an administrative area.

The purpose of this chapter is to describe the social activities and contacts of the disabled persons interviewed, and to discuss the role of local authorities in providing opportunities for social activities. What are the needs of disabled persons in this respect, and how far do statutory services meet the need? First, the ways in which the persons interviewed participated in normal social activities—meeting relatives, friends and neighbours, going out on shopping expeditions, on holiday, and to places of entertainment—will be described. Their supplementation or replacement by statutory provisions will then be considered. The provisions discussed here are confined to the work of welfare officers, occupation centres, voluntary and statutory social clubs, special transport services, and arrangements for holidays. Employment and housing provisions are discussed elsewhere in the report.[1] It must be remembered that the persons interviewed were all registered with local authorities. As such, they belonged to that group of disabled persons to whom statutory provision designed specifically for the disabled were limited.

1. Contact with relatives, neighbours and friends

The differences in their expectations of regular social contacts between persons living alone, in two-person households, and with two or more other persons, were small. (See Table 17.) But the absence of regular weekly contact with at least one relative, friend or neighbour was of far greater consequence to persons in single- and two-person households, than to those in larger households. Those living alone who had no such contacts were severely incapacitated and received considerable help from domiciliary services: home helps and district nurses provided their only regular social contacts.[2] Of the

1. See Chapters 5 and 6 respectively.
2. Less than half of the persons living alone saw a relative at least once a week. Contact with relatives has been shown to be far more frequent among *elderly* persons living alone: 'Three-quarters even of those living by themselves saw at least one relative every day; some of the others had no relatives.' Townsend, P., *The Family Life of Old People*, Pelican Books, 1963, p. 53.

eleven people living in two-person households who had no regular social contacts, five saw relatives several times during the year. But the others appeared to be cut off by distance from the rest of the family.

However, there were differences between persons in the three types of households in the source and frequency of their social contacts. Generally, relatives were less important as sources of social contact for persons living alone or in larger households, than for those living in

Number of persons who had at least weekly contact with a relative, neighbour, or friend

Type of household:

Persons seen at least weekly	Persons living alone		Those living in two-person households		Those living with two or more persons		All	
	No.	Per cent	No.	Per cent	No.	Per cent	No.	Per cent
Relatives only	4	(7)	7	(8)	9	(12)	20	9
Relatives, and neighbours as well	21	(39)	41	(51)	31	(40)	93	44
Neighbours only	25	(46)	22	(26)	24	(33)	71	34
Total having contact	50	(92)	70	(85)	64	(85)	184	87
N =	54	(100)	81	(100)	76	(100)	211	100

two-person households. But one factor was common to all households —the importance of neighbours for providing opportunities for contact with persons beyond the household. In fact, this, rather than the provision of help emerged as the major role of neighbours, in their relationships with the disabled persons interviewed. And whatever the size of their household, social contact with neighbours was recognized by the persons interviewed as essential to their morale.

Mr. Anderson, aged sixty-five, lived with his wife and three adult children in a council flat in Shoreditch. 'I gave up work ten years ago when I had a stroke. I'm paralysed down the left side. I haven't opened my left hand for ten years. I came home from work for dinner one night and I went out like a light. I thought someone had hit me over the head. They can't do nothing for me, it just takes time. But I'm as fit as a fiddle in myself. But I don't get lonely. I can knock next door and have a talk to Mrs. Bradshaw any time. And everyone round here knows me. I stand in the door, and then I have a walk up and down, and they say, 'Hullo, Bert, you're still sticking it then?' and I say 'Yes,' and we have a talk.'

Even those who were visited regularly by relatives or friends felt isolated if they were surrounded by immigrants, or had recently lost the support of an old and trusted neighbour. The difficulties involved in replacing old neighbourhood contacts were considered to be immense, but fear of isolation drove most people to make an effort to promote contact with neighbours.

Those who had previously experienced little neighbourhood contact reported that after the onset of disability they were astonished by the kindness and sympathy of neighbours.

Only a little more than half of the persons living alone and in the larger households saw two or more persons from outside the household each week, but almost three-quarters of those living in two-person households did so. Of course, not everyone was dependent solely on relatives *or* neighbours for social contacts, but there were differences in this respect between the three types of household. Only two-fifths of those living alone, compared with two-thirds of those in two-person households, and almost half of those in larger households saw relatives *and* neighbours at least weekly. Again, those living alone, or with two or more persons were less likely than others to see someone from outside their homes daily. (See Table 18.)

TABLE 18

Frequency of social contacts with persons from outside the household of persons in each of the three types of household

Type of household

Frequency of social contact	Persons living alone		Those living in two-person households		Those living with two or more persons		All	
	No.	Per cent	No.	Per cent	No.	Per cent	No.	Per cent
No one seen at least once a week	4	(8)	11	(12)	12	(15)	27	13
Persons seen between one and four times each week	19	(35)	10	(12)	20	(26)	49	23
At least one person seen daily	31	(57)	60	(76)	44	(59)	135	64
Total	54	(100)	81	(100)	76	(100)	211	100

Generally, contact with neighbours was more frequent than with relatives. In most cases, daily contact with neighbours supplemented less frequent contacts with relatives. As many as three-quarters of those with close contacts with neighbours saw them daily, compared with a little more than half (60) of those who had regular contact with relatives. The difference between the frequency of contact with relatives and neighbours was more marked for persons living alone or with one other person, than for those in larger households.

Regular contact with relatives was not necessarily restricted by distance. Some disabled persons were visited at least once a month

150

by relatives who lived as much as a two hour journey away but who had the use of a car: such relatives were usually adult children or siblings. Others were themselves able to visit relatives in their own vehicles. The importance of motor cars in promoting close family ties even when relatives are scattered has been noted in other studies.[3] But car ownership among the persons interviewed was not common. Only sixteen per cent of the persons in the sample belonged to households which had the use of a car.[4] Of these, the majority—twenty-four (11 per cent of the total sample)—had Ministry tricycles. Only one of the persons interviewed had been granted a car by the Ministry. But some of those who were dependent upon tricycles found that their own transport was not always suitable for social occasions since it did not accommodate other members of the household. Where no private transport was available, contact was sometimes restricted because relatives were themselves elderly or incapacitated. Fares, too, limited regular contact between relatives, particularly where people were dependent upon state benefits.

Like cars, the telephone is a recognized medium for the maintenance of close links with a scattered family. As many as twenty per cent (43)[5] of the disabled persons interviewed lived in households where a telephone was available. For the persons in the sample, the telephone was primarily a means of summoning aid in an emergency. A number of people had the telephone to reassure a close member of the family, and in some cases a relative had paid for its installation. Some households had been forced to give up the telephone when the chief wage earner became dependent through disability on state benefits. In each case this was the most regretted economy which disability had forced on the household. Most of the persons interviewed felt that severely disabled persons should either be given a phone, or receive a government grant towards the payment for one.

Of course, most people kept in touch with relatives by letter, usually at Christmas. Some elderly people reported that another member of the family, usually an older sister, took it upon herself to write to the whole family. Meeting members of the family for Christmas and at birthdays appeared to become increasingly important with age. Some elderly persons who were interviewed shortly after their birthday proudly displayed flowers from relatives on the sideboard. A few people were eager to show photographs of relatives who had gathered

3. Rosser, C. and Harris, C., *The Family and Social Change*, Routledge & Kegan Paul, 1965, p. 222. Also, Willmott, P., and Young, M., *Family and Class in a London Suburb*, Routledge and Kegan Paul, 1960, p. 79.
4. Compared with one in four of the persons interviewed by Rosser and Harris, and 18 per cent of the working class persons in their sample. The disabled persons interviewed belonged to a group for whom it is official policy to provide transport.
5. The same proportion of persons in Rosser and Harris's samples were found to possess telephones. *The Family and Social Change*, p. 107. For the importance of the telephone in helping to maintain regular family contacts, see also, Willmott, P., and Young, M., *Family and Class in a London Suburb*, Routledge and Kegan Paul, 1960, p. 79.

to celebrate their golden wedding anniversary. But mobility difficulties usually prevented disabled persons from attending family weddings and funerals.[6] The participation of the persons interviewed in such occasions was usually limited to the receipt of wedding photographs and written accounts of funerals.

Lack of regular contact outside the household was reported to be a major factor in causing depression by the persons interviewed. Altogether, half (106) of the persons interviewed said that because of their disability they became more depressed than most non-disabled persons. Not all (29) felt able to name a specific cause of their depression, and others (17) considered it to be part of their condition or an inevitable result of their treatment. But more than half (57) felt that the social limitations imposed by disability were to blame. The importance of contact with persons beyond the home was clear: almost one-fifth of those who became depressed identified their lack of such contact as the main cause of their depression. Another tenth (12) blamed frustration arising from incapacity for normal activities. Other people were still more specific: almost one-fifth (16) isolated their inability to get out, and a further tenth (11) their lack of occupation, as the major cause of their depression.

2. *Going out*

How far were the persons interviewed able to go out and to occupy themselves? Only twenty per cent (42) of those in the sample were able to go out as far as they liked, but of these more than half (22) were entirely dependent for their mobility on their own motorized transport. As many as thirty-five per cent (75) of the persons interviewed reported only limited mobility out of doors. The majority of them were able to get to the local shops. But there were some who were unable to go beyond their immediate neighbourhood, and a few who could walk only to the garden gate. By far the largest proportion of persons in the sample—forty-five per cent (94)—were unable to go out alone at all.

Of course, even severe mobility difficulties did not necessarily prevent people from going out. Many people were taken out in cars and wheelchairs and thus participated in all family outings. But not everyone was lucky enough to have someone to take them out regularly. More than a quarter (25) of the persons who were unable to go out alone lived on their own, and most of these experienced difficulty in finding someone to take them out.

Mrs. Gipson said, 'I've had that wheelchair on the National Health for three years, and do you know how many times I've

6. The importance of such occasions for reaffirming links with the family have been stressed by other studies, for example, Rosser, C., and Harris, C., *The Family and Social Change*, p. 224. Also, Young, M., Willmott, P., *Family and Kinship in East London*, Pelican Books, 1962, p. 84.

been out in it? Twice. My nephew took me down to Whitechapel market in it. He's the only relative I've got round here, and he's on my husband's side. What's the point of having the chair? What good is it doing underneath the draining board, eh?' Within a year, Mrs. Gipson sent her wheelchair back.

Even those in two-person households often had the same difficulty, particularly when the second person in the household was elderly or incapacitated.

But there were often other problems to be overcome besides lack of mobility. Some people found the process of getting ready so exhausting that they were rarely able to enjoy themselves once they were out.

Mrs. Guierson said, 'I hate going out. It takes ages to dress in the wheelchair. And I have to put knickers on if I go out. That's very difficult. Then there's the baby to see to. My husband's very good, and he manages most of it. Then he has to take us both out. My husband's got two babies—me and John. By the time I get there I'm whacked. Then I start to worry about whether the baby will play my husband up. And I feel guilty that we have to depend on him so much. It isn't right when he's at work all hours. I don't enjoy myself because I keep feeling he's ever so tired.'

Others were deterred from going out by the difficulties presented by public lavatories.[7] About one-tenth of the persons interviewed (23) had never overcome the feeling that a stigma was attached to disability, and therefore went out as little as possible. But most people had been forced either by necessity or the insistence of relatives to overcome such difficulties.

Mrs. Stanton, aged fifty, lived with her husband and two dependent children in a terraced house in the South London dock area. She had rheumatoid arthritis. 'We have to visit my husband's brothers and sisters every week. He's got twenty because his Dad married twice. Then there's his grandmother, she's still alive. They're a wonderful close family. All my side have gone now. I used to hate going out, not being able to walk. And my hands have gone a funny shape. I used to be ever so proud of them. I got depressed about it all last year. That was when my sister died. She lived with us, you see. But my husband *made* me go out. His family insisted on dragging me round there, and one of them always comes round here. So I got used to the chair, and now I value going out

. Recent studies have focussed on the problems of access to public buildings for the disabled. But public lavatories presented the only problems of access which seriously worried the persons interviewed. See for ezample, Bruce-Lockhart, F., *London for the Disabled*, Ward Lock, 1967. Copp, J., *Disabled Person's Guide to Cambridge*, Cambridge Public Health and Welfare Department, 1967. Goldsmith, P. S., 'Public buildings, access for the disabled,' *Architects' Journal*, March 20, 1963, pp. 627–642.

more than I did before the arthritis got me. I really look forward to going out. It isn't just something else you do: it's special because you can still do it.'

Given the low rate of car ownership among the persons interviewed, public transport was an important factor governing ability to go beyond the immediate neighbourhood. But as many as forty per cent (85) of the persons in the sample were unable to use any form of public transport even with help. A smaller proportion—thirty-five per cent—were able to use some form of public transport with help, but only a quarter (52) used all forms without any help, though most of these reported some difficulty. On the whole, trains presented fewer difficulties for the persons in the sample than buses or coaches. Buses were reported to be the most difficult form of transport to use.

Even so, almost half—90—of the persons in the sample had been out the day before they were interviewed, and another third (64) had been out that week or the previous week. But more than one fifth had not been out for more than a month. And there were people —eight per cent of the sample (16)—who had not been out for more than a year. Less than one-third of the persons interviewed (60) expected to go out every day, and a further fifth said that they usually went out twice a week. Weekly or fortnightly outings were reported by about one-third—64—of those interviewed. But as many as ten per cent said that they went out only a few times each year, and a further seven per cent expected to go out even less frequently.

Few people reported regular outings beyond their immediate neighbourhood. By far the highest proportion, forty-one per cent (86) said that they usually went to the local shops. Indeed, almost as many, thirty-six per cent (77), reported that their last outing had been a shopping expedition. Relatives, pubs, parks, cinemas, friends, or churches were each visited regularly by five per cent or fewer of the persons interviewed. For a small minority of people (four per cent of the sample) visits to the hospital outpatients departments and doctors were the sole occasions on which they went out.

People were asked which of a short selection of public places they had visited within the previous twelve months. The largest proportion—twenty-seven per cent (58)—reported having been to a park. However, in most cases such outings were made only during the summer. Visits to churches and pubs were more likely to be regular as many as twenty-two per cent (47) had been to church, while twenty per cent (42) had been to a pub within the previous twelve months. In contrast, only eight per cent (16) of the persons in the sample had visited a cinema and six per cent (12) had attended theatres or concerts. Two people reported that problems of access prevented them from going to cinemas and theatres, but most of those who would

154

have liked to have gone to such places more often said that they simply could not get there or afford to go. However, the vast majority of people expressed little interest in these forms of entertainment. The places people would like to visit more frequently are discussed on page 158.) Few people visited a wide variety of places during the year. Only ten per cent (21) had visited three or more, and sixteen per cent (34) had visited two of the listed places during the previous twelve months. But more than one-third (71) had been to only one such place. However, a large proportion of persons in the sample— forty per cent (85) had been to no such public places in the previous twelve months.

How far were people able to compensate for not going out to ordinary public places for social contact?

Churches appeared to maintain some contact in a variety of ways with most of the people who could no longer attend services. Almost one-fifth (37) of the persons interviewed had attended church regularly before the onset of disability. Of these, all but four still maintained some link with the church. About half (18) of them were visited regularly by the clergy, though the frequency of visits varied from once a fortnight to twice a year. Only two people received communion at home. Almost as many (15) maintained their connection with the church through fellowship meetings, and, sometimes, Bible classes held at their own homes.

Clubs and Centres for the Disabled

Special clubs run by voluntary organizations provided the only opportunity for some housebound persons to participate in social activities beyond their own homes: six per cent (13) of the persons interviewed reported that their only regular outings were to disabled persons' clubs. Altogether, almost a quarter (50) of the persons in the sample belonged to at least one club run specially for the disabled. Few people below the age of forty-five belonged to clubs.

Occupational centres administered by local authorities were not as important as clubs for providing opportunities for social participation. Only thirteen per cent (28) of the persons interviewed attended a local authority occupation centre, a surprisingly small proportion considering the importance attached to this service by the Ministry of Health.

It was ironic that whereas most housebound persons (20) were taken to centres once or twice each week, those who were able to travel alone attended daily. Most of the people who went to centres only once a week said that they would like to go more often. For most people, the value of visits to centres lay in the simple pleasure of getting beyond their own homes. A number of people reported that regular visits to centres were responsible for arousing their interest in life after the onset of disability.

Mrs. Guierson said, 'I go to the Centre once a week. It takes me one and a half hours to get there in the coach. Then we have a cup of tea. So that only leaves a quarter of an hour for work before we have dinner. I get impatient waiting for the lady who dishes out the work, I'm afraid. I do basket work. There's not much choice. I'd like to go more often. I got upset at first when I saw one spastic girl, but I'm better now. You have to start again when there's some one new like that. It's a pity there aren't more youngsters there. don't look forward to going, but I'm alright when I get there. Be fore I just stayed at home. It gives you something else to talk about a first hand experience rather than just hearing about things second hand. I'm getting back to my old self now. I can even crack a joke now. I got to the point where I couldn't manage in a crowd, couldn't join in a conversation—there was nothing to talk about I'm getting back to living now. I don't get so depressed now because I see others much worse than me.'

It was recognized that dependence upon social activities provided by statutory or voluntary bodies entailed important drawbacks. To begin with, those who went to clubs or centres were deprived of the right to exercise any choice of companions. Not all of those attending centres found their companions congenial. A more important draw back was the difficulty which most people experienced in adjusting to participating in social activities with other severely disabled persons. Not everyone had successfully overcome their initial horror of seeing other very severely disabled persons. Three people were so distressed that they had given up attending clubs and centres. Because they had little choice, most people were willing to continue to attend centres

Feeling varied widely on the advisability of disabled persons mixing mainly or solely with other disabled persons on social occasions However, only a minority of people in the sample—eighteen per cent (39)—were in favour of disabled persons seeking companions among the disabled. The reason most frequently given was that only a disabled person could fully understand the problems arising from disability. One man said, 'The disabled, they're the only people that got time for you.' But the vast majority of persons interviewed—seventy-nine per cent (166)—declared themselves to be in favour of mixing socially mainly with non-disabled persons. Some people felt that there were important practical advantages in having non-disabled friends. Mrs. Atkinson said, 'If you're disabled you should have someone you can rely on, someone to give you a bit of help.' But the most common reason given was that groups of disabled persons tended to talk about their disabilities. One woman said, 'At the club

156

you're always hearing about their operations.' Most people wanted to forget about disability and its problems: 'It takes you out of yourself if you're with the able-bodied.' It was on these grounds that special clubs and centres for the disabled were usually criticized.

Mr. Grantham, said, 'I think it's a mistake to collect the physically handicapped together. I know that organizations that try to do things for the disabled do it. But it may not be good for them pyschologically. This applies to old age pensioners, too, I think. When they go to these clubs they're only seeing themselves in a mirror. This is what happens at the Centre. You feel together too much.'

Younger people appeared to show little interest in the special social provisions for the disabled. All except the very severely disabled seemed to maintain close contact with their non-disabled friends.

Nevertheless, most people were aware of the difficulties which faced disabled people who attempted to participate in ordinary social activities, and mix freely with non-disabled persons. Few people overlooked the possibility of rejection. Mr. Kenton said, 'I think the disabled should have ordinary friends. But you have to realize that not everyone would want you.' It was widely acknowledged that a social life restricted to the company of other disabled persons in many ways tended to be less demanding. But people were still prepared to reject it in favour of maintaining wide contacts among non-disabled persons.

Mr. Brown said, 'I used to be a keen athlete before I had polio. Plenty of running and that. And I used to organize hikes for the kids round here every weekend. When I came out of hospital I decided I'd have to have a sport where I could be equal to everyone else. I'm not a spectator. After a few tries at swimming I decided that was no good. I'd never be able to compete with normal people, and I hate being surrounded by disabled people. I think you've got to live in the world as it is on your own terms. That's why I never joined the IPF. When I was in hospital a bloke from the IPF came to see me and asked me to join. I tried to explain why I couldn't. He said 'It will be very difficult out on your own, you know. You won't have anyone to help.' I told him that I knew that, but I was determined to try. I felt sorry for him because his daughter had died with polio, but I was determined not to join. Once I got a car I realized that this was it. Once in the car I'm the same as anyone else. I drive in rallies. And I go down to races with my mates—we help out there a bit. They wave the flags, but I can't do that because I can't leap back. So I sit in the starter's box and I've got the very important job of blowing a horn to warn people to get ready for the start. It's only a little thing, but I like to think its important. Mind you, I enjoy the rallies most. I've won a couple of times, and then they let me. I know that but they don't realize it. I accept that kind of thing. They're bound to do it, so there's nothing you can do. They mean it very kindly, and I don't suppose I'd win otherwise.'

People varied widely in their reaction to the possibility of going out more often. Only a minority—twenty-nine per cent (61)—reported that they did not wish to go out more often, either because they were too ill to enjoy themselves, or because they were already satisfied. In contrast, another ten per cent (21) were so anxious to go out more often that they were not prepared to specify where they would like to go—anywhere would do. It was striking that only five per cent (10) specifically mentioned that if they could go out more often they would like to go to a club or centre for the disabled. But the majority —fifty-five per cent—were keen to visit ordinary places, such as shops, parks, and pubs. In fact, as many as thirty per cent (63) said that if they could go out more often they would like to visit shops. Women in particular missed regular visits to the West End. A further ten per cent felt that they would like to go to the park more frequently. Between one and three per cent wished to visit cinemas, theatres, pubs, churches, relatives, friends, football matches or cricket matches more frequently.

In discussing a service to meet their social needs, most people suggested volunteers to visit and take disabled persons out regularly to shops and parks. That current special provisions for the disabled did not appear to meet many people's social needs, probably helps to explain the relatively low proportion of persons who were in touch with voluntary organizations—twenty-four per cent (51). Demand for existing voluntary services was low, too: only half as many people again (25) said they would like to be put in touch with a voluntary organization.

4. Holidays and other social activities

Some of the persons interviewed reported considerable difficulty in going on holidays. Only forty-five per cent (94) of those in the sample had been on holiday the previous year, while a further sixteen per cent (33) had had a holiday within the last five years. Thus more than one-third (39 per cent) of the persons interviewed had not had a holiday for six or more years. Of course, not everyone wanted a holiday. Some people felt that the problems arising from disability could be overcome satisfactorily only in familiar surroundings of their own homes. Mrs. Rellen said, 'I've not been for the last three years because

158

I was in hospital. But I don't really want to go. I'm happier doing for myself at home.' Others said that they were not well enough to enjoy a holiday. Mr. Belper said, 'I haven't had a holiday for years. You have to be a little bit alive to enjoy strange surroundings.' But in general, even the most severely incapacitated persons said that they felt they would benefit from a holiday. However, most felt that they could not afford one.

Many of those who went on holidays which they arranged themselves experienced difficulty in finding suitable accomodation. Hotels and guest houses were reported generally to have only upstairs bedrooms. Some people overcame this difficulty by renting private accommodation, but this was not always successful.

Mr. Kenton said, 'We still manage to make holidays a family concern. We rented a cottage in Cornwall last year. I had to travel by train, it's all I can manage. Of course, coach is cheaper. I had to sleep downstairs in this cottage. It was all a bit of a job, but I told them it was O.K.'

Other people visited relatives, but even this arrangement was not necessarily entirely satisfactory.

Mrs. Johnson said, 'I went to relatives near Southend last year. They fetched me in the car. They were very good. I got taken out every day in the car and I didn't have to pay a thing. But I seldom have a holiday. I'm afraid of being a nuisance. When I have a fit I might knock something over.'

Special holidays are provided by many voluntary organizations and local authorities for disabled persons. But for those persons interviewed who went on holiday, almost two-thirds (56) arranged 'orthodox' holidays or stayed with relatives. More than two-thirds (24) of those who went on special holidays for the disabled, stayed at special camps or in homes under the sponsorship of local authorities. The remainder (13) went on holidays arranged by disabled persons clubs. Everyone who went on holidays arranged in this way were grateful for the opportunity of going away, and reported favourably on the facilities at camps and homes.

Mr. Rogers said, 'Last year I went to a holiday camp. The welfare did it all. They collected me in the school coach, it was door to door. The camp was lovely, all on the level. There were four of us in one little room which wasn't so good, but the toilets were ever so nice. It was lovely country. We had entertainment every night, there was bingo and a band. I won two cans of beer. Someone came round every day to take us out. All the ladies who looked after us were Red Cross nurses. I only paid £2 5s. 6d. I think the welfare paid the rest. It was the first time I've been on holiday in my life. I couldn't afford to go, and I'd be nervous on my own.'

But an important drawback in the provision of special holidays was reported to be that families were generally not catered for. Usually only the disabled person was able to go.

Some of the criticisms of special clubs and centres for disabled persons were applied to special holidays. People who refused the opportunity to go on special holidays but were unable to make satisfactory arrangements of their own said that most people did not *have* to spend their holidays in company which was not of their own choosing. Moreover, not everyone enjoyed the large gatherings of people which were inevitable in camps and homes, or even the kind of holidays provided by camps. Furthermore, there were people who said that they would be unable to enjoy themselves surrounded by large numbers of severely disabled persons.

Mrs. Beskin said, 'I haven't been for a holiday for years, only convalescent. There seems no point. I can't walk far because I can't get my breath. I'm afraid of being taken bad if I go on my own. But I don't want to go with the handicapped. The sight of all those poor people would make me miserable.'

For some of those who went on them, special holidays were an important source of income in kind. The provision of special holidays was a means tested service. Only four people reported that they had paid the full cost of their special holiday, while another four had paid nothing at all. Of the remainder (29), the majority had paid relatively small amounts—£2 or £3—towards the cost.

Because the opportunities for participation in social activities beyond the home were severely restricted for many of the people interviewed, the availability of entertainment within the home was particularly important. Reading played only a small part in most people's lives. The majority of people reported reading little more than the morning paper. But fifteen per cent (31) of the persons in the sample were keen readers, and took books from the library at least once a fortnight, and in some cases every day. Mobile libraries were more important than relatives or friends for bringing books to people who were themselves unable to go to libraries: thirteen people depended on the mobile library, but only five people had books brought to them by someone else. Altogether, four people said that they would like the mobile library to visit them but two of them lived in rural areas beyond the range of the service.

For most people, wireless and television, particularly the latter, were the most satisfactory forms of entertainments. Moreover, they provided a reliable illusion of contact with the outside world. All but three of the persons interviewed had either a wireless or a television. One woman said, 'I live for my television. That's all I've got in life.' Many people expressed similar sentiments. Almost three-quarters of those in the sample had both a wireless and a television. Another fifteen per cent (33) had only a wireless, and nine per cent only a television. In some circumstances local authorities and voluntary organizations gave wireless and television sets to disabled persons. Eight people had been given television, and three people wireless sets by their local authority. Another person had received a wireless set from a blind persons' organization. Sets appeared to be granted according to their availability rather than standard assessments of need.

5. *Provision of services*

Thus statutory provision affected only a minority of the persons interviewed. Moreover, it was felt by some of those who benefited from them that services were sometimes misdirected. Yet the bulk of local authority services specifically designed for the disabled are intended to meet social and occupational needs. Provision is made under Section 29 of the National Assistance Act. Until 1948, the role of government was restricted to making it easier for disabled people to get to work, and providing money for the industrially injured, war pensioners, and those entitled to sickness benefit. Such services as existed to meet the need for social activities were maintained by voluntary organizations, as they had been in the previous century. A survey of the work of voluntary services for the disabled immediately before local authorities entered the field, reported that provision was 'scattered, uneven, and unco-ordinated.'[8]

Circulars inviting local authorities to submit plans for the provision of services, and containing model schemes, were sent out by the Minister of Health in 1951.[9] But it was not until 1960 that welfare schemes for the disabled became mandatory. During the intervening period, when legislation was permissive, the establishment and development of schemes was uneven. By 1953, seventy-seven schemes had been approved and nearly all the local authorities with schemes had begun to compile registers.[10] Two years later there were 101 approved schemes.[11] In 1960, there were still eight local authorities which had no schemes, and two of these had no plans for one.[12] Only after 1960, when schemes became mandatory was complete national coverage achieved.

8. Clarke, J. S., *Disabled Citizens*, George Allen and Unwin, 1951, p. 185.
9. Circular 32/51, dated 28 August 1951. Comparable action was taken in Scotland by the Secretary of State in Circular 14/51, dated 21 April 1951.
10. *Report of the Ministry of Health for the year ending 31st December 1953*, Cmnd. 9321, London, H.M.S.O., p. 185.
11. *Report of the Ministry of Health for the year ending 31st December 1955*, Cmnd. 9857, London, H.M.S.O., p. 137.
12. *Report of the Ministry of Health for the year ending 31st December 1960*, Cmnd. 1418, London, H.M.S.O., p. 119.

There was no uniformity of provision even between areas where schemes were established. From the first, there were variations between local authorities in the administration of schemes. In many places the voluntary bodies continued to provide most of the welfare services, but on an agency basis, with grants from the local authorities. By the end of the 1950's there was a general tendency among local authorities to end their agency agreements, and administer directly most of the welfare services for the disabled. The Younghusband report forecast the rapid extension of the process under the pressure of increasing demand for the services.[13]

Even with the trend towards the termination of agency agreements, co-ordination between voluntary and statutory authorities remained important. First, the speed at which the different local authorities reached the various stages in the transition from agency agreements to direct provision varied. Second, even in areas where the transition was complete, it was usual for voluntary organizations to supplement the services provided by the local authorities. Joint committees were regarded as the most suitable instruments for facilitating co-operation between voluntary bodies and statutory authorities,[14] but their development was slow.[15]

The growth of services and the enthusiasm they generated gave rise to new dangers. Those providing the services tended to concentrate on the development of special skills to meet the needs of the different classes of disabled persons. Services began to grow apart and develop in isolation. Towards the end of the 1950's a reaction became apparent. The Younghusband Committee was able to state that 'the existing sectionalization of these services no longer makes sense administratively, in economy, or from the point of view of social work.'[16]

What was the purpose of the new services, and what form did they take? The Piercy Committee based its definition of the purpose of the services for the disabled on the Minister's initial Circular:

'In every case the chief object of a welfare service must be to ensure that sufficient aid is given to any handicapped person requiring help to enable him thus aided, to have some share in the life of the community. The handicapped person should be enabled not just to live in the community but be able to contribute to it by

---

13. *Report of the Working Party on Social Workers in Local Authority Health and Welfare Services*, London, H.M.S.O. 1959, para. 1037.
14. *Report of the Ministry of Health for the year ending 31st December 1954*, Cmnd. 9566, London, H.M.S.O. p. 137.
15. *Report of the Ministry of Health for the year ending 31st December 1955*, Cmnd. 9851, London, H.M.S.O. p. 138.
    Report of the Ministry of Health for the year ending 31st December 1956, Cmnd. 293, London, H.M.S.O.
16. *Report of the Working Party on Social Workers in Local Authority Health and Welfare Services*, London, H.M.S.O. 1959, para. 553.

work, if that be possible, and by playing a part in whatever social life exists around him.'[17]

Two years later, the form of the services was outlined by the Ministry of Health.[18]

The piecemeal establishment of schemes over a decade was unlikely to produce a uniformly comprehensive service. Indeed, the unevenness of development was acknowledged early on by the Ministry of Health: 'already the diversity of pattern within a general framework, which is characteristic of local government in this country, is beginning to emerge.'[19] But apart from the models provided by the original Circular, no standard was set by the Ministry against which the performance of local authorities could be measured. Ministry evaluations attempted little beyond noting 'steady progress' in the development of services, and occasionally reporting 'slow progress' in 'some areas'. No procedure was apparently developed to determine local needs empirically and thereby assess the services. Indeed little attempt was made even to quantify and compare provision regionally or over time.

In the absence of empirical data, the development of the services was based largely upon the recommendations of the Piercy and Younghusband Committees. Without attempting an objective assessment of the services, the Piercy Committee was able to state that it was 'clear that only the fringes of the field have yet been touched . . . and on the evidence received there is no doubt that there is a need for fuller and better provision and scope for considerable development.'[20] As a result, the Ministry issued a circular two years later.[21] But its guidance was of a general nature: the publication of the Piercy Report and 'Help for the Handicapped', encouraged the recognition of the need for comprehensive care for the disabled and for teamwork among all those providing services.[22] The Younghusband Committee was likewise without empirical data, but felt justified in focusing on more specific areas of need. Social isolation was identified as the chief hazard faced by disabled persons, and greater efforts to bring the disabled into the community and to prevent their segregation were recommended.[23]

In fact, it was the rate of development of services, rather than their pattern which varied. In essence, remarkable similarities between local authorities was apparent in the content and aims of ser-

---

17. *Report of the Committee of Inquiry on the Rehabilitation, Training, and Resettlement of Disabled Persons*, Cmnd. 9883, London, H.M.S.O., 1956, para. 107.
18. *Ministry of Health Report for the year ending 31 December 1958*, Cmnd. 806, London, H.M.S.O., p. 251.
19. *Report of the Ministry of Health for the year ending 31 December 1955*, Cmnd. 9857, London, H.M.S.O., p. 138.
20. *Report 1956*, Cmnd. 9883, London, H.M.S.O., para. 106.
21. *Circular 16/58*.
22. *Report 1958*, Cmnd. 806, London H.M.S.O., p. 251. See, Nicholson, J. H., *Help for the Handicapped*, National Council of Social Service, 1958.
23. *Report 1959*, London, H.M.S.O., para. 608.

vices. The pattern was pre-determined by the initial voluntary provision. Local authorities were expected mainly to develop an existing pattern rather than to investigate need and design services accordingly. The basic aims and direction of the services remained largely unquestioned. The major problem was considered to be the achievement of an acceptable level of provision everywhere, though the acceptable remained undefined.[24]

Even the ten-year plan for the health and welfare services[25] established no criteria for defining needs. Therefore, no attempt to estimate success in meeting need was possible. Indeed, even the possibilities of comparison of local authority provisions were limited.[26]

6. *The Extension of provision*

The persons interviewed saw their needs largely in terms of the physical and financial help required to enable them to participate more fully in ordinary activities.

Most people thought that the first priority was to ensure some kind of contact with the outside world. To this end it was suggested that telephones should be provided free to severely and very severely incapacitated persons living alone or with one other person who was elderly or infirm. Where similarly incapacitated persons lived in larger households, a grant should be made towards the cost of the telephone, particularly when such persons were alone for a large part of the day or night.

Mobility difficulties were common among the persons interviewed. It is not surprising, therefore, that the more generous provision of vehicles by the government was regarded as an important method of overcoming the segregation of the disabled from daily life. It was suggested that all those whose mobility was so restricted that the use of public transport was dangerous or impossible, should be eligible for a government vehicle if they were capable of driving. The provision of small adapted cars was advocated rather than tricycles, which were held to be socially isolating. It was felt that where a disabled person with restricted mobility purchases his own vehicle, he should be subsidized at the same rate as a person who received a government vehicle.

Not everyone with severe mobility difficulties was able or wished to drive a vehicle. For them, the need appeared to be for special transport arrangements to be made, and financial help to cover the cost of these to enable them to attend family gatherings or to visit friends and relatives. The role of the welfare officer was seen to be

24. *Report of the Working Party on Social Workers in the Local Authority Health and Welfare Services,* London, H.M.S.O., 1959, para, 549.
25. *Health and Welfare. The Development of Community Care. Plans for the Health and Welfare Services of the Local Authorities in England and Wales.* Cmnd. 1973, London, H.M.S.O., 1963.
26. For some regional comparisons based on IMTA statistics, see Appendix 3, p. 199.

crucial here. In fact, if welfare officers were to undertake the necessary arrangements it would entail an extension of the role they already played in arranging special holidays. It was recognized that such a scheme would require closer contact between welfare officers and registered persons than was currently the case.

Severely incapacitated persons living alone or with another elderly or infirm person wished to visit shops, pubs and parks more frequently. It was felt that voluntary societies might initially provide the manpower and structure necessary for such a service, but it was admitted that probably a full scale service would require statutory provision. It was pointed out by a few people that at present far more was spent per head on those disabled persons who could than on those who could not drive, in enabling them to overcome restricted mobility and the consequent limitation of social life.

For severely and very severely disabled persons who spent most of their time at home, it was suggested that television and wireless sets should be provided and the licence paid, either by central or local government.

Some of the persons interviewed felt that those efforts already made in a few cases to provide help in arranging ordinary holidays, and special transport and financial assistance for those who required them should be extended. In particular, younger severely disabled persons with their own families found the special holidays provided by local authorities and voluntary associations innappropriate.

This is not to suggest that current provision should be scrapped. On the contrary, people saw their suggestions for change as an extension of these provisions. Moreover, it was readily acknowledged that for some people, the arrangement of special activities for disabled persons met a real need.

7. Summary

The present pattern of services which exists to meet the occupational and social needs of disabled persons was established by local authorities after they had been invited to submit schemes to the Minister of Health in 1951. Basically, the services reflected existing provisions made by the voluntary societies—advice with personal problems, the provision of craft instruction and other occupational activities, often in special centres, adaptations to the home, the supply of special aids, and the provision of holidays and outings. Provision was, and remains, uneven because complete national coverage was achieved only after schemes became mandatory in 1960. Apart from models initially agreed by the Ministry of Health, no standard criteria for measuring local authority performance in this field have been laid down. But in terms of the numbers of persons on the registers of the disabled, and the provision of special centres, it is clear that the provisions of local authorities vary enormously.

The object of the services was said to be to prevent severely disabled persons becoming socially isolated. How far did disability limit the ordinary social and occupational activities of the persons interviewed, and how successful were local authority services in supplementing them?

Only two-fifths of those living alone had daily contact with a relative, neighbour or friend, compared with almost two-thirds of those living in two-person households and a little more than half of those living with two or more persons. But the proportions of persons having at least weekly contact with someone beyond their own household was much the same for each type of household. As many as fourteen per cent (29) of the persons interviewed could expect no such weekly contact. Neighbours were the most important source of social contact for the persons interviewed. The absence of neighbourhood friendships promoted a sense of isolation even when relatives visited regularly. Neighbours were less important, and relatives correspondingly more important as sources of social contact for those living in two-person households than for others.

Where families were dispersed, contact between relatives was promoted by car ownership. But a below average proportion of persons in the sample belonged to households where a car was available—sixteen per cent. And in most cases where the vehicle was provided by the Ministry of Health, the disabled persons usually had to travel alone. Some people were unable to use public transport, while others complained about high fares. As many as twenty per cent of the persons in the sample were able to keep in contact by telephone, but the majority of them in fact used their telephone mainly in times of emergency. Most people felt that disabled persons ought to be granted free telephones in case of emergencies. Like other people, those interviewed kept in touch with relatives by letter, usually at Christmas, but their attendance at family occasions such as weddings and funerals was limited by mobility difficulties.

More than half (106) of the persons interviewed felt that their disability caused them to become more depressed than most people. More than half (57) blamed the social limitations imposed by disability. Particularly important causes were held to be the lack of outside contacts, inability to go out, and lack of occupation. Only one-fifth of those interviewed were able to go out without restriction, while almost half were unable to go out unaccompanied. Persons living alone or in two-person households experienced particular difficulty in finding someone to take them out. In addition, there were problems of exhaustion, access difficulties to some public facilities, particularly lavatories, and a feeling of stigma. Even more important were the difficulties involved in the use of public transport: forty-five per cent were unable to use any form of public transport even with help. In spite of these difficulties, almost half of the persons interviewed had been out the previous day, though eight per cent had not been out for more than a year. Only one-third expected to go out every day, and almost one-fifth only a few times a year or even less. In most cases, visits were restricted to shops, though pubs and churches were also important. Few people went to public places of entertainment such as cinemas and theatres. In most cases problems of mobility rather than access prevented more frequent visits. On the whole, churches appeared to be successful in maintaining contact even with housebound persons.

Although almost a quarter of those interviewed belonged to special clubs for the disabled, only six per cent reported that their only regular outings were to such clubs. Only thirteen per cent of the persons interviewed attended local authority occupation centres. Although they were appreciated, special provisions of this kind were reported by many people to have a number of important drawbacks. To begin with, there was little choice of companions. More important, some people found it difficult to adjust to the company of other severely disabled persons. The majority of those who wanted to go out more often said that they would like to visit shops, parks or pubs, rather than special clubs or centres. Similar criticisms were made of holidays run specially for disabled persons by local authorities and voluntary organizations. But again, the problems affected only a minority of the persons interviewed: of those who had been on holiday the previous year, only one-third (37) went on special holidays.

The restrictions placed on the social activities of many of the persons interviewed by mobility difficulties increased the importance of home entertainments. For a minority (15 per cent) reading was the most satisfactory form of occupation, though only six per cent depended on mobile libraries and another two per cent required this service. Television and the wireless were the most important forms of entertainment: only three people had neither television or wireless, though three quarters of those interviewed had both. Some people (11) had received sets from their local authority or a voluntary organization, but provision of this kind was small in scale and unsystematic.

Broadly speaking, the action of local authorities and voluntary organizations in making provisions for the occupational and social needs of the disabled affected relatively few of the persons interviewed. The provision of 'special' activities tended to segregate people even more from the general community, and restricted their choice of activity still further. Although some people felt more secure among disabled persons, the majority expressed a wish to participate in 'ordinary' activities.

167

The purpose of this small pilot study was to explore the daily lives of disabled persons. Three major problems required investigation—that of mobility and self sufficiency, the problem of occupation, and difficulties arising out of household and outside relationships. How far did these vary according to age and incapacity?

Theoretically, all the crucial questions seem to hinge on whether the disabled should be integrated into society or segregated from it. Theories of disengagement and segregation were explored by examining the structure of contemporary relationships between disabled persons and the rest of society. Thus the object of the research was to describe the roles and social relationships of disabled persons according to their levels of incapacity.

For a number of reasons, only tentative conclusions may be drawn from this study. First, the study was small in scale. Second, only persons on local authority registers of the physically handicapped were included in the study. Third, it must be assumed that changes have occurred which have affected the disabled since the interviews were completed in 1965. Moreover, the study is based on the subjective accounts of the persons interviewed. Finally, it was restricted geographically. It is the purpose of the first part of this chapter to assess these limitations in more detail. Thereafter, general conclusions will be discussed relating to physical capacity, income, employment, housing, social activities, help at home, and family life.

Only a small number of persons were interviewed—211. These represented about two per cent of the persons registered as belonging to the general classes of the physically handicapped by local authorities in the areas studied. Although the study was restricted to persons registered as physically handicapped, forty-five different clinical conditions were reported by the persons interviewed, the most common being arthritis, polio myelitis, amputations and multiple sclerosis. Although the registers of deaf, blind, mentally handicapped and mentally ill persons were not sampled for the study, some of the persons interviewed had these disabilities. That by no means all physically handicapped persons were registered is clear from the wide variation between local authorities in the proportion of persons registered. Thus the experience of the persons interviewed cannot be representative even of physically handicapped persons in the areas studied.

The age structure of the sample meant that the problems of young disabled persons remained largely unexplored. Probably the age and sex structure of the sample was determined by the content of local authority services. Although the age range of the persons interviewed was wide—sixteen to ninety-two years, eighty-four per cent were aged forty-five years or more, while forty-two per cent were above the age of sixty-four years. More women (130) than men (81) were interviewed.

How far have the circumstances of disabled persons changed since 1965? The reform in London government which took place while interviewing was in progress, has not resulted in uniformity of provision. In the areas studied, services are now provided by as many as twenty local authorities. The proportion of persons per thousand population registered varied in 1968 from 1.6 in Bexley to 6.0 in Southwark (excluding the City of London). Even between areas with similar rates of registration there may be a difference in expenditure of as much as 133 per cent: for example, in 1968, Islington registered 5.8 persons per thousand population, and spent on each of them an average of £28 a year, whereas Tower Hamlets, with a registration rate of 5.1 spent an average of only £12 a year on each registered person.[1] Moreover, the multiplicity of local authorities created a wide variety of means tests for services for disabled persons. In an attempt to reduce the confusion, the London Boroughs Association set up a working party in 1967 to make recommendations for a common basic assessment scale for payments for various welfare services. But the scale is intended only as a guide.

Since the study was completed there has been an expansion of local authority services for the disabled. The number of persons registered as physically handicapped in England and Wales has risen from 3.6 to 3.9 per thousand population, while annual average expenditure on each person registered has risen by one third—from £19 6s. 0d. to £31 0s. 0d. But wide variation between local authorities persists. Among London boroughs the expansion has been even more startling. In 1965, 3.3 persons per thousand population were registered as physically handicapped in London boroughs, compared with 4.9 in 1968. Average annual expenditure per registered person has risen sharply, from £19 6s. 0d. in 1965 to £66 0s. 0d. in 1968.

---

1. See, The Institute of Municipal Treasurers and Accountants, *Welfare Services Statistics*, 1965–66 and 1967–68.

Since 1964-1965 there has been a considerable rise in income. Between 1964 and 1968 average weekly earnings of male manual workers rose by thirty per cent. The basic rates of state benefits have risen sharply too. But on the whole there has been little change in basic benefit rates as a proportion of average weekly earnings. (See Figure 3.)

FIGURE 3

Some state benefits expressed as a percentage of average weekly earnings of manual workers (a)

	Unemployment and sickness benefit (b)	100 per cent industrial injuries disablement injuries (c)	National Assistance /Supplementary benefit (d)
1963	19.9	34.0	19.8
1964	19.1	32.7	18
1965	20.5	34.7	19.6
1966	19.8	33.3	20.0
1967	19.1	32.8	19.6
1968	20.2	32.6	19.3

(a) Wages refer to April, benefits to June every year.
(b) Refers to basic rates for single person.
(c) Refers to basic rate for 100 per cent disablement.
(d) Refers to basic rate for single householder.

During the period since 1964 the proportion of unemployed persons increased from 1.4 per cent on 13 July 1964 to 2.1 per cent on 10 February 1969. Moreover, long term unemployment increased.[2] Disabled persons suffered more than others: the unemployed among those on the Department of Employment and Productivity's Disabled Persons' Register rose from 7.4 per cent in July 1964 to eleven per cent in February 1969.[3] Whereas the rate of unemployment among registered persons was four times higher than the national average in 1964-65, the proportion was five times higher by 1969.

The problem of rehousing disabled persons in suitable accommodation has become more acute in some areas since 1965. It is becoming increasingly difficult for some local authorities, particularly those in central urban areas to give priority to disabled persons in new housing schemes.

It was impossible within the resources available to assess the objectivity of the information given by the persons interviewed. Nevertheless, the evidence of the persons interviewed is important, for it represents their view of reality, the consumer's assessment of the

2. See *Ministry of Labour Gazette, August 1964*. London, H.M.S.O., and *Employment and Productivity Gazette, March 1969*, H.M.S.O., London.
3. See *Ministry of Labour Gazette, August 1964*, London H.M.S.O., and *Employment and Productivity Gazette, March 1969*, H.M.S.O., London.

special provisions which the disabled are obliged to accept in so far as they are unable to comply with social norms.

The study was restricted to the administrative districts of the London County Council, the Middlesex County Council, and the Chelmsford and Maldon areas of Essex. Therefore the experiences of the persons interviewed may not be taken as representative of those of disabled persons throughout the country. In certain respects, people living in these areas on average enjoyed higher standards than those living elsewhere. For example, in 1965, thirty-eight per cent of the households in Greater London, compared with twenty-five per cent of those in the rest of the country had a total household weekly income of £30 or more. Men's weekly earnings, too, were higher on average in the South East than in other regions—£20 5s. 0d. compared with £18 8s. 0d. The standard of housing was generally higher. A higher proportion of persons in the area covered by the study lived in dwellings with standard basic amenities than was true of the country generally.

In the provision of special facilities for the disabled, the area studied was about average for the country as a whole: in 1965/66, for example, an average of 3.3 persons per thousand population were registered as physically handicapped in the London boroughs, excluding the City of London, compared with 3.6 per thousand in England and Wales; but the London boroughs and local authorities as a whole in England and Wales spent on average on each of the persons registered £19 6s. 0d. and £15 16s. 0d. respectively.

The persons interviewed suffered from a wide variety of clinical conditions, yet it is possible to isolate an experience common to most of them. In varying degrees they were segregated from the mainstream of life in so far as their choices were limited by disability, and material resources were insufficient to increase the opportunities for involvement.

The persons interviewed were limited in the first instance by incapacity for ordinary daily activities. Current methods of assessing disability make comparisons between persons with different clinical conditions difficult. The published percentage assessments relate primarily to amputations, and they may be the exception. However, comparison of some of these suggests that there is sometimes little relationship between clinical assessments and incapacity. Assessments made by medical practitioners based on schedules of the Department of Employment and Productivity are not assessment of overall incapacity.

For the present study an attempt was made to cut across clinical conditions by defining disability in terms of incapacity to follow ordinary activities. A list of twenty-four daily activities was devised, ranging from 'feeding oneself' to 'cleaning floors' which provided

171

a rough index of capacity. The scoring system was crude: those able to complete an activity without help but with difficulty and those unable to complete an activity without help were assigned scores of one and two respectively. However, when assessments were compared they appeared to be broadly reliable. But there were a few cases in which total scores required to be weighted because certain manifestations of disability, such as incontinence and deafness were not well reflected by the index.

The persons interviewed varied widely in their capacity. Between three-fifths and three-quarters of the sample could not clean floors, get up and down stairs, shop, cut their toenails and go out of doors unaided. By contrast, only thirteen per cent were unable to get about the house unaided, and only two per cent were unable to feed themselves. On the basis of information about activities on the index, as many as twenty per cent of the persons interviewed were categorized as very severely incapacitated. Another thirty-six per cent were severely incapacitated, while only thirteen per cent were slightly incapacitated. Incapacity tended to increase with age. Only a third of those younger than forty-five were severely or very severely incapacitated, compared with half of those aged forty-five to sixty-four years, and more than two-thirds of those aged sixty-five years and over.

The effect of disability was complicated for many people by the changes in capacity which they experienced over time. In some cases this was a function of the condition. Some people found that their disability was quickly progressive. Others reported progressive conditions, but experienced remissions, often for long periods of time. In other cases, variation in capacity was the result of external factors. Even people with apparently static conditions reported changes in capacity. The problems presented by pain and exhaustion were referred to again and again. Any demand made beyond those of a person's normal routine could prove to be intolerable. In a society which places a premium on independence it was understandable that many of the persons interviewed should have been intent on proving their self-sufficiency. But others, while they themselves followed this practice, questioned its value. It appeared to them that a narrowly defined independence was often bought at the expense of a wider choice of social activities.

Income was rarely sufficient to increase a choice range limited by incapacity. Indeed, the average weekly household income of the persons in the sample was only half of the national average—£12 4s. 1d. compared with £24 13s. 0d. A far higher proportion of persons interviewed than of the population generally lived at or near officially determined levels of poverty. As many as forty-eight per cent (100) of the households represented in the sample reported resources of below 140 per cent of the basic national assistance scale, comared with eighteen per cent in the United Kingdom generally. Whereas five per cent of households nationally had incomes below the basic national assistance scale, this was true of as many as fourteen per cent of households in the sample. Even the proportion of persons below pensionable age in the sample who belonged to households where the total income was below the basic national assistance scale—en per cent—was twice the national proportion.

To some extent the low incomes of the persons interviewed are to be explained by dependence on state benefits. As many as eighty-seven per cent of the persons interviewed depended on state benefits for all or part of their income: fifty-four per cent (65) of persons below pensionable age belonged to this category—three quarters of he men (35) but less than half of the women (23).

By tradition, the Poor Law provided minimum standards for those who were unable to maintain themselves in financial independence. When responsibility for relief was assumed by the National Assistance Board in 1948, and subsequently by the Supplementary Benefits Commission in 1966, relief remained a means-tested payment. Altogether eleven per cent of persons below pensionable age were entirely dependent on national assistance. National insurance against sickness and unemployment was established to make provision outside the poor law for those who are unable to maintain their financial independence and whose contribution record satisfies the Department's requirements. As many as thirty-two per cent (36) of those of working age were dependent primarily on sickness benefit (17 per cent of the total sample), but only two persons received unemployment benefit. Payments made under the Industrial Injuries scheme, like war disability pensions, are made according to a clinical assessment of the percentage of disability. The supplementary allowances available to those disabled as a result of service in the armed forces or at work go some way towards recognizing the social and economic effects of disability, but the amounts payable are small. Moreover only a minority of those with disablement benefits receive the supplementary allowances. But only seven per cent of those interviewed received war disablement pensions or industrial injury disablement benefit.

On average, the weekly income of employed persons was twice that of those who were dependent on state benefits. Even so, the average weekly earnings of persons in the sample was below the average for the area generally—£12 2s. 0d. compared with £16 7s. 0d. Moreover, only twenty-six per cent (29) of persons below pensionable age were in full time employment. Nor were low income households confined to those which were entirely or largely dependent on state benefits: about two-fifths of the households in the sample which received no income from state benefits had total incomes of less than 140 per cent of the basic national assistance scale.

Thus, for most people problems resulting from low income were added to those arising from disability. Many people found it impossible to replace clothing and household articles. Only three of those who depended upon national assistance had received small discretionary grants for this purpose. Those who were congenitally disabled or disabled from an early age had usually been unable to save for the replacement of household articles or clothing. People who had been disabled later in life spent their savings ensuring for their children expected opportunities. Altogether, as many as three-quarters (158) of the persons in the sample reported savings of less than £50, while only one-fifth had savings of more than £100.

Some people found that their conditions gave rise to needs which required additional expenditure, for example, on special diets, extra laundry expenses, and extra fuel. Some of those on national assistance received small discretionay allowances to meet such expenditure.

Among non-employed persons below pensionable age the demand for employment was high: more than half (42) said that they would like to work. Degree of incapacity clearly affected the choice of suitable employment. Although the majority of persons in full time employment were only slightly or moderately incapacitated one seventh were severely or very severely incapacitated. On the other hand, almost half of the non-employed seeking work were only slightly or moderately incapacitated. Travel facilities were required by one-third of those who wanted work. But over two-fifths of those seeking employment did not require special working conditions. All of these wanted full-time employment, and all but two of them were able to travel any distance to work provided they had their own transport. A further fifth, however, required work, mainly of an unskilled or clerical nature, within ten or fifteen minutes of home. The remainder required home work, although a few of them could have been taken to part-time open employment if transport had been available. The majority of people seeking work were unskilled. Yet it was precisely the suitable unskilled jobs with reasonable rates of pay which were so difficult for the disabled persons to find.

The special services designed to help disabled persons find employment had either failed those seeking work, or had not been contacted. Only two people had been to an industrial rehabilitation unit while one-seventh of employed persons had seen the Disablement Resettlement Officer. Only ten per cent of persons below pensionable age interviewed said that they were on the Department of Employment and Productivity's Disabled Persons' Register. Some people reported that their 'green card' gave them a sense of security, but others felt that it limited their choice of jobs still further. The majority of em-

174

ployed persons had found work through newspaper advertisements, friends and relatives. Some people reported employers who readily adjusted the working environment to their needs while others concealed their disability for fear of being dismissed.

Few people had benefitted from the special facilities devised to widen their choice of employment. Only one of the persons interviewed was in sheltered employment. Yet at least one of the sheltered workshops in the area studied had vacancies at the time. In fact, few people desired sheltered work. First, there was no factory-based provision of transport for employees. Second, the hours, conditions, and pace were said to be similar to those in open employment. Finally, wages tended to be below the average. Nor were people keen to undertake designated employment as car park and passenger lift attendants. Most people felt that such jobs lacked interest, were of low status, and provided low wages. Moveover, the limited choice of employment tended to result in segregation. Most people desired the provision of special transport, or a grant with which to buy transport so that they could travel to suitable work in open employment. For these reasons most people felt, on balance, that more complete registration accompanied by a more skilful advisory service was required, together with greater exploitation of the 'quota' system, which appeared to require careful vetting.

More than half (109) of the persons interviewed lived in council dwellings, compared with a quarter of persons in the area generally. The proportion of persons in privately rented dwellings was the same as in the area generally—twenty-five per cent. But less than a quarter (49) of dwellings in the sample, compared with forty-six per cent of those in Greater London and Essex, were owner-occupied. The limitation of choice in housing was reflected in the below average standard of much of the housing in which the persons interviewed lived. For example, the proportion of persons without piped hot water was twice that of dwellings in the area generally, while higher proportions of dwellings in the sample than in Greater London and Essex as a whole, had no fixed bath and an outside W.C. As might be expected, privately rented dwellings were the most and council housing was the least likely to lack amenities and have inadequate facilities.

The absence of standard housing facilities added still further to the difficulties of daily life in the home, and reduced capacity to participate in household activities. Even more important in this respect were unsuitable dwellings. As many as seventy per cent of the persons interviewed found it impossible to climb stairs, and the majority of the remainder experienced difficulty. Yet more than half lived in dwellings to which stairs were the only means of access, while almost as many had stairs to the kitchen, the bathroom, the W.C. or the bedroom.

Some people were unable to use certain facilities: five people reported that the W.C. was too low; one-fifth were unable to use the kitchen sink or taps because they were too high; one-fifth found the cooker too high to use; a quarter were able to use only some cupboards, while a further fifth were unable to use any. More than half of the persons who were unable to use any cupboards were housewives. As many as two-fifths of those with money-in-the-slot gas and electric meters were unable to reach them, and the majority of persons interviewed were unable to open the living room and kitchen windows.

Most people recognized that their command of suitable and adequate housing was limited by their incapacity. The search for another dwelling often required strength which was beyond that available for ordinary daily activities. Income, too, was recognized as being crucial. Most of the persons interviewed realized that their only hope of adequate and suitable housing lay with the local authority. Yet even successful applications to the local authority required a degree of persistence—to produce supporting letters from hospitals and doctors, and to visit the housing department—which was beyond some people. For most people there was little hope of swift re housing: almost half lived in their present dwellings for more than fifteen years.

Although almost all of those who had been rehoused by the local authority lived in adequate accommodation, by no means all had been suitably rehoused. Some lived on large inter-war estates, remote from public transport, shops, and other facilities. Some were dependent on lifts which were subject to frequent break-down. In all, half of those who had been rehoused found the location, and almost as many the dwelling unsuitable. Adaptations and alterations within the home often did much to make daily activities easier for the persons interviewed. A little less than half had had their dwellings altered in some way. But only two-thirds of these alterations were carried out by the local authority. Most alterations were modest in scale: rails were provided beside stairs and steps, near the bed, and in the bathroom and lavatory; lavatory seats had been raised and ramps constructed. Not everyone who had to pay for adaptations under the local authority means-tested scheme felt that they could afford to do so. As many as twenty-five per cent of the persons in the sample still required alterations to be made to their dwellings, but the majority of these had been told that their dwellings were unsuitable for alteration.

The possibilities of special standardized housing for the disabled are limited. Thus the evidence pointed to the need for good modern housing without steps, and the adaptation of kitchen and other facilities to meet the needs of each disabled person.

The choice of social activities of many of the persons interviewed was severely limited. More than a fifth of those in the sample had not been out for more than a month before the interview; of these, half had been out less than three times in the previous twelve months. Nevertheless, almost half (90) of the persons interviewed had been out the day before they were interviewed, and another third (64) had been out that week or the previous week. As many as forty per cent of the persons interviewed had not been to a public place of social activity or entertainment such as a park, cinema, theatre, pub, church or concert within the previous twelve months. Mobility difficulties most commonly caused social activities to be restricted. As many as forty-five per cent of the persons in the sample were unable to get about outside without help. Almost as many (forty per cent) were unable to use public transport without assistance. Yet only sixteen per cent of the persons interviewed lived in households where there was a car, compared with one in four of households generally. Most of those with private transport had a vehicle from the Ministry of Health—eleven per cent of those in the sample. Only one person had been issued with a car by the Ministry. Yet most of those with tricycles felt unsafe travelling alone, and complained that single-seat vehicles were socially isolating. It has been admitted by the Ministry that reliance for the most part on tricycles limits demand for Ministry vehicles.[4]

Most of the persons interviewed were not in a position to buy private transport. Household income was insufficient to compensate for incapacity in this way. Inability to pay for private transport meant that for many people social outings were impossible or rare, and that when they occurred they were exhausting. Yet most of the persons interviewed stressed the importance of 'getting beyond the four walls', of meeting other people 'to take you out of yourself', 'to forget your own troubles'. In general, low income restricted social activities almost as much as incapacity. Only ten per cent of the persons interviewed admitted that any stigma attached to disability led them to restrict their activities.

Nor did ownership of a telephone compensate most people for the dearth of social contacts outside the home. Of the persons interviewed, the same proportion as nationally lived in households where a telephone was available—twenty per cent. The telephone was important mainly as a means of summoning help. Most people thought that severely disabled persons should be given a telephone or receive a special government grant for one. Few of those who had a telephone actually paid for it themselves: in most cases it was paid for by a relative.

Although most people were able to get out only with difficulty as

---

4. For the Minister's statement, and the categories of persons to whom eligibility for cars was then extended, see Parliamentary Debates, Commons, *Hansard*, Volume 741, 15 February 1967, column 524.

M

many as seventy-seven per cent of the persons interviewed saw someone from outside the home at least once a week, while sixty per cent saw two or more persons each week. But there were persons—thirteen per cent of those in the sample—who saw someone from outside the household less than once a week, and one-seventh of these lived alone. Indeed, of persons living alone, only a little more than half saw someone daily. Generally, daily contact with neighbours supplemented less frequent contact with relatives. Persons living alone or with one other person depended far more on neighbours for regular contact with those outside the home than was true of persons living in larger households.

The importance of contact with persons outside the household for disabled persons is officially recognized: local authorities have powers under Section 29 of the National Assistance Act, 1948, to establish schemes to promote social activities for the disabled. Some voluntary clubs are subsidized by the local authority and have the use of local authority special vehicles. Such clubs provided the only opportunity for regular outings for six per cent of the persons interviewed. Altogether, almost a quarter (50) of the persons in the sample, most of them above the age of forty-five, belonged to at least one club run specially for the disabled. Younger people, particularly those who were not very severely incapacitated, appeared to be successful in maintaining contact with non-disabled friends.

Occupational centres administered by local authorities were less important than clubs. Only thirteen per cent (28) of the persons interviewed attended a centre, a surprisingly small proportion considering the importance attached to this service by the Department of Health and Social Security. Most of those who went to centres were grateful to be taken beyond the household, and some people reported that centres had been responsible for arousing their interest in life after the onset of disability. But local authority provision did not extend the choice of disabled persons. First, such provision largely denied the choice of companions. Second, some people experienced difficulty in adjusting to the company of severely disabled persons. People were critical of holidays arranged by local authorities and voluntary associations for the same reasons. The aim of such services was a minimum provision which in effect segregated disabled persons from others in their social activities. Special provision of this kind was recognized as a substitute for the real thing. The majority of persons interviewed said that if they could go out more often they would like to go shopping. However, a substantial minority of those interviewed—eighteen per cent—preferred to be among disabled persons than others. Having been identified and categorized by society, they were relieved to accept the limitations imposed by society on their activities. In view of the pressure to adopt the role assigned to them by society, it is striking

178

that such a large proportion of those interviewed accepted it unwillingly. Most people felt that the ability to buy private transport and help would increase their choice of social activities enormously. The evidence substantiated this belief: where people lived near a wide range of relatives or friends, and received help from the people with whom they lived, it was noticeable that they were able to enjoy a wide range of contacts and activities outside their own homes.

Essential personal and household tasks were often carried out only with considerable pain and effort, and sometimes not at all. All but five of the persons interviewed required help with at least one of our listed personal or household tasks, while more than a quarter (57) did so with nine or more such tasks. Yet help was not always available within the home. Broadly speaking, those living alone required as much help as those in other households.

The source from which help in the home was obtained varied with the type of household. Persons who lived alone depended predominantly on local authority welfare services. Those living in two-person households depended mainly on relatives for help, but received considerable help from welfare services as well. Few persons in other types of household received help from welfare services; they depended almost entirely on relatives for help. Generally speaking, relatives were the most important source of help. But for those living alone, neighbours and welfare services were both more important than relatives. On the whole, local authority services were substitutes for family help: they were not sufficiently developed to play a well defined supporting role where disabled persons lived with their families.

Recipients of domiciliary services tended to be persons living alone or with a frail or elderly person and were usually severely or very severely incapacitated. But this was not invariably the case. Not only was there no guarantee that the domiciliary services would be obtained as a substitute for help normally available from the family; there appeared to be no standard criteria by which services were allocated to play a supportive role in situations where no family help was available. Furthermore, the extent of help provided by domiciliary services for the disabled persons interviewed appeared to be governed by no objective assessment of need in terms of functional capacity and extent of other help available.

Help from local authority services tended to be even more inflexible than that from other sources. Moreover, the help available was limited in kind and scope.

The most important single contribution to help in the home from statutory services was made by the home help service. Even so, only a little more than a quarter (57) of the persons interviewed had a home help. The period of help given to recipients varied from one to ten hours each week. But almost half of the recipients interviewed were helped for only four hours or less each week and only about seven per cent of the total sample were helped for eight or more hours. In the majority of cases, the home help's activities were restricted to cleaning and shopping. But a small minority of persons in the sample received extensive help. Although thirty-eight per cent of the persons interviewed were unable to cook, only four per cent received meals on wheels. No provision was made at weekends. More than a quarter (55) of the persons interviewed required help with bathing, but only one person was helped by a bathing attendant, and another five per cent by the district nurse. Although the majority of people —ninety per cent—were unable to do their washing at home, only three of them benefitted from a local authority laundry service. Fourteen per cent of the persons interviewed were visited by a district nurse. District nurses primarily undertook medical duties, but for about one-third of recipients of the service nurses helped in other ways, too. Almost two-thirds of the persons in the sample were unable to cut their own toenails, yet only ten per cent were in receipt of the home chiropody service.

In spite of the wide variety of services available to help disabled persons, as many as seventeen (eight per cent) of persons interviewed received no help with at least one personal task which they were unable to do themselves. In fact, there was considerable unmet demand for statutory services. Of those who were in receipt of the home help service, as many as two-thirds (35) said that they would like help for longer hours, while almost one-third wanted additional jobs, usually of an occasional nature, undertaken. In addition there was considerable demand for services from people who did not receive them at all. A further ten per cent of the persons interviewed said that they required help in the home. Only a further five people said that they required a district nurse and six people meals on wheels: demand for the latter appeared to be limited by the reputation of the service. Altogether, another twenty per cent of the persons interviewed said that they required home chiropody; ten per cent said that they would like a bathing attendant; and as many as twenty-seven per cent required the borough laundry service.

The existence of some services such as chiropody, bathing, and laundry services was not widely known. Most people did not apply directly for a specific service: their difficulties became known usually to doctors or medical social workers who referred them to such appropriate services as they knew to exist in the area. Furthermore, most of the persons interviewed were aware of the pressure on local authority domiciliary services, and restricted their demands for help accordingly. Requests for help were not lightly made. Of those who said that they would like help from a local authority service, the majority lived alone or with an elderly or infirm relative, or were severely or very severely incapacitated. In most cases the amount of help asked for was modest. For example, of those who required a home help, more than half (13) said that they required help only once a week, and the remainder twice a week. Most people (17) said that they needed only two hours, and the remainder (five) four hours help each week. Finally, insistence on the importance of a narrowly defined independence by society generally, ensured that demand for help remained low.

Severe limitation of choice which resulted from disability gave rise to unhappiness for many of the persons interviewed. Even those for whom the major effect of the onset of disability was the temporary interruption of employment, usually experienced a permanent contraction of their promotion prospects. Those below pensionable age who were unable to work sensed a loss of status. Many people reported that they felt they were 'on the scrap heap'. Loss of independence gave rise to feelings of inadequacy. Guilt resulted from dependence on others. Some people were reluctant even to contact relatives more frequently in case it was thought that they were asking for more help. People who used local authority services bore an additional burden of guilt: they were dependent upon a service which was largely payed for by the community. Guilt was most intense among persons who were dependent upon national assistance. Most of them were anxious to justify their dependence on the state. Indeed, about five per cent of the persons interviewed were assessed as being eligible for national assistance, but refused to apply. Yet it was clear that there were officials who went to considerable lengths to convince people that they were receiving their 'rights', not charity. But the formalities attached to means-tested services and benefits, however humanely applied, resulted in loss of status.

Many of the persons interviewed believed that their difficulties caused them to become more depressed than most people. Altogether, half (106) admitted that disability resulted in depression. In some cases (17) depression was felt to be part of the condition. But almost half (57) felt it to be the result of the incapacitating effects of disability, and their consequent dependence on others. The acceptance of a life style which did not meet expectations was also seen to be important. Actual capacity often fell short of apparent capacity: an activity might be possible in isolation, but not as part of a necessary sequence or in addition to other difficult activities. Many people realized that they could have accomplished far more with the aid of adequate and flexible help, imaginative adaptations in the home, adjustments in the work environment, and a higher income.

Where disabled persons did not live alone, incapacity tended to limit the choice of other members of the household as well. Some men found their choice of employment restricted because they had to look after wives whose condition periodically deteriorated. Others with severely incapacitated wives were unable to work overtime. Some men had to adopt two roles—that of housewife as well as that of breadwinner. The presence of young children increased the burden on the father and the disabled mother's consequent guilt. As a final resort, to prevent the family being separated a father may give up work to look after the family in return for national assistance. The result may be a considerable loss of income as well as status.

For a man, disability almost always resulted in loss of potential as well as current income. Some had been forced to accept lower paid work while others had given up work altogether. Most men, particularly those with young families found that their savings were spent soon after the onset of disability in an effort to maintain their standard of living. Thus even when children became independent and the standard of living rose, it generally failed to meet former expectations.

Wives who replaced their severely incapacitated husbands as the main wage earner often experienced difficulties in maintaining jobs, particularly when they required time off work to care for husbands whose condition periodically deteriorated: thus low earnings alternated with state benefits. Husbands deprived of their role as breadwinner suffered considerable loss of status, though this was mitigated to some extent where roles were reversed in the household and the disabled husband was able to undertake some of the housewife's duties.

The burden of help required by severely incapacitated persons often strained relationships within the household. Of the persons interviewed, five per cent were divorced or separated, while a further ten per cent reported that their marriages were under considerable stress. In particular, elderly or infirm persons found the help required of them in caring for severely incapacitated persons, burdensome. The limitation of activities imposed by incapacity on a disabled person, often extended in some measure to other members of the household as well.

In spite of their difficulties, most of the disabled persons interviewed enjoyed a warm family life. Some people had a wide variety of interests, and many continued to be involved in the activities of home and neighbourhood. Even the most isolated and severely incapacitated persons felt a passionate attachment to their life at home. Indeed, the major preoccupation of the persons interviewed, and of those who cared for them, was to ensure that they lived at home for as long as possible. Some people had already been faced with the possibility of moving to an institution. But the experience had strengthened their determination to delay admission until there was no choice.

Much of the discussion to date has expressed the problems relating to disability largely in administrative terms. More recently, central government has been under pressure from a number of independent organizations to place greater emphasis on the financial relief of the disabled. The object of the present study was to consult the consumer and enquire into the conditions and aspirations of the disabled. It has shown that the problems posed by disability are complex. And attempts to find solutions will inevitably involve a reappraisal of some of the basic concepts of our society. For perhaps the most important problem to emerge from the study is the difficulty of reconciling the expressed needs of the disabled and provisions made for them. Most disabled persons required help to enable them to participate as fully as possible with others in daily life. But the provisions made for them tended to segregate them from the rest of the community. Thus the aspirations of many of the persons interviewed and the objectives of social policy were in conflict.

THE ROLE OF LOCAL AUTHORITY
WELFARE OFFICERS

Welfare officers were in some senses the pivot of local authority welfare services for the disabled. To begin with, it was they who assessed people for registration with the local authority. Thereafter, welfare officers had the duty to visit the registered persons in their 'district' at least once a year. Additional visits were made as the need for them arose. Thus visits tended to be concentrated around times of crisis rather than to take place at regular intervals. During crises, welfare officers were seen mainly as referral agencies. It was their duty to provide from available services those which they considered to be necessary to maintain the disabled person at home — such as home helps, meals on wheels, adaptations to the home. As a consequence they were also asked to assess the point at which the disabled person could no longer remain at home and should seek admission to an institution.

It was clear that there was considerable disagreement among welfare officers themselves as to what their role should be. Some, particularly those who had attended Younghusband courses, felt that far greater emphasis should be placed on casework. They were aware that many of the psychological and social problems attendant on disability, which lay beyond the scope of avilable welfare services, remained unexplored by social workers. Some older welfare officers reacted sharply against the idea of extending their role to include more intensive casework. They tended to restrict deliberately their duties to obtaining for the disabled persons they visited those services which were readily available and, once conditions had again deteriorated, obtaining a place for the disabled person in an institution as quickly as possible. Other welfare officers adopted a position between these two extremes. They regarded an expansion of existing welfare services as of prime importance, and would have been largely content to act as referral agencies for these. In addition, they recognized that there was a demand among the people they visited for greater opportunities to talk about problems, and felt that more time should be available for this purpose. However, they tended to regard intensive social casework as an intrusion into people's lives which produced few practical results. In fact, however, the role played by welfare officers was determined largely by the number of persons they had to visit. At the time, these varied widely, but probably averaged about 350 persons in London. Intensive casework was, therefore, impossible to provide for more than a small minority.

A month was spent visiting local authority welfare departments in London, in the course of which welfare officers were accompanied on their routine visits to disabled persons. Accounts of some of these visits were selected for inclusion here, to illustrate various aspects of the welfare officer's duties.

1. *A first visit for registration*

Miss Grant, aged 86, had been referred to the L.C.C. welfare department by the organizers of a club for elderly persons in Bermondsey. She lived in one room at the back of a large terraced house in the South London dock area. The home help was present and said, 'Oh, thank goodness you have come. I'm so glad that someone has come who can sort the old girl out. She's as deaf as anyone can be, but you can make yourselves understood if you write everything down.' Miss Grant was usually bedfast. The welfare officer wrote down the questions, and the home help expanded on Miss Grant's answers. It emerged that the most important practical problem was the difficulty experienced by the home help in gaining entrance to the house each morning. As a result Miss Grant frequently waited until after 11 a.m. for the home help to cook her breakfast and light the fire. Miss Grant was unable to hear the door bell, she explained, and the people upstairs refused to answer. At the same time they refused to allow Miss Grant or anyone connected with her a key in case it was given to strangers. Miss Grant was sometimes deprived of her weekly visit to hospital because ambulance drivers were unable to get in. In the previous week, however, they had climbed the back fence, and then through a back window. Sometimes her meals on wheels were taken back because no one answered the door. (Miss Grant had meals five days a week, and on Friday dinners were left for her to heat up over the weekend.) Miss Grant would open the door herself if she happened to see people through the frosted glass of the door. The home help said that when she remonstrated with the people upstairs they told her that Miss Grant was too old and should be put away in a home. The home help persuaded Miss Grant to show the welfare officer a letter about a summons which had recently been served on her by the gas board. Miss Grant explained that she had sold the house two years ago to the people upstairs for £800 on condition that she could live in one room rent free. They had previously been tenants of hers, and had taken over the house without paying their gas bill. The home help said that until last Christmas she had been to the bank every week to collect £4 for Miss Grant. At that point the bank manager told her that there was only £1 9s. 0d. left. The home help had then gone to her supervisor who had put Miss Grant in touch with the National Assistance Board. Miss Grant said that she had previously lent the people upstairs £200 for decorating the house. They had promised her interest, but had repaid nothing so far. She admitted that there had been no written agreement. The welfare officer asked for the name of her solicitor and Miss Grant said that was in the sideboard. But after searching for 15 minutes nothing was found. The welfare officer explained that this would have to be sorted out by her supervisors. The solicitors would have to be found so that the legal position could be made clear. Then the council would act according to the wishes of Miss Grant. Miss Grant accused the people upstairs of searching in her sideboard, and the home help said that she had once lost some money. Ever since then she had persuaded Miss Grant to keep her money in a little bag attached to her garter. The home help said that Miss Grant used a bucket, which she emptied for her. She often came in to find the floor awash because Miss Grant tended to fall on the bucket. The welfare officer said that she would get a commode from Public Health. The welfare officer asked to see the lavatory. The home help led us down steep, broken stone steps which were without a handrail. At the bottom there were large stones on the floor which were used as stepping stones to avoid the water which collected in the basement. The lavatory was in what had once been part of a wash house. The window was a hole in the wall covered by wire netting. It was freezing even for someone wearing boots and a winter coat. The lavatory was set in concrete, and it had no seat. The welfare officer thought that little could be done to adapt such a place. She told Miss Grant that she would get a bell with a flashing light fixed for her on the door. She felt that this part of the house could be partitioned from the rest so that the people upstairs would have no fear of strangers in their house. A path could be made from the side fence to Miss Grant's back door, and then she could have her own key. (The visit lasted more than an hour.)

2. A visit to a registered person seeking a place in a residential home

This was the welfare officer's second recent visit to Mr. Black. As he was threatened with eviction, a medical social worker had called at the welfare department to see if the welfare officer could help to get him into a home. His flat was on the third floor. Mr. Black was deaf, and suffered from loss of balance and various internal troubles as well. He said that he was being evicted because his was the only flat in the house which had not been modernized and let out at a higher rent. However, their excuse was that he was dangerous and likely to cause a fire because a few weeks previously he had fitted a switch to one of their faulty electrical installations and this had caused smoke. The housekeeper, instead of enquiring into the trouble, simply called in the fire brigade. Mr. Black did not want to leave the neighbourhood because the few friends he had lived nearby. He had little hope of finding another flat in the area which was becoming popular and expensive. He could afford very little rent as he was on National Assistance. He felt his declining status keenly: he had previously been the manager of large and well known dance bands. He looked with regret at the photos around the walls which he had taken of fashionable Mediterranean resorts: photography and visits to such places had been his hobby. Born of central European parents, and sent to an institution at an ealy age by a stepmother, he had tried to overcome his lack of formal education by attending part-time courses. Until he had been forced to retire recently, he had never had a home of his own. His room here was small but neat, and his possessions meant a great deal to him. He asked what would happen to his furniture if he went into the home which the welfare officer had in mind. It was clear that he was reluctant to leave the flat. He asked her if he would be allowed to keep his photographs. She said that she thought he would, and that he would probably be able to take the ornaments and other small possessions which he had collected on his travels. He was not reassured. The welfare officer said that everyone in his situation faced the same problem. She explained that the application forms which she filled in were only to be looked on as a last resort. For the moment they would only secure a place on the waiting list. If they could prolong his stay in his present flat they would do so. She would continue to look for a suitable flat while she was in the district, and the medical social worker had also promised to do so. A colleague had told her of a flat which sounded suitable. However, this was twenty minutes' walk away from his present flat, and he felt that this was taking him too far away from his doctor and friends. Furthermore, it was not near a tube which was the only form of transport he could use. At least the home would be on a direct tube line into Town. Mr. Black was going to attend the L.C.C. club for the first time that day. He said he was looking forward to it, but did not sound enthusiastic. He felt he was not the kind of person who liked mixing with people unless he chose them carefully himself. The welfare officer said that it might be a success since it was designed for people who were interested in the Arts rather than snakes and ladders. She felt keenly the dearth of special housing which allowed people to keep their own furniture and as much independence as they were able to maintain. (The visit lasted 35 minutes.)

3. A visit to provide adaptations and a holiday

Mrs. Cottrell, aged 56, lived in a flat consisting of a living room which contained an alcove for her bed, a bathroom and kitchen. She was in the obviously laborious process of dressing herself when we called. The welfare officer called to inspect the progress of alterations to the new flat. Mrs. Cottrell had been rehoused when she could no longer manage her room above her shop. The new flat was purpose built for old people and the disabled, but was not intended to accommodate a wheel chair, and Mrs. Cottrell was dependent on her wheel chair. She showed me where the door between the kitchen and the sitting room had been removed to allow the wheel chair to pass from one room to the other. The alterations had been held up because

186

the firm concerned had gone out of business. The council meanwhile had discovered that the original estimate had already been exceeded, while only half of the proposed alterations had been completed. Originally, it had been intended to replace the present bathroom door with a swing door. Mrs. Cottrell was unable to take her wheel chair through the bathroom door. However, she and the welfare decided that there was an easier solution: if the bathroom door were to be removed and rails put up in the bathroom she could leave her wheel chair outside and pull herself on to the lavatory. The bath was already provided with rails and boards. Mrs. Cottrell said that she had trouble getting out of bed. The welfare officer decided that a board under the mattress might help since the mattress was sagging slightly. She also suggested blocks under the bed so that it would be easier to move to the wheel chair. She felt that a pulley would be useful for Mrs. Cottrell to pull herself up into a sitting position. For these alterations she took measurements and promised that she would get the equipment from the L.C.C. Mrs. Cottrell said that she also found difficulty in getting from her wheel chair to the ordinary chairs. The welfare officer thought that blocks might help here too. She explained what was needed, and Mrs. Cottrell decided that her son could probably make something suitable. Mrs. Cottrell said that she spent one day a week at the hospital. The welfare officer asked how she was getting on there. She replied that she had slipped back since her illness though the doctors still said that they were very pleased with her. She had no strength in the top part of her arms: she depended almost entirely on her hands and wrists. However, she thought that life would be easier if the home help were to come in the afternoon on the days when she went to the hospital, since she could then get her something to eat when she arrived home. As it was, she had to get up at 7 o'clock to be ready in time for the ambulance which came between 9.30 and 10.30. From then until about 4 in the afternoon when she was brought home, she had nothing to eat. She said that the home help people were trying to arrange something. The welfare officer asked when her son, who visited her almost every day, would be going on holiday. She said that she did not know, but that she could find out. The welfare officer explained that she was thinking in terms of a summer holiday for Mrs. Cottrell this year. Mrs. Cottrell said that this was very kind, but she was afraid to go as she would probably be a nuisance to people: she was helpless and took a long time to do even the simplest things for herself. The welfare officer assured her that she would be going to a home which catered for people who were unable to look after themselves. She added that people whom she had sent in other years had enjoyed themselves immensely and were now busy booking up for this year. She explained at great length that if Mrs. Cottrell had been able to look after herself, she would not be allowed to go there. If she would like to go it would seem a good idea to make her holiday coincide with that of her son. Mrs. Cottrell agreed, and said that she would love to go if the welfare officer was sure that she really would be no trouble. She said that since her last illness she felt that she ought to go away. It was explained that as she was on National Assistance and had no savings, the Council would pay all but three pounds of the cost of the holiday. Mrs. Cottrell also agreed that it would make a nice change to spend a few days now and again in the Centre when the warmer weather came. Afterwards, the welfare officer expressed annoyance about the alterations. She was cross that the situation had arisen at all. Mrs. Cottrell had been rehoused without her knowledge and the accommodation was unsuitable. Once in the lovely new flat, naturally Mrs. Cottrell would not move, and the expense involved in alterations was going to be somewhere in the region of £200. This, she felt, was expense which could have been avoided if welfare workers had been consulted about the subject. However, she was unable to offer suitable alternative accommodation, and agreed that little accommodation was built for those in wheel chairs. (The visit lasted 40 minutes.)

4. *A routine visit*

Little Miss Smith, aged 81, lived alone in a tiny room in a block of nineteenth century industrial dwellings in Soho. She said that her niece had just been in to clear up, but the saucepans on the stove were caked with stale gravy. The home help came in every day to clean and do the shopping. A bed was made up on the settee, the sideboard was neat, though heavy laden with oddments. Another settee behind the table was piled with washing, and Miss Smith sat herself down at our insistence on the only available chair. Behind her was the gas stove and sink. Beside the small fire there was a pail of coal. Miss Smith was very frail and wrapped in a cross-over pinny. The cracks of her hands, deformed with arthritis, were grimed with dirt. When the welfare officer asked her how she was keeping, Miss Smith said that the doctor had discovered that she had a cataract on her good eye. She said that she couldn't see me, but could see the welfare officer dimly when she stood under the light. The welfare officer asked if she would like to be visited by one of her colleagues who helped people who could not see. Miss Smith said 'No thank you, as the visitor from the Centre comes once a fortnight and someone from the church comes every week.' The welfare officer had obtained both of these for her, and said 'Isn't that nice, and don't you like them?' Miss Smith said she liked them both very much. She asked Miss Smith how she managed now that she could not see. She replied that she was all right. What about the fire? 'Oh, I light a match and toss it in when I have turned the gas poker on.' What about cooking? 'Oh, I can manage what little I need.' The welfare officer expressed concern about this and asked Miss Smith if she had ever tried Complan. She explained what this was and how to make it. Miss Smith asked if it was a powder, and said that W.O.P.A. had given her some. She struggled to the sideboard and rummaged about, saying that she could not find anything since her niece cleared away. At last she came to a small dirty packet. She said she had had it for about three weeks. It had not been opened because she did not know how to make it. The welfare officer made no attempt to show her how to make it, so I tried to explain the instructions. The welfare officer looked at her bed and remarked that the clothing looked rather thin; would she like more blankets? Miss Smith replied that she was not cold because she had to sleep in blankets for her spine. There was a terrible draught under the door near the bed: the door opened straight onto the pavement. I asked the visitor whether it would not be worthwhile actually offering the blankets physically. The welfare officer agreed that there might be something in this. (The visit lasted 15 minutes.)

DIARIES OF FOUR DISABLED PERSONS

The four diaries reproduced here cover a wide range of experience. The diaries are those of two younger, single persons living with their families, a middle aged housewife, and an elderly woman living on her own. Three of these diaries were written with great physical difficulty.

DIARY No. 1 (*Extract*)

Mr. Gleason, aged 28, lived with his mother and father in a council house in south-east London. He was a spastic and confined to a wheelchair. (Very severely incapacitated.)

Monday, July 6th

My mother woke me just before seven, as usual on a Monday morning. Half an hour or so later she washed and dressed me in the bedroom and then my father carried me downstairs to the living room. I then had breakfast which took about half an hour from 8.0 till 8.30 and consisted of a cup of tea, which I drank using a drinking straw, a boiled egg, which my mother had broken into a cup for me, some fruit and a slice of bread and marmalade. My father left for work at about 8.40 and then my mother brushed and combed my hair and got together the odd items I would need at the L.C.C. Day Centre today, things like straws, my spectacles and some small change.

The coach called for me at about 9.30 and, together with about seven others, I arrived at Dorset Road Centre shortly before ten. We had picked up one other person after me. We were assembling ceiling roses at the Centre this morning and, although I'm rather slow, I can manage the job alright. Apart from a break for a cup of tea soon after we arrived, we all worked on till lunchtime which is 12.30. I eat very little at the Centre as I take rather longer than most people and prefer to wait until I get home to have a bigger meal. After lunch we continued with the ceiling roses until was 3.30 and time to leave. I arrived home shortly before four and watched the end of the Test match on television. My father got home soon after five and he, mum and I had tea at six o'clock. I finished just before seven, had a short stand up holding on to the back of my wheelchair, then Mum and Dad brought me upstairs to my bedroom where I'm writing this diary.

Wednesday, July 8th

After writing my diary by hand for the past two nights I feel I would rather use the typewriter from now on as it does enable me to get things down much faster and I did find writing a little tiring.

This morning was a little different to the previous two I have described because I do not go to the Day Centre on Wednesdays. So today there was not the urgency to have breakfast quickly and get ready for the coach to call. All the same my mother woke me as usual shortly before seven and was back to wash and dress me at about

7.40. After my father had carried me downstairs just after eight I had breakfast. This morning I had an apple, which I ate with a spoon after my mother had grated it into a dish for me, a cereal and some bread and marmalade. Breakfast over at about 8.40 my father went off to work and I glanced at the morning paper while my mother cleared the breakfast things. I always like to plan something to do on my days off from the Centre and this morning I decided to write a letter to an old friend of mine who used to attend the Day Centre a few years back. Using the typewriter again, I started on my letter just after ten o'clock. As I began, my Aunt, who lives over the road, called in to see us. I soon found myself joining in conversation with her and my mother and I wasn't making much progress with the letter, but when I did get down to it I managed to type a page and a half and in fact finished it just on dinner time, which was one o'clock. I should mention that my mother and I had had a cup of coffee at about 11.15. For dinner we had a lamb chop which my mother cut up for me, and, of course, vegetables. I was able to take my time over this meal which also included black-currant tart and it was after two o'clock before I had finished. Soon after this my mother helped me to stand up holding the back of my wheelchair, as I have described before. I was standing for about fifteen minutes. We had our afternoon cup of tea at about 3.15 and then I looked through a few magazines. Soon after half past four I had a shave and it wasn't long before my father got home at ten past five. We had a cup of tea and then I had a light meal at six o'clock. I had another short stand up after this and then watched television until a quarter to nine when I started my diary. I am typing this in the living room and the time is now 10.15. I have just had my usual cup of coffee and a biscuit for supper and soon Mum and Dad will be taking me upstairs to bed.

Sunday, July 12th

After my mother had got me up shortly before nine this morning I stayed in my bedroom to have breakfast. This was because I wanted to use my tape recorder directly afterwards. I had breakfast at about 9.15 and was finished by a quarter to ten when my mother got my recorder out for me. I can operate it on my own and I put a tape on that I received from a friend in Cambridge a few days ago. I have been tapesponding (exchanging tapes) with this friend for nearly three years now and this morning I made notes on what he had said on the latest tape so that I can reply to it later in the week. I very much enjoy using the tape recorder and I also have a record player which I use quite frequently. When I had finished making notes on the tape my father carried me downstairs and we all had a cup of coffee. By this time it was nearly midday and I looked through the Sunday newspaper then I listened to the radio for a while. We had dinner a little later today, at about 1.45. It was roast pork, my favourite, and as usual I took my time over it. I had finished in about an hour but didn't do much before four except have a cup of tea. Shortly after four o'clock I started typing yet another letter. This was to a friend of mine with whom I correspond pretty regularly. When I had finished the letter I was just about up to date with my mail for the present. But I didn't finish it before tea which we had at six o'clock. After this I shaved, in readiness for the morning, and then continued with my typing. By this time it was 7.15. I didn't complete my letter until half past eight. Directly I had read it through, signed it and sealed it up, I decided it was high time I started making today's entry in my diary. The time now is half past ten, we have just had supper and soon Mum and Dad will be taking me up to bed.

I have tremendously enjoyed keeping a diary this week and hope I have included the information required without making it sound too monotonous. It has been a fairly typical week and therefore an apt one for me to describe, although, perhaps I should mention that, up until a few months ago, I did have a regular little job which I used to do at home. It consisted of putting nails into rubber bases to form flower-holders. I had been doing the work for five years and, although it meant a bus ride for my mother to collect it and take it back for me every two weeks, there was sense of satisfaction that I had a little job to do, and that I could earn a few shillings a week off my own bat. Even without this work, however, I think it will be clear from my diary that I am rarely at a loss for something to do.

DIARY No. 2 (*Extract*)

Miss Tanner, aged 21, lived with her aunt and cousins in a small flat in a block of nineteenth-century industrial dwellings in Poplar. She had polio. (Severely incapacitated.)

Monday, 7th September

I start my day at 7.30. My aunt came in to sit me up. (I cannot get up alone from a lying position.) I put my shoes and stockings on. I do this first every morning because when I am dressed wearing my spinal support I cannot bend to tie my shoes. I then went to the toilet and came out and had a wash. I put the kettle back on for coffee for breakfast, then I went and got myself dressed for work. I came out from the bedroom at 8.10 and sat down to eat the breakfast my aunt had got ready for me. I just quickly looked at the daily paper before I gathered a few bits and pieces together to take to work. At 8.35 I went to my garage which is just opposite the flats and my aunt came with me and carried my things as I cannot carry anything. It makes me lose balance on the walking sticks. I was settled in the car and ready for the off by 8.45. The car was in good form today and I arrived at the office at 8.55. First in the office I opened the windows. They just push out and hook on but if the weather is too bad I open the top windows with one of my sticks. I now have this to a fine art and can do it quicker than anyone climbing onto the office desks. By the time I'd opened the windows June, the typist, who is a great help to me had arrived and very kindly went and gathered my things from the car as I am unable to it myself. I had quite a few things to catch up on as I have been on holiday. First there was work and then 'goings-on' in the office. Already it's 10 a.m. and coffee time but I must get the cheques ready for the bank by 10.15—that done we had coffee then June came upstairs to the toilet with me at 10.30. We were back down again at 10.40 when she also tied my shoelace which had come loose. Now I must work and catch up so that I know where to start next, but when one is busy time goes so quickly and it's now 12.30 so I'm due for my lunch. There's plenty to do in my hour today but I must call home. I got home at 12.40 and had a glass of milk and a sandwich. Afterwards I left home at 12.55 to go to the jeweller to pick up a christening present I had left for engraving, I was pleased with the result and after collecting a repair for Hazel (office friend) I went back to work and arrived at just 1.30. Thank goodness I have the car, for without it I was unable to go out at all in my lunch hour. At 1.30 I started work but stopped when the others came back from lunch to show them the gift I had bought. It was a silver egg-cup and spoon and the name of the child had been engraved on the eggcup. After they had all seen it we started work again and Mr. Davies (cashier) carried the ledgers from the safe to my desk. 3 o'clock, it's teatime and we have no set break. We drink our tea while we work, according to how much we have to do. 3.15 and both June and Hazel came upstairs with me. There are about 20 steps to go up but they are shallow ones. I need someone with me to carry my stick on the way down. I use my right hand stick and the handrail and swing myself down and whoever is with me carries my other stick to the bottom of the stairs. We were down in the office at 3.25, I find the people in the office extremely helpful and willing to lend a hand. I worked until 5 o'clock then June carried my things to the car and I was on my way home. However the bridge was up so a great queue of traffic had built up and I turned off my engine and waited patiently (I work in the dock area and often get caught at either the lift up bridge or the swing bridge). It wasn't too long and I arrived home at 5.20. I tooted my hooter and my 11 year old cousin came and took my things from the car to our flat. I had my dinner which my aunt had ready and at 6.5 I had finished so I washed and got myself ready to go out. I was ready at 6.30 so popped into my friend Audrey to see her and two of my 5 sisters who babysit every Monday. I showed them my holiday photos and asked if the rest of the family was alright, then I came and got into my car and went to a very important meeting at the Salvation Army (I am a Young People's local officer and a very active member of the Salvation Army. My fiancé is also S.A. and we are to be married in our uniforms in March 1965. The meeting started at 7 o'clock and finished at 9 o'clock so I arrived back home at 9.15 and my 11 year old cousin Adrian saw me safely in the garage. I got myself ready for bed at 9.40 and started writing a letter to Fred my fiancé at 10 o'clock. I was finished at 10.20 and had a glass of milk, then went to the toilet and washed my hands, then I went to bed. I can get into bed alone if it's a low one. I sit on the bed and put my hands under my knees and fall backwards letting go of my knees when I'm on my back. If however the bed is high I have to have someone to pick my legs up and put them into the bed. When I was nicely settled I wrote a letter to my friends Rae and David at Ryde, I.O.W. They want Fred and I to go for a weekend but we are very busy just now so it will have to be in about 8 weeks time. I finished the letter at 11 o'clock and settled down to sleep. Lesley the cousin who I sleep with came to bed at 11.30 but I was too tired to talk so left her reading.

Wednesday, 9th September

At 7.30 my aunt came and got me up. I felt better than yesterday and was washed and dressed by 8.5. I ate my breakfast and had time to read the paper this morning but time goes so quickly and it was 8.40 and time to go to work before I had finished half the paper. Still I went and got the car out and was off to work. It is so nice to get to work under my own steam instead of relying on my boss to pick me up each day. I arrived at work at 8.55 and opened all the windows. Then got straight down to work. June came in about 5 minutes later so work stopped to catch up on the news of the evening before. June got me the ledgers this morning and I started doing a list of debtors. I really must get down to phoning them. I'll probably do it this afternoon. I've just phoned the parks Superintendent and I have an appointment to see him at 2 o'clock at the S.A. Hall. All this is in connection with our harvest this weekend. Now it is coffee time, 10 o'clock, and I've done the cheques. Must tell the boss I want a late lunch hour. At 10.30 June came with me and we were back by 10.40. It is alright for me to have a late lunch today. I made phone calls until 1.15 then I made my desk tidy and left for home at 1.25. I called at the butchers for 2 pork chops for June. The butcher served me and carried my chops out to the car. I popped indoors and ate the sandwich that my aunt had prepared. She's one in a million, she would do anything to help anyone. At 1.50 I left for the Army and the parks superintendent came true to his word at 2 o'clock. He has promised to send a lorry load of plants etc. on Saturday morning at 8.30. I must be there by 8.15. I thanked him and drove home for five minutes before going back to the office. I left home again at 2.20 and arrived at work at 2.30. I told June the good news about the plants. Already it is teatime. After tea I made some more phone calls and then June came upstairs with me. The heat of the afternoon has taken my energy and my legs are aching. The stairs are a terrible effort today and I often wish the toilet was on the ground floor but I suppose the exercise is good. We were gone about 20 minutes but I was glad to get down into the office and sit down. This afternoon has gone so quickly it is 4.45 and I just have the time for one phone call then it's home again. Now it is 5 o'clock and I hope I don't get a bridge. Well, I didn't get held up and I was home at 5.10. My aunt had done me another sandwich. I'm going swimming at 6.30 and I don't like to have a meal before swimming. I must do the lettering for the harvest. I can cut out Y.P. (young people) now and paint it yellow. That will leave the seven letters of harvest to do. I must make time to do them before Friday evening. I wish there were 48 hours in a day sometimes because I don't seem to have enough time to do all I'd like to do. The paint has dried and the Y.P. looks pretty good. It is 6.15 and I must go now. I want to call at the garage for some petrol. I only got one gallon because funds are low after our holidays. I arrived at the baths at 6.30 and Ann my sister-in-law, was waiting outside. She came and carried my swimming gear for me. My aunt had put it just inside. We went in and changed into our costumes. Ann gave my clothes to the attendant. The floor was rather slippery so I had to be very careful. It had taken 20 minutes to change. It was well worth the effort because the water was lovely. How independent I feel in the water, no walking sticks, no wheelchair, I stay in the water once I'm there because it's so difficult to get out that once is enough. We had a good swim and got out at 7.30. Ann got out first and I swam to the steps. I haul myself up and finally I pull myself half out of the water then lean over the bars so that my knees are on the top step, then I give one heave and I am up leaning against the bar. I have to stop there for a moment or two to gather my strength. Ann had my sticks waiting so I took these and Ann went on to get our clothes and put them in the changing locker. I told Ann to go home and not wait for me because I would be a long time. It took me from 7.30 to 8.5 just to get myself dressed. I feel so exhausted after swimming but satisfied I can do it. I carried my swimming gear in my teeth but, of course, a wet swimming costume is very heavy so I asked one of the girls who had been swimming to carry the gear to the car. The people around here are very good and although they look rather surprised they do anything for you. I called at my brother's for some photos and Ann had a cup of tea waiting for me. This was most welcome. I drank my tea then Ron, my brother, carried the photos to the car and I was off home at 8.25. When I got to the corner my aunt, cousin and two of my sisters were there waiting for me. They had the garage open and I drove in. We all went indoors, Doreen, one of my sisters, had come to cut my hair, and Joan, my eldest sister, come to see how I was. After Doreen had finished I washed my hair. This is a job I really hate doing. There isn't enough room in our kitchen for two people so I wash it myself. It takes me about 25 minutes to wash it and another 20 minutes to recover my strength and straighten up, I always have quite a bad backache afterwards. Doreen set my hair and then we decided on fish and chips for supper which my aunt and sister Joan went to buy. While they were at the shop we laid the table and made coffee. We had our supper and now it was time for Joan and Doreen to go. They both live a bus ride away. We said goodnight and then decided to clear the table and get it ready for breakfast time. We have the sideboard near the table so that I can put things in by leaning on my sticks, my aunt carries the dishes to the kitchen. Then I decided it was time I got ready for bed, it is 10.45 and I'm tired. It took me 25 minutes to change then I went into the toilet, I had just a quick wash and then went to bed at 11.20. I wish I could find five minutes where I have nothing to do at all.

Sunday, 13th September

I woke my cousin Lesley to get me up out of bed, I couldn't sleep last night, I ached too much. Now it is Sunday and the whole day is spent at the Salvation Army. I went to the toilet. My legs felt so heavy it was an effort to walk. I washed and dressed and this took me 45 minutes. I dressed in my 'Army' uniform. While I dressed my aunt cooked my breakfast. I had breakfast and made sure everything was in my briefcase. By now it was 9.45 and time I was leaving for Sunday School which starts at 10 o'clock. Adrian carried my case across to the car and saw me safely out of the garage. I went off and as it was Sunday there was not much traffic on the road. When I got outside the 'Army' I had to ask a passerby to take my briefcase across the pavement. I got out and locked the car and went into the hall. One of the children carried my briefcase to the table. I mark their cards and keep the records morning and afternoon. We had a good Sunday School and soon it was 11 o'clock and time for the Senior Meeting. We had a good start, then the leader of the meeting asked me to tell the young people a story. I did but my legs weren't as willing as my heart. I felt very tired today. I suppose it is the result of the preparation for Harvest. The meeting finished at 12 o'clock and after saying 'goodmorning' and shaking hands with everyone I left for home. My aunt had the dinner ready when I arrived home at 12.30. I went to the toilet, washed my hands, and served the dinner, our kitchen is not big enough to lay out plates and serve dinner so the plates and dinner are brought into the living room and I serve the dinner while my aunt carries pots and pans to and from the kitchen. We had our meal and I washed up. I do this every Sunday as it is not fair for my aunt to be the only one to do anything on Sundays. So I wash and my cousin Lesley dries. I took about 20 minutes today. My back is awfully painful. I hoped hard that I would last the day as arranged. I popped into my friend Audrey and found she wasn't feeling too well, and was lying down. We chatted for about 10 minutes, then I went back indoors. My brother's baby was being christened and they asked me to be Godmother. Of course, I was very happy about this. I washed and got ready to go because it was a half hour journey in my little car. Now it was 2.40, so I left for my destination. It was quite strange because my usual Sunday afternoon is a big rush back to the 'Army' for Sunday School where we get on average 65 children. We have wonderful times there. However, it was different this Sunday and I had to go to Manor Park. The road wasn't too busy and I enjoyed the drive. I got to my brother-in-law's at 3.5. My first thing was to hold the baby. She's a lovely babe and very cuddly. Ann (my sister-in-law) dressed the baby very nicely. She was in white lace. The christening was at 4 o'clock. The church was just round the corner but for me it seemed miles. We arrived at the church and I was quite exhausted. It had taken about 15 minutes. We sat in the church and the ceremony began. It was very nice and the vicar made certain remarks concerning the seriousness of Godparents. Now the walk back to the house. We arrived back and had tea and also some photos taken. Now it's 6 o'clock and I must get ready to go back to the Army. I was leading the meeting that Sunday night. I left the house at 6.10 and arrived at the Army at 6.30. I shook hands with quite a few people in the hall, then went to the toilet and afterwards on to the platform to get my things ready for the meeting. Our meeting starts at 6.45 and we had some good harvest songs and hearty singing. The atmosphere in the hall was really lovely. However the day was telling on me and after the offering I had to give the rest over to the Corps Sergeant Major and I sat through the rest of the meeting. It was a good end to our Harvest Sunday and although I didn't feel too well I did enjoy it. The meeting finished at 8.30 and after saying goodnight and shaking hands I left for home. How I treasure my car on occasions like these, for I just get in and go instead of waiting for someone to push my wheelchair. I got home at 9.10 and Adrian saw me into my garage. He also carried my briefcase indoors. I put my bonnet away and went to see if Audrey was better. She was and she made me a cup of tea which was welcomed. I went back home and got my things ready for Monday night. The Sunday School are doing a Harvest demonstration for their parents and everything must be on hand. Now it is time for a glass of milk and a very much looked forward to bed. I went to the toilet and then got myself undressed for bed. I ached from top to toe and it was a painful effort to take my shoes and stockings off and put my pyjamas and bedsocks on. That took me 35 minutes and at last I am in bed. My cousin Lesley wasn't ready for bed so lay reading up a very big play for the Sunday School to do at Christmas. It has a cast of 40 children and 12 adults. Now it is time for sleep and Lesley had turned the light out. Sleep did not come very easily. However I slept some of the night.

In my usual week I also have a girls' handicraft club, a brass band and songster practise, I play tenor or flugel horn in the band and sing treble in the Songster (singing brigade) but due to the harvest preparation I had to let these go this week.

DIARY No. 3

Mrs. Lexington, aged 46, lived with her husband and daughter in a pre-fab in Hammersmith. She had polio and was chairbound. (Severely incapacitated.)

Monday, 6th July

6.50 a.m. Teasmade alarm wakes me up (the teasmade is a luxury we bought year ago). I pour out the tea for hubby and myself. Then when he is nearly ready to go o work I get up and dress, wash and then back to bedroom to make the bed. A quick dust round this morning. Then wheel myself into the kitchen, up onto the long stool, wash my cups etc. Prepare for the evening meal. Sweep the kitchen floor, dust the living room, push the carpet sweeper over the carpet and generally tidied up. 8.45 make a cup of tea for the driver and escort of the coach, which takes me to the L.C.C. Centre for this morning. We leave here about 9.20. After picking up the other people we arrive at Warwick Row about 10.45. Once there I start on my job of making white felt beatles string bags—very popular at the moment. Sandwich and a cuppa or lunch. Then I start home again. 2.15 p.m. arrived home again at 3.15. Drag the carpet sweeper over the hall carpet and dusted. Wrote some thankyou letters to the committee members of the Central Middlesex branch of the B.P.F. for a lovely day at Middleton on Sea yesterday. 5 o'clock start cooking the evening meal. Hubby and daughter home soon after six. Hubby washes up the things after the evening meal, while I get on with my knitting tonight. 10.50 after another cup of tea and a biscuit off to bed and I hope to sleep.

Tuesday, 7th July

6.50 alarm and tea as usual. While waiting for Hubby to go to work I read my daily portion of the Bible. Then into the bathroom in my chair for a bath. Wash up cups etc. Back to the bedroom to make the bed and clean the room out. It is very awkward as my chair won't go round the other side of the bed, so I have to hold on to everything within reach and work with one hand only. 10 o'clock that's done. Thank goodness. Now into my chair to sweep the kitchen and clean the living room and hall. 11.45 Remploy come to collect last week's work and brought a packing job for me to do. (Plastic circus figures to put in transparent bags. I think for cereal packets). I feel a bit tired. So stopped to have a snack before starting this job. Had my snack sitting on the kitchen stool, then I can wash up and cut Hubby's sandwiches for work tomorrow. (They keep fresh in the fridge well wrapped up in greaseproof paper.) Also I can wash out my stockings etc. and throw them up onto the drying rack then straighten them out with a long stick. 1.15 p.m. Start Remploy's work now until ambulance comes to take me to hospital. 4.20 The ambulance came, but when I arrived at Hammersmith Hospital the clinic was finished and the doctor gone, so home again, without any treatment until next week. I feel pretty fed up about this as I'd hoped to have the plaster off today.[1] 5.30 Time to start cooking the sausages and tomatoes for Hubby and daughter Joyce. 7.30 Hubby washes up and I get on with Remploy's work. It's a good film on T.V. tonight (The Room at the Top). Must see the end of it, and then to bed for a little read. (I love reading) until Hubby comes in at 11.30 p.m.

Wednesday, 8th July

The usual routine except that, today, I cleaned out my daughter's bedroom. Now both bedrooms have had their weekly turn out. 11.15 a.m. The housework done I made a layer cake sandwiched together with mock cream and iced on top. I feel I've done enough but must get ready for the evening meal and cut Tom's sandwiches for tomorrow. 12.30 Remploy arrived with more work. The same packing job. One o'clock I have my dinner, wash up, start work. Then a friend comes. I made her a cup of tea. She could only stay an hour. 5.15 Start the evening meal. Hubby always washes up after that. So I can get on with Remploy's work. My daughter goes out to the pictures. 10.30 a cuppa and biscuits now she has come home. So another day ends.

Thursday, 9th July

The day starts as usual at 6.50. Then after Hubby has gone I dust and tidy the bedroom. As I had not quite finished Remploy's work yesterday I finished that.

<hr/>

[1] Mrs. Lexington's arm had fractured when her chair pulled away from her husband and hurtled down some steps.

10 o'clock I wash over the kitchen floor with a mop. How I wish I could get down on my knees to do it. Then give the living room and bathroom their weekly turn out again mopping the bathroom floor. After tidying myself up I prepare the potatoes etc. for the evening meal, cut Hubby's sandwiches and have my dinner. 1.15 Remploy arrive with the same job to do again and collect the finished work. 5.15 Switch on the stove to cook the meal. 6.15 p.m. Hubby and daughter home. We have our meal watching the T.V. at the same time as usual. 7.30 Hubby washes up and I get back on the job which is 6/- per 1,000 bags—one plastic figure sealed in a bag. 10 o'clock a cup of tea and a biscuit. 11.15 and so to bed. I forgot to mention the Butcher delivers the meat and we got enough shopping last weekend to last the week. That's the best of having a fridge, a must, if at all possible for the disabled.

Friday, 10th July

Not so much housework to do today. It gets a bit tiring by the end of the week. So a general dust up and mop through. Then prepare a saucepan full of potatoes ready for the weekend cooking and put in the fridge. As we don't get up very early on Saturdays and Sundays this saves time. 12.30 had my dinner, then finished the work in hand for Remploy's and am now waiting for them to come and collect. So until they turn up I have a little rest, listening to Woman's Hour and doing some knitting. 5.30 Remploy have just arrived with more work. Not much time to do any before getting the evening meal. 7 o'clock Tom and Joyce work late on Fridays so meal is later. Then on to Remploy's work until cup of tea time. 11.30 and so to bed.

Saturday, 11th July

My daughter goes to work Saturday mornings. But as Hubby is always home then he does the housework, while I do the weekly wash in my Hotpoint machine and cook the dinner. Then Hubby hangs the washing in the garden if the weather is fine. We have dinner about one o'clock. After I've washed up we get ready to go out, to do the rest of the shopping. Usually my friend does most of it during the week, but she's been away on holiday for the last fortnight and I've missed her very much. 5 o'clock We all have tea together and spend the evening watching television, and I like to knit and do the crosswords in the daily papers, or odd jobs. 10 o'clock we have supper. Fish and chips as a Saturday treat. Off to bed at 11.30.

Sunday, 12th July

I had breakfast in bed. Then after washing and dressing enjoy the Salvation Army service from St. Ives. Then out to the kitchen to prepare and cook the dinner. While the dinner was cooking and having to sit on the stool for that I did the weekly ironing. 1.15 We had dinner, then I wash up and my daughter dried the china and put it away. Hubby tidied round the place. This afternoon we sat and watched televison. 5 o'clock we have tea. Then Hubby and I went to the Baptist Chapel. We always attend. As there are about 12 steps to go up and down the young men there are so good. They carry me, chair and all up and down, every time I go, and always make fun doing it. It was a lovely service and we enjoyed it very much. Everyone at Chapel has always been very kind to me, and I have attended there from childhood. My daughter's boy friend walked home with us. 9.30 We have a cup of tea and biscuits. 10.30 So ends another happy weekend and now off to bed. I wonder if I dare say that I would rather like a hairdresser and a chiropodist to be able to call on disabled people in their own homes. But all the same, things are much better now than they used to be years ago.

DIARY No. 4

Mrs. Griffin, aged 82, lived alone in a flat on a block of nineteenth-century industrial dwellings in Bermondsey. She had twice weekly visits from her son who worked in the City, but lived in Kent. (Very severely incapacitated.)

Monday, 6th July

Got my legs out of bed at six o'clock. It takes me 20 minutes to get my callipers on. Then I get my crutches and get out to the toilet[2], wash my hands, put kettle on, grill a small rasher of bacon and half of a tomato. Have my breakfast, then get dressed. Then I fix myself up against the sink and wash up. Then I have to sit down because my legs are shaking. Then I wait for my home help to come. 9 o'clock she makes my bed and cleans the kitchen. Then we have a cup of coffee, and she goes to other old people at 12 o'clock. Egg and toast and rice pudding for dinner then I sit in my armchair and read a book. At 4 o'clock a cup of tea, bread butter and jam, listen to wireless. At 9 o'clock glass of milk and a biscuit, have a wash. Take a heart and sleeping tablet and in bed by 10 o'clock, sleep till about 5 o'clock.

Tuesday, 7th July

Up at 6.30. Done the usual things. Had toast and marmalade for breakfast. Washed up and waited for home help to come. She helped me to bath, made my bed. We had coffee. I had to rest for an hour. At 12 o'clock steamed fish and milk pudding. Then washed up. Did some needlework. At 4 o'clock a cup of tea, bread and butter. My son came in from the office at 5.30. He put money in electric and gas meters, and stayed for one and a half hours. Then I read some of my book, listen to wireless. At 9 o'clock a glass of milk and biscuits. Had a wash. 9.30 took heart and sleeping tablets. In bed at 10 o'clock. Sleep till 4.30.

Wednesday, 8th July

Up at 6.30. Did the usual things. Toast and marmalade for breakfast. Washed up, some help came at 9 o'clock. She made my bed and cleaned the bedroom. We had coffee. At 12 o'clock she left. Had egg salad, biscuit and cheese. Sat in my armchair. At 4 o'clock had a cup of tea, bread, butter and jam. A neighbour came into me in the evening to tell me about a silver wedding she had been to, what they had to eat and drink. She stayed for 2 hours with me. After she had gone I listen to the radio. At 9 o'clock glass of milk and biscuits. Then had a wash and took tablets. In bed by 10 o'clock.

Thursday, 9th July

Up at 6.30 and did usual things. Had toast and marmalade. Then washed up and waited for the home help. She made my bed, cleaned the windows, cleaned the dresser down and had a cup of coffee. Then she went. I did some mending. At 12 o'clock I had stewed lamb. Then washed up and sat down in my armchair. I had a read at my book. At 4 o'clock got a cup of tea, bread, butter. My niece and her husband came to see me. I was pleased to see them. They live at Beckenham, Kent, so that passed the evening away for me. At 9 o'clock I had a glass of milk and biscuits. Then had a wash, took tablets and so to bed at 10 o'clock. Why I make it 10 o'clock each night I must not take tablets till that time.

Friday, 10th July

Up at 6.30. Did the usual things till the home help came. She cleaned the living room and helped me to bath. Then she got all the weekend shopping in. We had our coffee then I had a rest. At 12 o'clock I had poached egg, chips and milk pudding. Then I washed up. Sat in my armchair. At 4 o'clock I made a cup of tea, bread and butter. My son came in from the office at 5.30 and stayed with me till 7 o'clock. Took my washing to his wife. After he had gone I listened to the radio. At 9 o'clock I had a glass of milk. Then had a wash and took my tablets. And so to bed.

Saturday, 11th July

Up at 6.30. Did the usual things. Had toast and marmalade for breakfast. Then had a wash, got dressed, and washed up. No home help now till Monday. Managed

---

The W.C. was on an open balcony.

to do my bed but had to sit down for a while. At 12 o'clock had spam and salad, chee
and biscuits. Then sat in my armchair and had a read of my book. At 4 o'clock I mac
tea and bread and butter. Then I washed up and listened to the radio. Had a qui
day. Did not see anyone. At 9 o'clock had a wash. Had a glass of milk. I think I to
you I cannot get out. It is nearly 4 years since I went out. It is nearly 10 o'clock,
taking tablets and off to bed.

Sunday, 12th July

Up at 6.30. Did the usual things. Had bacon and tomatoes for breakfast. Done t
best I could for myself. No home help so it takes me a long time to do things as
cannot do without my crutches. At 1 o'clock I cook chop, peas and potatoes, mi
pudding. One of the neighbours came and had a cup of tea with me. She came ba
from her holiday yesterday from the Norfolk Broads and had a lovely time. When s
went I listened to the radio. At 9 o'clock I had a wash, then a glass of milk. I to
my tablets and so to bed. I hope you will be able to read my writing. I am a bit shak
I think I told you I am going on for 83, so will close.

VARIATIONS BETWEEN LOCAL AUTHORITIES IN THEIR PROVISIONS FOR PHYSICALLY HANDICAPPED PERSONS

For a number of reasons the local authority registers of the general classes of the physically handicapped do not reflect incidence of disability. First, special schemes for the disabled were established gradually over a period of almost a decade. Although many local authorities used their permissive powers in the early 1950's to set up schemes under Section 29 of the National Assistance Act, 1948, it was not until after 1960, when such provision became mandatory, that complete national coverage was achieved. Therefore, to some extent, variation between local authorities in the proportion of persons registered as physically handicapped reflects the different stages reached in the development of schemes. Second, there is no uniformity between local authorities in the basis on which registers are compiled. In some areas it is the policy of the local authority to register all disabled persons who are brought to the notice of welfare officers. In other areas, only those persons are registered who can be helped by the services available. Third, the content of the registers is changing over time. Since 1960, there has been a net decrease in the number of children below the age of 16 of 1,329, while of those aged 16–64 there has been a net increase of 26,124, and of those aged 65 and over of 45,087. The increase in new registrations in successive age groups has become more marked since 1960.[1]

Nor does registration reflect volume of service. For example, in 1965–66, Glamorgan and West Bromwich each registered 6.9 persons per thousand population. But whereas it is estimated that West Bromwich spent on average about £21 on each person registered that year, Glamorgan spent a little more than £11.[2]

There is wide variation between local authorities in both registration and expenditure. For example, in 1965–66, the number of persons per thousand registered as physically handicapped ranged from 0.7 in Cheshire to 10.1 in Kingston-upon-Hull.[3] In the same year, average expenditure on each registered person ranged from almost £53 in Bristol to less than £2 in Durham County. On average, local authorities registered 3.6 persons per thousand population, and spent a little more than £15 16s. on each registered person. There was some difference between counties and county boroughs in average registration. On average, county boroughs registered 4.5 persons per thousand population, compared with 3.3 in London boroughs, and 3.1 in counties. Average expenditure, too, varied. On average, a little more than £17 was spent on each person registered in county boroughs, but more than £19 in London boroughs, and only £12 5s. in counties.

---

1. *See, Annual Report of the Ministry of Health for the year 1966*, Cmnd. 3326, London, H.M.S.O., p. 33.
2. See, *The Institute of Municipal Treasurers and Accountants, Welfare Services Statistics, 1965–66*.
3. These and subsequent estimates exclude the City of London, Tynemouth, Cambridge and Ely, and Huntingdon and Peterborough, for which only partial information was published.

Local authorities with above average rates of registration and expenditure were not necessarily those with an above average percentage of the penny rate product for England and Wales.[4] Only one-third (20 out of 61) of local authorities with a rate of registration above the average also had a higher than average percentage of the total penny rate product. Less than one-third of local authorities with expenditure above average also had a penny rate product which was higher than the average percentage of the total product. Indeed, only a little more than one-third of those local authorities where the penny rate product was above the average percentage of the total penny rate product for England and Wales had neither expenditure nor registration above the national average. For example, West Bromwich, where the penny rate product which was only 0.19 per cent of the national total, registered 6.9 persons per thousand population and spent on average more than £20 on each registered person. Again, Barnsley, with a penny rate product of only 0.14 per cent of the total for England and Wales, registered 4.7 persons per thousand population, and spent on average over £30 on each registered person. Yet Kent, with a high penny rate product—2.27 per cent of the total for England and Wales—registered only 1.5 persons per thousand population, and spent on average only about £12 on each registered person. Similarly, Coventry. with a penny rate product which was 0.62 per cent of the total for England and Wales, registered only 1.5 persons per thousand population, and spent on average a little more than £5 on each person registered.

It is clear from comparable statistics for 1967–68 that wide variations between local authorities in their provision for physically handicapped persons remain, though registration and expenditure has increased markedly, particularly in the London boroughs.[5] As with all local authority statistics, these and the succeeding analysis must be treated with caution.

4. For the penny rate product see, Ministry of Housing and Local Government and Welsh Office *Rates and Rateable Values in England and Wales, 1965–66.*
5. See, The Institute of Municipal Treasurers and Accountants, *Welfare Services Statistics, 1967–68.*

Local authorities categorised according to the number per thousand population registered as physically handicapped, and ranked according to average expenditure per person in 1965–66.

Local Authority	Number per 1000 Registered physically handicapped 1965–66[a]	Annual average expenditure per person registered physically handicapped 1965–66[a]		Penny rate product expressed as a percentage of the penny rate product in Eng. & Wales in 1965–66[b]
		£	s.	
7.0 or more persons per thousand population registered physically handicapped				
Merioneth	7.8	17	16	0.04
Kingston upon Hull	10.1	15	0	0.41
Bath	7.3	12	16	0.15
Preston	7.2	5	2	0.23
6.0 to 6.9 persons per thousand population registered physically handicapped				
West Bromwich	6.9	20	15	0.19
Cardiff	6.6	12	5	0.56
Southwark	6.0	12	4	0.82
Burnley	6.2	12	2	0.11
Glamorgan	6.9	11	6	1.06
Wakefield	6.2	9	12	0.11
Lincoln, Holland	6.6	8	9	0.13
Wallasey	6.9	6	13	0.17
5.0 to 5.9 persons per thousand population registered physically handicapped				
Exeter	5.3	28	3	0.22
Rotherham	5.1	18	1	0.16
Oldham	5.3	15	13	0.15
Burton on Trent	5.7	11	13	0.10
Sussex West	5.6	9	7	1.11
Caernarvon	5.9	8	16	0.15
Wigan	5.7	7	19	0.13
Gloucestershire	5.1	7	16	0.85
Birkenhead	5.1	6	16	0.22
Salford	5.9	3	10	0.22
4.0 to 4.9 persons per thousand population registered physically handicapped				
Dudley	4.7	34	14	0.13
Islington	4.1	31	14	0.88
Barnsley	4.7	30	3	0.14
Reading	4.3	21	13	0.32
Wiltshire	4.1	21	6	0.75

Local Authority	Number per 1000 Registered physically capped 1965–66[a]	Annual average expenditure per person registered physically handicapped 1965–66[a]		Penny rate product expressed as a percentage of the penny rate produced in Eng. & Wales in 1965–66[b]
		£	s.	
Leeds	4.6	20	1	0.96
York	4.1	19	2	0.17
Barking	4.5	18	19	0.47
Lewisham	4.4	18	7	0.55
Doncaster	4.7	17	10	0.18
Enfield	4.9	16	18	0.82
Cardiganshire	4.7	16	2	0.06
Monmouthshire	4.1	14	3	0.44
Lambeth	4.1	14	3	0.89
Lincoln, Lindsey	4.3	12	16	0.70
Newport	4.7	12	1	0.22
Leicester	4.2	12	1	0.62
Bolton	4.1	9	6	0.24
Tower Hamlets	4.0	8	3	0.65
Radnorshire	4.6	7	19	0.02
Great Yarmouth	4.0	7	9	0.16
Lincoln, Kesteven	4.2	7	0	0.18
St. Helens	4.3	6	9	0.17
Greenwich	4.1	5	2	0.58
Stockport	4.1	3	17	0.24
Cornwall	4.8	3	11	0.49

3.0 to 3.9 persons per thousand population registered physically handicapped

Local Authority	Number per 1000	£	s.	Penny rate %
Worcester	3.7	48	10	0.13
Sheffield	3.1	42	14	1.00
Stoke on Trent	3.1	26	15	0.44
South Shields	3.4	26	8	0.14
Westminster	3.0	25	13	4.80
Camden	3.3	23	13	1.49
Bournemouth	3.1	22	9	0.46
Liverpool	3.3	19	15	1.17
Bradford	3.1	19	2	0.43
Waltham Forest	3.1	17	9	0.54
Croydon	3.8	16	10	0.88
Manchester	3.1	16	0	1.26
Bedfordshire	3.7	15	11	0.58
Lincoln	3.4	15	5	0.12
Gloucester	3.1	14	13	0.13
Brighton	3.7	13	16	0.53
Essex	3.4	13	8	2.09
Norwich	3.5	12	14	0.25
Halifax	3.5	12	13	0.12
Newham	3.7	12	12	0.67
Hammersmith	3.3	12	11	0.64
Buckinghamshire	3.6	12	4	1.36
Berkshire	3.3	11	5	0.90
Southampton	3.6	11	5	0.52

Local Authority	Number per 1000 Registered physically handicapped 1965–66[a]	Annual average expenditure per person registered physically handicapped 1965–66[a]		Penny rate product expressed as a percentage of the penny rate product in Eng. & Wales in 1965–66[b]
		£	s.	
Nottingham	3.3	10	11	0.68
Sutton	3.5	10	5	0.43
Denbighshire	3.7	10	2	0.24
Dorset	3.7	9	13	0.61
Plymouth	3.6	9	9	0.40
Dewsbury	3.5	8	15	0.07
Rutland	3.3	8	5	0.04
Anglesey	3.4	6	17	0.06
Sussex East	3.8	5	17	0.93
Sunderland	3.0	5	14	0.31
Cheshire	3.7	5	3	1.89
Southend on Sea	3.5	4	19	0.38
Hastings	3.1	2	17	0.13

2.0 to 2.9 persons per thousand population registered physically handicapped

Local Authority	Number per 1000 Registered physically handicapped 1965–66[a]	Annual average expenditure per person registered physically handicapped 1965–66[a]		Penny rate product expressed as a percentage of the penny rate product in Eng. & Wales in 1965–66[b]
Gateshead	2.1	52	9	0.15
Bristol	2.9	52	8	0.97
Kensington and Chelsea	2.6	37	4	1.15
Darlington	2.7	36	0	0.17
Kingston upon Thames	2.6	35	2	0.45
Bootle	2.9	30	11	0.12
Walsall	2.8	29	2	0.19
Brent	2.2	27	16	0.92
Harrow	2.3	27	7	0.52
Smethwick	2.8	27	1	0.12
Warrington	2.5	25	2	0.15
Derby	2.1	24	17	0.31
Luton	2.5	23	9	0.44
Hillingdon	2.1	22	12	0.76
Richmond	2.5	21	15	0.49
Ealing	2.6	20	18	1.07
Herefordshire	2.9	20	16	0.20
Nottinghamshire	2.9	20	2	0.98
Surrey	2.6	19	17	2.34
Barnet	2.5	19	17	1.01
Rochdale	2.2	19	11	0.12
Breconshire	2.8	19	16	0.06
Wolverhampton	2.9	18	13	0.36
Havering	2.7	18	5	0.55
Yorkshire East Riding	2.8	18	2	0.34
Redbridge	2.9	17	13	0.59
Birmingham	2.6	17	1	2.27
Derbyshire	2.4	15	10	1.14
Hertfordshire	2.6	14	2	2.30

Local Authority	Number per 1000 Registered physically capped 1965–66[a]	Annual average expenditure per person registered physically handicapped 1965–66[a]		Penny rate product expressed as a percentage of the penny rate produced in Eng. & Wales in 1965–66[b]
		£	s.	
Newcastle upon Tyne	2.9	13	18	0.56
Northumberland	2.2	13	0	0.71
Bury	2.5	12	12	0.09
Warwickshire	2.3	12	10	0.99
Pembrokeshire	2.0	10	17	0.16
Suffolk East	2.9	10	7	0.32
Portsmouth	2.7	10	5	0.44
Merthyr Tydfil	2.8	9	19	0.06
Somerset	2.5	9	19	0.86
Salop	2.0	9	6	0.51
Hampshire	2.0	9	5	1.63
Solihull	2.0	8	19	0.21
Blackpool	2.6	8	10	0.37
Westmorland	2.0	8	8	0.10
Ipswich	2.0	8	7	0.23
Huddersfield	2.6	7	12	0.19
Middlesborough	2.8	7	9	0.23
Lancashire	2.6	7	1	3.55
Yorkshire West Riding	2.6	6	14	2.05
West Hartlepool	2.6	6	12	0.11
Eastbourne	2.2	4	8	0.16
Devon	2.7	4	8	0.92
Norfolk	2.4	4	7	0.52
Worcestershire	2.6	2	12	0.82
Durham County	2.3	1	9	1.37

0 to 1.9 persons per thousand population registered physically handicapped

Blackburn	1.9	48	16	0.15
Carlisle	1.6	45	5	0.12
Suffolk West	1.1	36	4	0.18
Oxfordshire	1.2	29	9	0.37
Bexley	1.6	26	4	0.49
Grimsby	1.5	21	19	0.16
Flintshire	1.6	20	18	0.30
Montgomeryshire	1.0	20	17	0.04
Carmarthenshire	1.5	20	2	0.19
Leicestershire	1.2	18	10	0.75
Canterbury	1.3	16	16	0.07
Southport	1.2	15	18	0.18
Staffordshire	1.7	15	12	1.81
Oxford	1.2	13	0	0.32
Northants	1.8	12	10	0.50
Northampton	1.6	12	10	0.25
Kent	1.5	11	19	2.27

Local Authority	Number per 1000 Registered physically handicapped 1965–66[a]	Annual average expenditure per person registered physically handicapped 1965–66[a]		Penny rate product expressed as a percentage of the penny rate product in Eng. & Wales in 1965–66[b]
		£	s.	
Yorkshire				
North Riding	1.5	11	0	0.71
Barrow in Furness	1.0	9	11	0.09
Cumberland	1.9	6	18	0.33
Coventry	1.5	5	16	0.62
Swansea	1.9	5	15	0.32
Chester	0.7	4	5	0.14
Isle of Wight	1.8	3	1	0.17
Bromley	1.8	2	17	0.73
Mean	3.6	15	16	0.58
Median	3.1	12	16	0.38

a. Based on I.M.T.A., *Welfare Services Statistics 1965–66*.
b. Based on Ministry of Housing and Local Government and Welsh Office, *Rates and Rateable Values in England and Wales, 1965–66*.